Adult ADHD Tools

Executive Functioning Workbook, Mastering Concentration, Organization and Cleaning

Adult ADHD Tools

Executive Functioning Workbook, Mastering Concentration, Organization and Cleaning

CALVIN CAUFIELD

TABLE OF CONTENTS

Book 1. Mastering Concentration for Adult ADHD **15**

Introduction 17

Chapter 1. Understanding Adult ADHD 21

How Adult ADHD Works 22
Understand Your Brain and Typical Brain Functions 24
Causes Of ADHD 26
Myths About ADHD 27
Types of ADHD 31
Symptoms 32
Effects 33
The plus side of ADHD 35
Diagnosis 38
What treatments work? 39

Chapter 2. Overthinking and Mental Performance 43

Who Is An Overthinker? 43
Is Overthinking A Mental Illness? 45
The link between ADHD & overthinking 46
Side effects of ADHD overthinking 47
How you can use your overthinking tendencies to your advantage 51

Chapter 3. Learn the Principles of Calming Your Thoughts 55

Why am I always overthinking? 55
What happens when I can't quiet my mind? 57
Mastering the art of keeping calm 59
Meditation and relaxation techniques for keeping calm 64

Chapter 4. Improving Focus and Concentration 69

Focus vs Concentration (Similarities and Differences) 69
Does ADHD Make it Hard to Focus? 70
Strategies and Concentration – Building Techniques 71
Focus Exercises For People With ADHD 73
Does Medication Help To Improve Focus? 75
Guided Meditations To Help Improve Focus 76
Foods That Help Improve Focus 81
Hyperfocus In ADHD And How To Manage It 82
Should I Consider Neurofeedback Therapy? 84

Chapter 5. Strengthening Your Memory 87

ADHD And Memory Issues 87
Does Mind Mapping Work? 88
Principles Of Mind Mapping 89
How To Apply Mind Mapping For ADHD 90
Executive Dysfunction And ADHD 91
Core Executive Functions Skills That You Need 92
ADHD-Friendly Tips To Strengthen Your Memory 94
Online Memory Tools That Work 95
ADHD-Friendly Mental Exercises 97

Chapter 6. Curb Overthinking 99

The Destructive Nature Of ADHD Overthinking 99
Identifying Your Overthinking Triggers 100
Strategies For Overcoming Overthinking 102
Mindfulness Meditation For Overthinking 107

Chapter 7. Mind Declutter Guide 109

Can I Be Organized Despite My ADHD? 109
Why Is Decluttering Difficult For Me? 113
The Mindblowing Benefits Of Decluttering One's Mind 114
How To Declutter With My ADHD Brain 115

Chapter 8. Simple Exercises and Mindfulness Techniques 119

Take Things One Day At A Time 119
How To Make Your ADHD Work For You 123
Fun Exercises For People With ADHD 125
Mindfulness Worksheets 127
Simple Visual Exercises For People With ADHD 130

Conclusion 133

Sources: 135

Book 2. ADHD Organization and Cleaning 149

Part 1.

Making Organization and Cleaning Easy – Even With ADHD 150

Introduction 151

How to use this book and what you'll learn 156

Chapter 1. ADHD – According to Science 159

Why ADHD Makes Cleaning and Organizing So Difficult 161
You Can Have ADHD and an Organized Home 164
Progress, Not Perfection – The Importance of Self-Compassion 165
Key Takeaways 167

Chapter 2. Getting Started Overcoming Common ADHD Challenges 169

Let's Start By Not Making Your Symptoms Worse 170
Identifying Practical Strategies that Work with Your Brain 173
Find a home for important items 181
Get Motivated – Let's Talk About Your Why 182
Tap into Your Reward System 183
Stay Motivated – Even When You Don't Feel Like It 185

Chapter 3. Habit Building for People with ADHD 193

Choosing the Right Strategies for You 193
Understand your Goals 194
Be Specific 195
Habit Stacking 196
Start Small and Build from There 197
Make it Work for ***You*** ***198***
Be Flexible 198
Make it Rewarding All the Way Through 201
The Only Failure is When You Stop Trying Altogether 202
Apply What You've Learned 202
Use Your Resources 203
Key Takeaways 204

Chapter 4. Decluttering with ADHD. Clearing the Mess, One Doom Pile at a Time 205

Didn't Organize, Only Moved 206
How Did it Get this Bad? 207
But There is Hope 208
Reiterating the Foundation 208
Where to Start 210
Keep Going for the Quick Wins 215
Your Ongoing System to Stay Decluttered 218
How to Recognize When it's Accumulating Again 220

Work with yourself rather than against yourself 221
Less is more 221
Key Takeaways 223

Part 2. Organizing Room by Room 224

Chapter 5. Your Simple Organization System. How to Make Organizing Automatic and Easy 225

What do we mean by organizing? 225
Bringing back the basics 226
Getting organized 228
Putting it All into Action 230
Stay on Task and Don't Let Perfectionism Derail You 235
Maintaining Organization 236
Assess and reassess your storage strategies 239
Key Takeaways 240

Chapter 6. The Living Room 243

Chapter 7. The Bathroom 247

Chapter 8. The Kitchen 251

Chapter 9. The Bedroom 257

Chapter 10. The Home Office 261

Chapter 11. Laundry and the Laundry Room 265

Chapter 12. Storage and Hallways 269

Part 3. Cleaning Room by Room 272

Chapter 13. Your Cleaning System 273

How Often Should You Clean 273
What Supplies You'll Need 274
The Secret to Never Getting Overwhelmed by Cleaning Again 275
Don't Skip Out on the Details 280
Schedule Your Cleaning in Advance 283
Don't be afraid to ask for help 284
Managing Boring Tasks & How to make cleaning more fun 285

Chapter 14. How to Clean Each Room 287

The Living Room 287
The Bathroom 289
The Kitchen 290
The Bedroom 291
The Home Office 293
Laundry and the Laundry Room 294
Storage and Hallways 296

Conclusion 299

Sample Calendar 299
Daily Weekly Organizer 301

References 303

Book 3. Executive Functioning Workbook For Adults With ADHD 307

Introduction 309

I wish someone had told me 310
The Role of Medication in Improving Executive Functioning 312
The Beauty of Neuroplasticity 313
How EF Skills Make a Difference in Your Daily Life 314
What to Expect 315
How to Use This Book 315
What is Executive Functioning 316
How EF Skills Develop 317
The EF Skills You'll Learn 317
Executive Function Skills Assessment 325
Let's Get Started 327

Day 1. Honing Your Attention and Focus 333

Don't Neglect the Obvious 334
Give Your Focus a Workout 335
Let's Talk About Hyperfocus 340
Shaping Your Perspective 344
Recognizing Your Unhelpful Thoughts 348
Who Doesn't Like Games? 355

Day 2. Enhancing Working Memory 361

Multi-Tasking Versus Monotasking 363
ADHD and Autopilot 366
Simple, But Effective 368
You'll Need a Planner 370
Mnemonics Have Been Helping You For Years 374

Day 3. Mastering Task Initiation 379

The Role of Perfectionism in ADHD 381
Your Patterns Matter 384
How CBT Applies 387
What To Do First? 391

Day 4. Applying Time Management 395

When Our Perception is Off 396
Creating Focus Bursts 400
Before You Know it, an Hour is Gone 402
The Importance of Planning 403

Day 5. Enacting Essential Organization Skills 407

Organization Essentials 409
The Role of Habit Building 410
The Importance of Decluttering 414
Getting Organized – It Starts at Home 420
Progress, Not Perfection 425

Day 6. Taking Command with Impulse Control 427

Your Self-Concept Matters 429
Awareness is Key 432
Impulse Control Tactics 439
Feeling Your Success 444
Stick With It 447

Day 7. Developing Flexible Thinking 449

How Flexible Are You? 450
Why Does Cognitive Flexibility Matter? 454
Play Video Games 458
Positive versus Negative Self Talk 460
Time to Start Training 463

Day 8. Strengthening Your Emotional Regulation 465
Self-Soothing Strategies 466
Solve 474
External Reminders 476
Using Imagery 479
Persistence Pays Off 480
Conclusion 483
Acceptance and Self-Compassion 483
Next Steps 484
Your Next Month 485
Remember to be Flexible 490
Resources 490
Embrace Your Success 491
Thank you 491
References 493

BOOK 1.

Mastering Concentration for Adult ADHD

Mindful techniques with simple exercises to calm your thoughts from an anxious mind, improve focus and stop overthinking

---

INTRODUCTION

When I was first diagnosed as being neuroatypical it was a momentous 'aha' moment. Retrospectively there were so many things throughout my life that now suddenly made sense. All my life I had asked the question 'why'. Why do I struggle with things that others seem to have no problem with?

Why do I struggle with something as simple as remembering appointments or paying bills on time? Why do I struggle with keeping my home neat and tidy, when I really want to, but just cannot seem to be able to – which all boiled down to my struggles with *concentration*.

Being diagnosed with ADHD finally gave me the answers to all these questions I've had for so many years. It's one of those moments where, when you're given an answer to a problem you've been having and you feel like you're so dumb for not having been able to see it. Because it's so obvious. Hindsight is 20/20.

I've spent a lot of time over the last couple of years scouring the internet for information relating to ADHD. Watching countless hours of YouTube videos, reading so many research papers that I figure I deserve an honorary doctorate, reading self-help and psychology books, going for therapy, and finding the right cocktail of medication.

It has been a journey.

I wanted to write this book so I could share all my knowledge and experience with you. I know what it feels like to be given information and not quite know what to do with it. So I wanted to write a guide or manual of sorts that you can use on a day-to-day basis to help you cope with your own symptoms.

This book is not just for people who suffer from ADHD, but also for parents of children with ADHD, partners of individuals with ADHD, and friends of those with ADHD. This book will help you both better understand yourself and your loved ones who suffer from ADHD.

This book is divided into three parts. The first part focuses on all you need to know about ADHD, how overthinking affects your overall performance and the rudiments of calming your thoughts.

The second part expressly discusses ADHD-friendly strategies to improve your focus and concentration, and how to put an end to overthinking tendencies.

The third and final part of the book covers a full guide for decluttering your mind, and more strategies for living with ADHD

I wanted to make sure this book gives you practical guidance, tools, and strategies that you can implement on a daily basis to help you better your own concentration skills. To this end, it was important to me that I include important information relating to comorbid symptoms that can have a negative effect on our ability to concentrate, such as overthinking.

We start off with a bit of background on the science of ADHD. We explore the different areas and functions of your brain involved and how ADHD affects these areas and functions. E.g. ever wondered why it's so challenging for you to keep up with paying monthly bills or organize your home? This is where those questions are answered.

Next, we'll cover the more technical aspects of ADHD. We'll have a look at some of the most popular myths that have been making the rounds over the last few decades, the causes of ADHD, symptoms of ADHD, effects, treatment options, and the official diagnostic criteria as per the Diagnostic and Statistical Manual of Mental Disorders.

These chapters are aimed at giving you a deeper understanding of how your neurodivergent brain differs from a neurotypical brain, and answer the question as to why you struggle with the things you struggle with.

One of the important topics we cover in the chapters after that is '*overthinking*'. I think this is such a crucial part to cover as I personally know just how debilitating the non-stop chatter in my mind can be at times, and the mental health struggles that follow as a result of being stuck in the overthinking loop.

The rest of the book is all about providing you with useful information and practical tools and strategies to overcome difficulties like memory issues, time-blindness, executive dysfunction, organizational difficulties, etc.

Throughout the following chapters, I provide you with exercises that have been invaluable in helping me improve my concentration, focus, and organizational skills over the years. I've personally tried all of these techniques and included multiple resources throughout the book.

Imagine going through this book and finally gaining control of your thoughts and thinking patterns that used to run amok in your head. Imagine finally being able to organize your home and work environments in a way that suits you best and makes it easier for you to accomplish your tasks.

Going through the exercises I provide you with and putting in the time and work necessary to better understand both your symptoms and yourself as an individual can help you overcome the difficulties akin to ADHD.

I want you to be able to reign in those thoughts that run wild in your head. I want you to be able to successfully organize your home and celebrate your space, rather than beating yourself up for not being able to keep some form of order.

I want you to be able to harness some of your ADHD superpowers and use them to your advantage, both in your personal and professional life.

That is something else you will discover as you progress through the book; you have certain superpowers that ADHD gives you that neurotypicals do not have. It's just a case of discovering and harnessing those superpowers.

I teach you how to use skills like mindfulness meditation in a way that works for someone with ADHD, rather than the mainstream techniques that are taught. How to declutter both your space and your mind, and how to tune into your senses to help combat intrusive thoughts.

I want you to be able to use this book as a practical guide and workbook on 'how to ADHD'. There's absolutely nothing wrong with having a neurodivergent brain. The problem is just that nobody ever taught you how to employ these skills to ensure your brain works with you instead of against you.

All that is left now is to dig in and discover the wonder that is your beautiful, magnificent, neurodivergent brain!

CHAPTER 1.

UNDERSTANDING ADULT ADHD

ADHD is, within itself, a fairly complex condition to try to make sense of. Though in this book my aim is not to bamboozle you with highly technical terms derived from some scientific journal under the guise of wanting to educate you on the inner workings of the neuro-atypical brain. No, in this book I aim to share research-based, peer-reviewed, scientifically-proven tips, tools, and techniques that are simple and easy to understand. These are tools I have used myself that have helped me to calm my overactive brain, master my concentration, and sharpen my focus skills.

As a neuro-atypical myself, or '*neurospicy*' as I like to call it, I have decades of experience in being *the odd one out.* Living in the margins is no easy feat, and a struggle that the majority of this blue planet's population will never understand. I choose to see my neurospicy brain as a superpower. I've learned how to harvest that superpower by implementing various tools and skills. I'm not promising a quick fix here. It takes time, practice, and patience to master these tools and techniques.

I can also just about guarantee that the words *time, practice,* and *patience* just made your brain go: "*No thank you. We don't want any patience here thank you. Nasty, uncomfortable things.*" Not to worry. With enough practice and science to back us up, we can do this!

How Adult ADHD Works

The first time I remember hearing the term ADHD was in the 1990s. There seemed to be a big rise in diagnoses at the time. Several factors could have accounted for this, e.g. better diagnostic criteria to help doctors make diagnoses, more parents were aware of the condition and reporting their child's symptoms, and a general rise in educating the public on it.

I remember back then people believed that it was only children who could be diagnosed with the condition. I think there are still a great number of people who might still believe that today. In fact, I know of people who still believe the condition to be made up.

It's no wonder people who suffer from ADHD feel ashamed about it. Most neuro-atypical individuals are taught to 'buck up' and stop being lazy. Just apply yourself!

Thank goodness for medical advancements in non-invasive imaging tools like Magnetic Resonance Imaging, or the MRI machine. A study published in Radiology, a monthly peer-reviewed medical journey owned and published by the Radiological Society of North America, showed that an MRI scan can not only differentiate between a 'normal' brain and an ADHD brain, but also ADHD subtypes. We'll get to the subtypes a bit later.

In the next section, we will have a look at how the brain works. In the meantime, it will be helpful for you to understand that ADHD is a neurodevelopmental disorder that affects certain functions like the ability to hold one's attention, impulse control, and executive functioning. Executive functioning refers to those skills that help us to control our behavior, juggle tasks, learn, and plan. A simple example would be following a daily schedule, which would take planning and execution. Individuals who suffer from ADHD notoriously struggle to keep up with everyday tasks like washing dishes, doing laundry, paying bills, etc.

For most of history, the disorder has mainly been diagnosed using subjective evaluations. You are given a questionnaire to fill out, and based on your answers a diagnosis is given, or not. The advancement of MRI scans makes this an exciting time to be alive as it now shows without a shadow of a doubt that ADHD is a brain disorder. Which makes it sound like there's something wrong with your brain and I do not mean that at all. It just means that your brain functions differently from the typical brain. Ergo *'neuro-atypical'*. This of course doesn't mean that it makes it easier to live with the condition.

It is estimated that ADHD affects 5% – 8% of children and 4% of adults. This means that we, as neuro-atypicals, will always be more than significantly outnumbered. People just don't care, whether they mean to or not, as the majority of the human population will never understand what it is like to be different from the norm. One might argue that if you cannot understand what it's like to have a certain experience, that you cannot be held responsible for not taking people who have that same experience on a daily basis into consideration.

I disagree. I believe that you can choose to consider others no matter your experience. I do not know what it is like to be neurotypical, yet I've been forced to have to fit in and act like one all my life. The minority will always be forced to fit in with the majority. I don't have to though. In fact, I choose not to.

I choose to see my atypical brain and how it affects my functioning as a superpower to be honest. I'm intelligent and extremely creative, I can work on a number of projects simultaneously, and I can understand complex ideas very easily.

According to a paper by (Sedgwick et al., 2018) on "*The positive aspects of ADHD*," they found that specific positive attributes related to ADHD include:

- High levels of energy and drive
- The ability to hyper-focus
- Exceptional creativity

- Agreeableness/ individuals putting others' needs before their own
- Great capacity for empathy
- A willingness to always assist others

I believe that people with a neuro-atypical brain have their own superpowers. You just need to do some inner work to discover them, if you haven't yet.

Understand Your Brain and Typical Brain Functions

The brain is a brilliant and still-mysterious pink meat computer that weighs just 2% of your total body weight, yet relies on the majority of the body's glucose for fuel. Various brain functions such as memory, learning, and thinking are closely linked to glucose levels available to the brain, and how efficiently the brain uses this fuel source.

Numerous studies published on the National Library of Medicine's website, (Arnsten, A. F., 2009) and (Gehricke et al., 2017) have found that certain areas of the brain can be smaller in people with ADHD. Certain sub-areas of the prefrontal cortex are associated with impulse control. This can be especially challenging for young children, as our brains are not fully developed until our mid-twenties. So for a child with ADHD, the struggle doesn't only lie in the fact that their brain is literally still developing, but they also have to contend with a deficit in impulse control due to slower developing regions in their prefrontal cortex as a result of changes in blood flow to those areas of the brain compared to their peers. Imagine for a moment what that must feel like.

Research suggests that there are regions of the brain that might never catch up in adults with ADHD[1]. MRI scans have shown no evidence of a difference in overall brain volume when comparing the brains of children with and without ADHD. Although, scans have shown differences in specific areas of the brain, as mentioned above. These scans were able to differentiate between ADHD and non-ADHD brains with 73.7% accuracy and discriminate between ADHD inattentive and ADHD combined subtypes with 80% accuracy.

We now know that there is a great genetic component linked to ADHD. A child born to one or more than one parent with ADHD is very likely to develop ADHD themselves. Though it is still unclear to what extent environmental factors play a role.

Different areas in the brain are also affected in a person with ADHD. These include:

- **The frontal lobe** – which is responsible for expressive language, voluntary movement, and executive function
- **The basal ganglia** – responsible for motor control, executive function, and emotions
- **The anterior cingulate** – responsible for attention allocation, mood regulation, and emotional expression
- **The temporal lobe** – responsible for processing auditory information and encoding memories.
- **Parietal regions** – responsible for sensory perception and integration.

Next, let's talk about neurotransmitters.

Neurotransmitters are the messengers of the brain. They carry important information from one nerve cell to the next muscle, gland, or nerve cell. There are many different neurotransmitters and I bet you've heard of a few of the main ones like Serotonin, Dopamine, Endorphins, etc.

The main neurotransmitter involved in ADHD is Dopamine. It's responsible for various functions such as motivation, motor control, arousal, executive function, reinforcement, and reward. People with ADHD typically have lower levels of dopamine – which can cause mood swings, difficulty concentrating, sleep disturbances, low motivation, and more.

Dopamine also regulates the brain's reward system. When we engage in pleasurable activities like eating food, having sex, shopping or scrolling through social media, it leads to a rise in dopamine levels in the brain. This makes us feel good, which is why Dopamine is known as one of the four 'feel good' hormones.

Though in the case of a person with ADHD, those levels will soon drop again and leave your brain needing another hit. We already know that the brain of an individual with ADHD looks and functions differently from that of an individual with a neurotypical brain. Neurotransmitters like Dopamine are transported via neural pathways in the brain. Billions of neurons act as little messengers passing along information throughout the brain and the rest of the body via the nervous system, which is made up of the brain and spinal cord.

An ADHD brain has some faulty messengers, which means that less Dopamine is passed along the messaging chain than should be. Hence the lower levels of Dopamine. Medications like Adderall and Ritalin help to ensure that more Dopamine is transported via these neural pathways by having more of it being picked up along the way.

In a non-ADHD brain, this process of balancing chemicals happens naturally. When a non-ADHD individual does something pleasurable Dopamine is released and gradually balances out again. In an individual with ADHD Dopamine is released but then soon drops back to below normal levels again, which leaves you feeling deflated and like you need to do things like scroll through social media or engage in risky behaviors to get those levels up again.

The good news is, there is help. We're getting to that.

Causes Of ADHD

We have come a long way in gaining a deeper understanding of the inner workings of ADHD. Though we still do not know what exactly causes the condition. There is a strong genetic component to it, meaning that if one or more parents suffer from ADHD, the chances that their child will also develop the condition are greater than for someone who does not have a parent/s who suffers from ADHD. We are still exploring other potential contributing factors such as:

- **Environmental factors** – being exposed to toxic elements in the environment, e.g. lead, during pregnancy or at a young age.
- **Physical brain injury** – either as a developmental issue or as a result of physical trauma.
- **Alcohol and/ or tobacco use during pregnancy** – as we all know by now, these things can cause abnormal developmental issues in a developing fetus.
- **Premature delivery** – a premature delivery is anything before a 37-week gestation period. The earlier a child is born the greater the risk of developmental issues or physical disabilities.
- **Low birth weight** – some babies are tiny and develop without any issues. Though a low birth weight can cause a number of serious health problems for babies.

There is no 'one size fits all', which makes it difficult to pinpoint a cause. There is no single gene that causes mental illness. The average human being has between 20000 and 25000 genes, and any combination of genetic mutations might cause genes to express in a different way leading to some or other illness. So you can imagine how hard it is to try and pinpoint a single cause.

Scientists have, however, identified a number of different genes that could have an effect on the development of ADHD.

Myths About ADHD

There have been many myths about ADHD. Though some myths just won't die and have followed the condition around for decades. In this section, we are going to explore some of the most famous myths that have stood the test of time, despite mounds of evidence against them.

MYTH #1
ADHD ISN'T REAL. IT'S JUST SOMETHING THEY MADE UP

You might hear people say something like *"we're all a little ADHD."* That's like saying that everyone who's taller than the ground is tall at some point. If you're standing next to someone shorter than you are, you're tall. But if you're standing next to someone who is seven feet tall, they're tall all the time. Not just some of the time, and it probably affects their lives on a daily basis – just like ADHD. Although the name may have changed over the years, it is the most researched mental health condition in the world today. It is very real, with very real evidence to support it.

MYTH #2
ADHD IS JUST A BEHAVIORAL ISSUE

False. Whilst it might seem like a case of laziness or bad behavior from the outside, just remember that behavior is directly affected by the functioning of different structures within the brain and genetics. Research has concluded that there is a direct link between ADHD and lower levels of Dopamine, and it's highly genetic. This means this myth is well and truly busted.

MYTH #3
ADHD ONLY AFFECTS CHILDREN

Though some individuals may grow up to experience fewer symptoms to the point of impairment, most people never *'grow out of it.'* Many people aren't diagnosed until much later in life, and long-term studies of children with ADHD show that it is a lifespan disorder.

MYTH #4
ADHD IS CAUSED BY EATING TOO MUCH SUGAR

False, but it can make symptoms worse. Historically there have been conflicting results from studies relating to the effects of sugar intake on ADHD. Though, in a 2019 review of studies (Del-Ponte et al., 2019) results showed that a high intake of refined sugar and saturated fat can increase symptoms of ADHD.

MYTH #5
ADHD IS CAUSED BY PLAYING TOO MANY VIDEOGAMES

False, but it can make symptoms worse.

MYTH #6
ADHD IS CAUSED BY BAD PARENTING

False, but it can make symptoms worse.

MYTH #7
YOU HAVE GOOD GRADES, WHICH MEANS YOU CAN'T HAVE ADHD

False. Many gifted students have neuro-atypical brains. One of my all-time favorite historical figures, Albert Einstein, is believed to have suffered from ADHD.[2]

MYTH #8
YOU'RE NOT BOUNCING OFF THE WALLS SO YOU CAN'T HAVE ADHD

False. Not all individuals who suffer from ADHD are hyperactive. There are different variants/ subtypes of ADHD, which we'll still get into. Some are more mentally restless.

MYTH #9
ONLY BOYS GET DIAGNOSED WITH ADHD

False. Studies delving into understanding ADHD in females have only gained more interest in recent decades. Though some data do suggest that the diagnostic rate stands at around 13.3% for boys as opposed to 5.6% for girls. Females are a lot better at masking their symptoms, which often leads to being diagnosed much later in life.

There really are a lot of these myths that aren't there.

MYTH #10
EVERYONE'S A LITTLE ADHD

Whilst everyone might experience getting a little hyperactive or distracted at times, people who have been diagnosed with ADHD have to meet at least 5 of the diagnostic criteria outlined in the DSM-5, since childhood, at a level where it interferes with everyday life.

MYTH #11
MEDICATION CURES ADHD

Medication can be very helpful in managing your symptoms, but it is just scaffolding. As soon as the medication wears off, the symptoms return.

MYTH #12
CHILDREN WITH ADHD ARE OVER-MEDICATED

Studies have actually shown that the prescribed medication for children with ADHD are either adequate, or undertreated.[3]

More myths are making the rounds out there, but these are the most commonly discussed. Now if you hear them out there in the world you'll know the truth.

Types of ADHD

As both research and diagnostic criteria have evolved to include symptoms experienced in adolescence and adulthood, mental health professionals are gaining better insight into how symptoms might present themselves with additional samples listed in the manual.

There are currently three major types of ADHD:

- **ADHD, combined type** – this is the main type of ADHD, which includes experiencing hyperactivity, impulsivity, being easily distracted, and having difficulties paying attention.
- **ADHD, predominantly impulsive/ hyperactive type** – classified as the least common type and only includes symptoms related to impulsivity and hyperactivity. This type of individual doesn't experience difficulties paying attention or being easily distracted.
- **ADHD, predominantly inattentive/ distractible** – This type was formerly known as ADD, though the term is no longer in use, and only includes symptoms relating to difficulties paying attention and being easily distracted.

Symptoms

Now that we have a better understanding of the different types of ADHD, let's have a look at some of the symptoms that people generally experience.

As there are different types of the condition, symptoms can also be organized into two categories. One category relates to inattention and distractibility, and the other to hyperactivity and impulsivity. Many people experience symptoms that fall into both categories, but this isn't always the case. As with the different types, you might experience symptoms that predominantly fall into one category or the other.

Symptoms that fall into the inattentive category:

- Struggling to stay focused or being easily distracted.
- A tendency to make mistakes quite often, e.g. in schoolwork for children, or at work for adults.
- Struggling to organize tasks. If a task is boring to you, you struggle to focus and get easily distracted doing other things.
- You have a dozen tabs open on your computer, listening to music, doing research, and shopping. Then suddenly realizing you're hungry and walk into the kitchen forgetting what you wanted to do.
- You struggle to listen to instructions as your brain wanders off to other places, which makes it hard to carry out said instructions.
- You misplace things all the time.

Symptoms that fall into the category of hyperactivity and impulsiveness:

- You struggle to sit still when you're expected to do so. E.g. in class for children, or in meetings for adults.
- You're constantly fidgeting, e.g. picking at skin, fidgeting with your hands, picking at your lip, tapping your fingers, etc.

- You really struggle with the concept of waiting your turn. Whether it's standing in a queue or in conversation.
- You are a chatty Cathy. You can talk to anyone, anywhere, about anything, and can often dominate conversations.
- Excessive physical movement, e.g. struggling to sit still, tapping your foot incessantly, etc.
- Feeling like you're always on the go. Like you have a machine inside of you. You struggle to just relax.

Effects

If you suspect that you might have ADHD it is important that you see a physician to seek a diagnosis and treatment as soon as possible. While ADHD might not get worse, the impact on your life does. Untreated ADHD can wreck your credit (impulsive spending), affect your grades (inattention), and create serious problems in your relationships.

If you're thinking that you don't want to take medication, that's ok. Medication is not your only option and many people with ADHD find other ways to cope. We'll talk about that a bit later.

There's also absolutely nothing wrong with taking medication as recommended by a medical professional. If it helps you and gives you a better quality of life, by all means. You need to do what works for you.

Here are just some of the effects someone might experience if their ADHD goes untreated.

- Social isolation. It can be an immense struggle when the people around you do not want to understand your symptoms and judge you for them. This can often lead to social isolation, which has a negative effect on one's mental health.
- Struggles with performing at school or work, which can lead to a decreased sense of self-worth.
- Compulsive eating. Having ADHD means you struggle to set a limit on what you consume sometimes. Eating junk food will

give your brain a spike in dopamine, which it's generally low on, which in turn, makes you feel good. It's a vicious circle.

- High levels of anxiety. Many individuals with ADHD are also diagnosed with an anxiety disorder. Having this feeling of an internal motor that's constantly driving you might make you feel anxious and on edge.
- Substance abuse as a byproduct of impulsivity or 'thrill-seeking."
- Living with ADHD can be very stressful and chronic stress takes a toll over time with issues relating to digestion, breathing, muscle aches and pains, heart problems, and more.
- Sleep problems.
- Employment problems. It's common for people with ADHD to struggle with holding down a job. Although workplaces differ, most of them expect you to be on time, attentive, organized, and focused on the tasks you are given. This can be challenging for someone with ADHD.
- Impulsive spending can be a real issue as it often lands people in a heap of debt.
- Financial issues due to not being organized and perhaps not paying bills on time, spending too much on things you hadn't budgeted for.
- Screen addiction is a real thing and although a lot of us have this problem these days, when your brain is low on dopamine it makes it harder to tear yourself away when you get little hits of the good stuff with constant image changes, comments, graphics, and games.
- Sexual problems can cause real issues in your relationship. Getting distracted during sex can be a real mood killer. It is important to have excellent communication with your partner. It's also important to choose a partner who is willing to try to understand your difficulties relating to ADHD as to not take it personally.

- The element of impulsivity can make it harder to control your emotions and/or how you respond to situations. Having emotional outbursts can affect your relationships both at home and at work.
- Depression commonly also goes hand-in-hand with ADHD. It only makes sense that if you have to struggle with things that come so easily to others, along with judgment from the outside, that it will cause you to feel down in the dumps at times.
- People with ADHD tend to have a shorter life expectancy due to risk-taking behaviors and a tendency to get into accidents.
- Family disruptions due to them not understanding your symptoms or taking your diagnosis seriously. People tend to get frustrated with family members with ADHD and often discount their symptoms.
- Teen pregnancies are quite common due to impulsivity and teens' inability to control their wants or needs. This also goes in hand with delinquency and teens dropping out of school.
- Poor performance at school and work.

Reading through this list may make you feel a little overwhelmed and thinking it's a losing battle. It's not all doom and gloom though.

People with ADHD also have certain *'superpowers'* that set them apart from the rest of society.

The plus side of ADHD

My best friend suffers from ADHD (inattentive/distractible type formerly known as ADD) and I have experienced first-hand how certain everyday tasks can be an absolute challenge for her. Though when it comes to creativity and the ability to hyperfocus and complete a project meticulously and with incredible detail, she's superhuman.

Even though she might struggle to pay attention for extended periods of time or get distracted easily when it comes to doing something she enjoys her abilities soar above anyone else's I know.

She was recently tasked with doing her company's newsletter as the person who was in charge of marketing, and the newsletter had resigned. I know that graphic design is something she loves to do, but even I didn't realize just how good at it she is! Perhaps because her job never presents her with opportunities to showcase her creative talents.

She told me that she had been tasked with creating the new monthly newsletter for her company and how excited she was. She spent hours on that newsletter, even staying behind in the office after hours because she had entered a state of hyperfocus. I often phoned her to remind her to go home as it was after hours and I knew if I didn't phone her she'd sit in that office until midnight without realizing it.

When she completed it and sent it over to me for a little friendly 'what do you think', I was absolutely blown away. I mean really blown out of the water. It was the most creative, striking, and professional-looking newsletter I have ever seen. I myself have done some graphic design work in the past and was super impressed and proud of my friend. The way she designed the layout along with pairing colors and fonts just worked.

Everyone in her office was equally impressed with her skills and as a result, she has been given a promotion to work in the marketing department, handling all of their creative content. How awesome is that?

With this bit of inspiration in mind, here are a number of other positive attributes related to ADHD that you might be able to identify in yourself:

- Excellent problem-solving skills. When your brain goes at lightspeed jumping between thoughts it also helps run through many different potential solutions to a problem.
- Imagination and creativity. Many historic creatives are believed to have had ADHD, including Pablo Picasso, Leonardo da Vinci, and Vincent van Gogh. Individuals who are neurodivergent can think outside the box and be wonderfully creative.

- People with ADHD tend to be deeply compassionate and empathic. Having such a unique understanding of what it means to 'be different' really gives people with ADHD an ability to show compassion for the struggles of others.
- A wacky sense of humor that will brighten up any room.
- Perseverance. It takes strength to live in a world that doesn't care to understand you, and that adds to one's ability to overcome obstacles on a daily basis.
- A keen sense of observation. People with ADHD very often notice small things that others might miss.
- Masters of multitasking. Although there are studies that show that multitasking is ineffective, many people with ADHD thrive when engaged in multiple tasks at once because their brains work differently from most.
- Hyperfocus, which is the ability to really hone in and focus on a subject or task. Especially one you enjoy. Someone with ADHD can focus on and dig up information about a subject you might have never even heard of. When harnessed, you can accomplish much more much faster than neurotypicals.
- Like the Energizer bunny, you never run out of power. You can keep going 'till the cows come home.
- People with ADHD have had to face many obstacles in their life and as a result, they've learned how to look on the bright side. They tend to have a real zest for life.

So you see, even though being neurodivergent comes with its own set of challenges, it also comes with a whole list of positives and abilities that others might not have. Each of us is unique with unique minds.

I personally believe that being unique is something to be celebrated.

Diagnosis

To receive a diagnosis of ADHD, you, or your child, have to display certain symptoms as set out in the Diagnostic and Statistical Manual of Mental Disorders 5. The first step towards getting a diagnosis is to undergo a clinical assessment. If you suspect you, or your child, might have ADHD you may want to bring it up to your GP or therapist, or psychiatrist.

An assessment can only be conducted by a trained and licensed professional such as a specialist psychiatrist, pediatrician, or other trained professionals.

The stages of assessments potentially involved before coming to a diagnosis might include:

- Clinical assessments.
- Assessment tools and rating scales.
- And clinical interviews with the individual or parents and teachers, etc.

Let's look at the diagnostic criteria[4] for the different types of ADHD.

Only a licensed professional can make a diagnosis after conducting an in-depth clinical interview. If you recognize yourself in any of the symptoms below, take it as a sign to see a professional and get a proper diagnosis, not as a diagnosis in itself. Below are some common symptoms of ADHD.

- More than six months of struggling with attention/concentration to the level where it is interfering with your work, academic, or social life.
- Often failing to pay attention to detail or making regular mistakes when it comes to your work or private life (e.g. missing out on paying bills or forgetting to pay bills altogether on a regular basis).
- You often struggle to pay attention when you find a task boring, e.g. lengthy meetings, conversations, lectures, etc.

- Your environment is mostly messy, almost all of the time. You struggle to keep things organized and in order.
- You often lose interest in certain tasks and leave halfway through, like when you're busy with house chores, etc.
- You are often easily distracted by noise and activity in your immediate environment, e.g. people walking by your office throughout the day.
- You do not like activities or tasks that involve you having to pay attention for an extended period of time or that you find boring, like sorting out your budget or taxes, etc.
- You very often misplace or lose things. Even things you use every single day like your house keys or your wallet, etc.
- You often find yourself fidgeting, tapping your foot, picking at your skin, etc.
- You struggle to sit still, especially in situations where you are expected to do so, e.g. meetings.
- You've been told that you talk a lot and that you talk over people all the time.
- You often interrupt others when they're mid-sentence or have difficulties waiting your turn.

These can all be signs of ADHD, but again, you need to see a licensed professional so they can conduct a thorough assessment and go through your symptoms with you.

What treatments work?

There are more treatment options available to individuals with ADHD today than ever before. As I've mentioned earlier on, medication is no longer your only option. That being said, medication can also be extremely useful in treating your symptoms.

Whether you've just received a diagnosis or are reading this book to understand and help your child, a partner, or a family member, there's always something new to learn. Here are a number of options that you can explore for yourself.

STIMULANT MEDICATION (IT IS ALWAYS BEST TO SPEAK TO YOUR DOCTOR ABOUT MEDICATION)

Currently, the most widely prescribed medication for the treatment of ADHD is a type of medicine known as 'stimulants'. These medicines appear to both boost and balance brain chemistry by either inhibiting or increasing the release of certain neurotransmitters. There are currently two types of stimulants namely Amphetamines and Methylphenidates.

Some examples of amphetamines include Adderall, Dexedrine, and Vyvanse. Some examples of methylphenidates include Concerta, Ritalin, and others.

It is important to note that it might take some time to find the right dose and to keep communicating with your specialist if you find that your current medication or doses aren't working for you.

Other medications like anti-anxiety and antidepressant medicines might also be prescribed in combination with ADHD medication. As we've discovered previously, there are a number of conditions that generally go hand-in-hand with ADHD.

THERAPY

I would say that therapy is non-negotiable. Seeking out a therapist who has the experience and a special interest in helping individuals with ADHD can be life-changing. Therapeutic frameworks used might include CBT (cognitive behavioral therapy) or DBT (dialectical behavioral therapy), social skills training, and many more.

Seeing an occupational therapist can also be helpful as they can equip you with various tools that you can implement to help you cope with the challenges that your symptoms tend to cause. Understanding your personal sensory profile, for instance, can help you set up your environment both at home and the office to better cope with any sensory sensitivities you might have.

Other possible treatments may also include diet and supplements. People with ADHD tend to sometimes have a problem with junk food and sugar intake. This can lead to all kinds of other health issues, so making sure you are eating a healthy diet and taking any supplements necessary (only as prescribed by your doctor) can be helpful in treating your symptoms.

In the end, it's all about finding what works for you. We're all different, and what works for me won't necessarily work for you. It can take some time having to experiment with different medications and therapeutic treatments, but in the end, it's an investment you make in yourself.

In the next chapter, we'll explore the wondrous world of overthinking. If you're anything like me, you're probably chuckling to yourself and thinking: "*Bring it on, I'm a pro at this one.*"

CHAPTER 2.

OVERTHINKING AND MENTAL PERFORMANCE

Who Is An Overthinker?

If you are someone who is in possession of a neurodivergent brain, it is almost a guarantee that you are an overthinker. Though what neurotypical individuals refer to as overthinking might just be *thinking* to us neurospicy individuals.

Nevertheless, let's have a look at what makes someone an overthinker. To overthink is to spend too much time thinking about or analyzing something. Which is subjective in my personal opinion. I mean, what constitutes '*too much time*?' The answer to that question is that it is an amount of time that would prove to be more harmful than helpful to you. In other words, if it interferes with your life or relationships on a day-to-day basis, it's too much.

If we look at it that way it makes sense that thinking, worrying, or analyzing something ad infinitum could potentially be perilous to one's health, both mentally and physically. Many of us are plagued by certain thoughts or concerns on a daily basis. What sets an overthinker apart from the rest is the constant worries and regrets. The 'what ifs' that uncontrollably swirl around in your thoughts. *What if she's angry with me? What if he thought I meant it in a way I didn't? What if they hate me for what I said? What if I don't do this and it ruins my life?*

Being an overthinker means you're living everywhere except here, now, and in the present moment. You're either stressing about the past or the future. Constantly analyzing your every thought, emotion, and behavior – as well as others.

It's exhausting, to say the least. I'd liken it to running a marathon a day, every day of your life. It's enough to cause you to suffer from high levels of anxiety coupled with all sorts of comorbid behaviors like either starving yourself or binge eating comfort food.

We can overthink situations that are both actual and hypothetical. For most people overthinking stems predominantly from social situations. Constantly worrying about something you said or did in the past or dwelling on something you still have to do. It can creep into every aspect of your life and have you ruminating on things that haven't even happened yet or might never even happen.

Here are some telltale signs that you might be an overthinker:

- You often struggle to fall asleep because it feels like your brain just won't shut down.
- You feel like you constantly relive your mistakes.
- You struggle with a lot of negative thoughts.
- You replay situations or experiences over and over in your mind.
- You constantly rehash conversations you had previously to analyze all the things you wish you hadn't said.
- You feel worried or anxious most of the time.
- You ask yourself a lot of "what if..." questions.
- You spend a lot of time worrying about things that are not within your control.
- You generally struggle to control your thoughts.

Sound familiar? You're not alone. I've been told that I suffer from analysis-paralysis for well over three decades. The good news is there are tools you can implement to help you navigate the urge to overthink and overanalyze. We'll be exploring these topics in the sections to come.

There are situations in which analyzing can be helpful, but those are solely situations you have control over. If you don't have control over something, you are torturing yourself without the possibility of a solution. Simply thinking about something over and over again isn't going to solve the problem you're experiencing.

Is Overthinking A Mental Illness?

Overthinking is not a recognized mental illness in and of itself. Though research [5] has shown that it is often linked to other mental illnesses such as Generalized Anxiety Disorder (GAD) and Depression.

Overthinking can sometimes be mistaken for generalized anxiety disorder, which is typically associated with excessive worrying that lasts for six months or longer, and difficulties controlling one's anxiety, which can cause difficulties in your day-to-day life.

Another aspect to take into consideration is a little thing called cognitive distortions.

Cognitive distortions are irrational or exaggerated thought patterns that cause an individual to perceive reality inaccurately. They're ruminative or repetitive thought patterns that continuously run on a loop in our minds that can lead to less-than-desirable outcomes in our lives. There are many different cognitive distortions but one such example is called *'catastrophizing'*. I'm sure you will have heard of this word before. Catastrophizing is when we blow something up in our mind, when it's not quite that way in reality. Here's an example. You have a friendly relationship with a coworker and every morning when you arrive at work you greet one another in a friendly manner and she always asks you how you are doing.

Yesterday she didn't ask you how you were and barely greeted you. Now in the world of catastrophes, your mind might leap to the conclusion that she's mad at you. You obviously did something wrong. Maybe it's because you took five minutes to reply to an email from her. After all, you were in the bathroom and now she's probably mad at you because you made her feel like she's not important...you get the gist. That, my friend, is catastrophizing.

Other types of cognitive distortions include:

- All-or-nothing thinking: *"I never do anything right."*
- Mind reading: *"My boss is angry with me. I'm going to lose my job."*
- Filtering/ focusing on the negative and discounting the positive. E.g., a friend pays you a compliment saying that your hair looks nice. In your mind, you're thinking, *"Thanks, but it doesn't change the fact that I'm still fat."*
- Comparing: *"All my friends have families, cars, jobs, houses. I'm such a failure."*

There are many more. These are just to name a few so you get an idea of what cognitive distortions are. I'm sure you're wondering how one overcomes these negative thought patterns? Well, we'll get into it in more detail later, but for now, let's just say the first step is self-awareness. Becoming aware of your thoughts on a daily basis and just genuinely observing your thinking patterns from a place of kind curiosity so you may tease out the when, where, how, and why of it all.

Ok, now that we know what overthinking is and isn't, let's explore the connection between overthinking and ADHD.

The link between ADHD & overthinking

Overthinking can be extremely debilitating. It can feel like you're kept hostage inside a cage within your mind. Unable to think your way out of it as your mind just focuses on this one intrusive thought. Even though it's making you miserable, it feels like it's impossible to stop.

Whilst all of us fall prey to overthinking at some point or another, it's usually considered a symptom relating to obsessive-compulsive disorder more than ADHD. Although OCD often coincides with ADHD, you don't need to have OCD to experience overthinking.

According to the Healthy Brains organization, our brains process 70 000 thoughts on average on a daily basis. That's 49 thoughts per minute!

Now imagine for a second what that looks like inside the brain of a person with ADHD who already feels like they wish their brain would just shut up sometimes. While most people might be able to process and move on from this one (usually) negative thought, someone with ADHD might be more prone to being stuck in that loop and continuing to ruminate on this one thought over and over and over again. If analysis paralysis were an Olympic sport, people with ADHD would be right behind team OCD.

The ADHD brain is fast. Really fast. Like no speed limits, 50-lane highways with 10 onramps, and exits on a closed loop. It never stops. It never slows down. It's exhausting.

The good news is that there are a number of ways to combat those nasty negative thoughts.

Side effects of ADHD overthinking

The side effects of overthinking for a person with ADHD are the same as for anyone else. The only difference between the effects of overthinking on a neurotypical versus a neurodivergent brain is that a neurodivergent brain becomes more easily consumed by negative thoughts. I like to call it 'tornado mind'.

Rarely, if ever, does overthinking bring joy, and having ADHD means that overthinking can lead to causing other comorbid conditions such as anxiety and depression. Some of the physical side effects you might experience include nausea, headaches, fatigue, difficulty concentrating, trouble sleeping, and changes in appetite.

Intrusive thoughts can be distressing and cause you to experience anxiety on a regular basis. I know a doctor who once told me that suffering from anxiety is like running a marathon a day, every day. I.e. It's extremely exhausting and takes a toll.

Suffering from ADHD can be stressful within itself. Adding being consumed by negative thoughts on top of that just makes navigating everyday life really, really challenging.

Overthinking can cause you to feel very lonely. You might misinterpret what someone said to you as being rude or hurtful. In turn, you cut yourself off from said person. This happens with this person, then that person, and before you know if there are no more persons.

Many relationships have fallen to the wayside due to overthinking and not choosing to communicate with others due to false beliefs caused by overthinking.

Because you tend to hyper-focus on the tiniest of mistakes you've made in the past, you lose confidence in yourself and your self-worth dives into a dumpster. You beat yourself up and punish yourself for no reason at all, thanks to overthinking.

It takes a toll on your immune system and mental health as well. Neuroscience has proven that our physical and psychological health can be influenced by what we choose to focus on, on a daily basis. Choosing to allow your mind to hyper-fixate on that tiny mistake you made a gazillion years ago can physically make you ill.

It affects the chemical balance of your body. Constantly focusing and building on hypothetical negative thoughts can lead to your brain being unable to differentiate between what is hypothetical stress and stress that needs to be acted upon. In essence, both need to be acted on, but a virus spreading throughout your body in the present needs more immediate attention than the stress of hyper-fixating on how you interpreted your boss' tone of voice in a meeting two months ago.

Overthinking can also stunt your creativity according to a neurological study conducted at Stanford University[6]. We might try to fool ourselves into believing that overthinking helps us to come up with solutions that are more creative. The science unfortunately shows that it may have the opposite effect.

The investigation came up with two different, surprising results. First, higher levels of cerebellar activity – which is the part of our brain right at the back, at the base of our skull mainly responsible for movement – were linked to higher levels of creativity. Second, better creative ratings were related to lower activity in the cerebral cortex –which is the outer layer of our brain, responsible for reasoning, emotion, language, and memory – despite the fact that more difficult drawings boosted activity in this region.

The results from this study thus showed that although more *effort* is required to produce creative results, executive-control regions such as the cerebral cortex (the thinking parts of the brain) might actually need to be *less active* in order to produce better creative results.

This proves why a brain that lacks executive-control functioning (i.e. the ADHD brain) leads to greater levels of creativity.

If I think back for myself, I'd say that I can relate to all of the above. I've certainly allowed overthinking to ruin some relationships. It's caused me a lot of anxiety. It's broken down my self-esteem and caused me many sleepless nights.

If you don't deal with your intrusive thoughts, they will potentially ruin your life. Or some aspects of it anyway.

OVERTHINKING AND YOUR PERFORMANCE

If a basketball player over-thinks a shot, what do you think is going to happen? They'll miss the shot more often than not.

I used to be a professional motorcycle rider. As a certified instructor, I taught many people how to ride a motorcycle whilst making sure they keep themselves safe. Well, as safe as you can possibly be on a motorcycle. One of the main concepts in motorcycle riding is that *where you focus, is where you go.* If you are constantly thinking about falling, you will fall. I can 100% guarantee that. If you're going into a corner and you get fixated on that guardrail, you will hit that guardrail.

As author James Redfield once said: "*Where attention goes, energy flows. Where intention goes, energy flows.*" Your life is controlled by what you choose to focus on.

When you focus on thoughts that tell you, you are useless and incapable–your brain and body will start believing them. Just like if you choose to focus on your strengths and abilities, your energy will flow toward acknowledging and appreciating your own strengths and abilities.

The poet, William Wordsworth, wrote: "*Your mind is the garden, your thoughts are the seeds, the harvest can either be flowers or weeds.*" I think this very aptly describes how important it is to be aware of what we allow ourselves to focus on. Your strengths are the flower seeds and your perceived weaknesses are the weeds. In the end, you will always reap what you sow.

Getting fixated on every little thought that goes through your mind can cause a myriad of problems for you. Questioning yourself at every turn causes you to sometimes take no action at all, or worse, engage in self-sabotaging behavior.

Imagine if you told your best friend what you believe about yourself sometimes. In other words, what if you said to her: "*You're useless. I can't believe you made that mistake again. You just never learn do you?*" How do you think that would make her feel? Yet, you do it to yourself.

When you break yourself down you can't possibly expect to perform in any area of your life. And I really mean it when I say *YOU* are breaking *YOURSELF* down. When someone says something in a way that makes you feel like they are judging you or belittling you, you don't have to take it on board. You have a choice. You don't have to buy every item you swim past. Even if the hagglers are trying to force an item upon you. You can choose to simply walk away. It's not always comfortable, but with practice, it gets easier.

We've all heard the maxim: you are your own worst enemy. It goes for all of us. What causes us great stress, self-doubt, fear, and anxiety is not outside of us but within us. If I chose to focus on every one of the 70 000 thoughts that go through my mind on a daily basis, I'd never be able to get any work done or make enough money to live. I'd be a wreck.

That's exactly what overthinking does. It wrecks your confidence. It wrecks your relationships. It wrecks your health. It's a filthy liar. Choose not to engage with filthy liars.

Choose to use it to your advantage instead.

How you can use your overthinking tendencies to your advantage

Overthinking is all about dwelling on problems. It would not cost you any more or less energy to swing that around and spend it on something that would be more useful to you, like opportunities and solutions. So, I'm not suggesting that you stop overthinking, but rather channel that overthinking elsewhere.

As someone with ADHD, you do have certain superpowers. Your brain is excellent at solving problems. It hates tedium, and this can be the place from where ingenuity and creativity flow. It loves novelty, which means you're really good at coming up with new ways of doing things. It loves exploring – again – essential for coming up with solutions.

You just need to learn how to best channel your superpowers to your advantage.

I know you're probably thinking *"sure, but HOW do I get off the hamster wheel that is overthinking"*?

Action. Action gets you off the hamster wheel. Deciding on ONE thing you can do right now to change the negative thoughts you're fixated on, gets you off the hamster wheel. And I know a lot of you were probably hoping for a different answer but, action begets action. Without action, you stay in the hamster wheel.

By choosing to take action and do just ONE thing to help get you out of that rut, will help build your tolerance for dealing with real and perceived negativity.

You can take your ability to hyperfocus and point it at something useful by following these simple steps to help you get the most out of a task or project you need to complete.

- Turn off all possible distractions like your phone or email and social media notifications on your phone/laptop/desktop. Make use of noise-canceling headphones if you have a pair.
- Take some time to set up your work environment for optimal productivity. Clear out any clutter on your desk.
- Take out your favorite stationery. Get a piece of paper or your notebook and write at the top what it is you want to focus on. Make a list of at least three things you want to accomplish for this hyperfocus stint below the title.
- Now add no more than three descriptions next to the points you listed on *'how'* you're going to achieve those goals.
- Set yourself a timer for 50 minutes and aim to focus on working on only one of the bullet points on your list until the timer goes off.
- Take a 10-minute break when the timer goes off. Go make yourself a cup of tea or take a walk outside. The point is to get away from your desk.
- After your 10-minute break come back and set your timer again for another 50 minutes.
- Rinse and repeat. Decide on one task to focus on, make sure your workspace is set up, get rid of distractions, set yourself a timer for work periods, and take breaks in between.

Your beautiful creative mind can come up with multiple solutions at the same time it would take someone to still try to figure out the question.

Use that to your advantage! Claim your superpowers. Because they'll never not be a part of you.

Also, the action that you decide to take doesn't need to be the ultimate solution. A mistake many of us tend to make is to be all-or-nothing. It either needs to fix every problem in your life, others, and the universe, or nothing.

This is obviously not very useful, nor is it realistic or sustainable. So let's focus those amazing superpowers on not indulging in all-or-nothing thinking either, shall we?

Even though having ADHD does come with its own host of problems and challenges, there are also a lot of positives to be garnered for the greater good. Starting with yourself of course.

If there's only one lesson that you take away from this chapter, I hope that it is hope. (See what I did there).

Knowing that you have all these amazing superpowers available to you should leave you with a sense of hope. Many who have come before you have had to face the same problem and they ultimately learned how to overcome it. And so can you.

CHAPTER 3.

LEARN THE PRINCIPLES OF CALMING YOUR THOUGHTS

Why am I always overthinking?

Because your brain works faster than non-ADHD brains, on average, you can experience more thoughts that are negative. Although we think 70 000 thoughts a day on average, I don't think that accounts for neuro-atypical brains. I certainly feel like I think more than that a day. My brain *NEVER* shuts down, sometimes to the point where I wish I could just find a little off switch. Even if it was just for one day. Or an hour even. Heck, I'll settle for a few minutes.

Ok, technically none of our brains ever shut down because when that happens you are technically dead. But you know what I mean when I say my brain never shuts down. I guess a more accurate way of explaining it would be for me to say that my mind never shuts up.

Overthinking is a widespread problem that many of us experience. It happens when our minds are caught in a cycle of constant worries and thoughts, which causes tension and anxiety. We tend to overthink due to a variety of reasons, such as low self-esteem, fear of rejection or failure, previous experiences, and a propensity to dwell on negative thoughts. Overthinking can also be brought on by a lack of mental stimulation, a lack of direction, or boredom.

ADHD interferes with the brain's capacity to control impulses and attention, resulting in disorganized thinking and excessive behavior. This disorganized attention can make it difficult for us to control our thoughts, which can result in overthinking. Additionally, those of us who have ADHD may also feel more tension and anxiety, which might make us more prone to overthinking. In addition, we could experience issues with poor self-esteem, perfectionism, and a need for control, all of which can make the overthinking problem worse.[7]

Because we're able to deeply analyze things at speed, a simple rejection from a girl you've just asked out might develop into you thinking about a previous relationship that failed and before you know it, it's mutated into categorizing every failure you've ever had by date, time, and severity.

We're exceptionally good at doing research. The details matter to us. ALL OF IT! So if I'm going to start down the path of considering how my other failures possibly led to my most current perceived failure... well, this might take a while.

To add insult to injury, you probably also struggle with organizing things and your living space is in a state of organized chaos. Organized being the operative word here. You also struggle with remembering appointments and can experience time blindness, which sometimes causes you to miss appointments.

Every time any of these things are pointed out and commented on you cringe because you already feel bad about having ADHD due to the fact that you've been scolded all your life for not sitting still, or for accidentally dropping and breaking something (more than once), or for not paying attention when others expect you to.

As an adult, you now also have to contend with being judged for what others perceive to be your shortcomings. Like not having a super organized apartment or house. (*Just because it's in a state of organized chaos doesn't mean it's not clean by the way.*)

For being late to events on occasion due to time blindness. For struggling to keep up with personal hygiene. Can we please stop pretending as if everyone takes a shower twice a day and therefore we should as well? It's a myth, people!

Your brain is just wired differently. I'm sure you've heard that a thousand times before. It's true though, and as we've learned, that means that a lot of positives come with it.

Yes, you might have more of a tendency to fall prey to overthinking. Though some people with ADHD have the opposite problem where they don't pause to think or reflect on what they experience due to inattentiveness. They jump from one experience or event in their day to the next without learning from the experience. If you don't pause to think, you don't learn from the experience, and you don't take the time to put effort into finding a solution, you're essentially stuck in an infinite loop.

Overthinking means you do stop to contemplate an experience. Which means you can learn from it. Which means you can change your response to it. So there is hope.

What happens when I can't quiet my mind?

Mindfulness is the buzzword of the decade. In this fast-paced noisy modern world of ours, we must take some time out on a regular basis to practice quieting our minds. Like mini holidays for your hard-working brain essentially. Mindfulness is more of an umbrella term that includes various techniques for practicing quieting your mind. There are a number of practices that can help you practice mindfulness like meditation, techniques involving the senses, yoga practices, breathing exercises, and more.

In modern psychology, it has been found that overthinking is often associated with the need for a sense of control. Gifted individuals also tend to have a lot of channels in the brain that can lead to overthinking. [8] A need for control coupled with a potential for perfectionism unfortunately usually results in struggles with symptoms of anxiety and depression. As if not being able to shut down your mind isn't enough, you now have to contend with feeling overwhelmed about overthinking as well.

I feel exhausted just thinking about it. I so often wish that I could install an on/off switch that will allow me to turn off my mind with the flick of a button. Wouldn't that be nice? It would be such a relief to not have to think. Even in my dreams, my brain is going at a hundred miles an hour. It would be so amazing to just not have any thoughts even if for just a few minutes. I'm betting you can probably relate.

Overthinking is often a result of our mind not being able to find a solution. If the bottom line is that overthinking is all about control, it means that when we are facing adversity our mind tries to find a solution. If a solution isn't found fast, our thoughts get stuck in a loop due to the overwhelm linked with not being in control. [9]

When we feel like something is not within our control and it causes us to feel anxiety, that feeling of anxiety can be extremely uncomfortable. It's a visceral sensation of "I do not have a solution, I don't know what to do, and it's freaking me out." This can lead to physical sensations like heart palpitations, rapid shallow breathing, the sweats, feeling flustered, etc. Or what is more commonly known as an anxiety attack.

The urge to want to escape anything that feels uncomfortable to us is only natural. This includes feelings that we find uncomfortable. This is where your brain might 'detach' from your body (metaphorically of course), and escape into your thoughts. If you're rummaging around your thoughts to try to find an answer, you don't have to sit with the discomfort of your feelings.

It's when we are unable to truly just sit with our feelings and process why we are experiencing these emotions that we start looking for answers elsewhere. We fool ourselves into thinking that if we consider every possible scenario we're allowing ourselves to come up with solutions and that will make us better prepared for the next time something happens. Though in reality all we're doing is blocking cognitive processes from doing what they're supposed to whilst causing overstimulation.

The effects of ruminating can have devastating consequences for our overall health. When we're not allowing ourselves to work through these uncomfortable emotions we experience like fear, rejection, anger, sadness, etc. it can quite literally make us sick. Just think about it this way – if you have a wound and you don't do what you need to in order to help it heal, what will happen to that wound? It will fester and get infected, maybe even land you in the hospital.

Similarly, shoving down thoughts and/or feelings that make us feel uncomfortable or even hurt us, or entering a loop of overthinking, can lead to symptoms of depression, addiction, eating disorders, and self-harm.[10]

Mastering the art of keeping calm

I think the first step toward practicing the art of calm is to be able to identify what we are feeling, and more importantly, *why* we are feeling what we are feeling. So often, an overwhelming emotion might come up and we immediately try to get rid of it by either trying to ignore it or ruminating on the discomfort we're experiencing.

One of the greatest lessons I've learned over the last few years is that my mind and body seem to be happier when I'm doing things for myself. Meaning that it's more fulfilling when I exercise because I want to look after my own health, instead of exercising because I worry about what other people think. Or, it's easier to stick to a routine because I want to reach my goals, rather than engage in the culture of 'busyness' for the sake of fitting in.

I have found that the same goes for calming my own mind. It becomes a bit easier when I approach my anxieties and feelings of overwhelm with an attitude of curiosity, openness, and kindness toward myself with the aim of wanting to better understand why these thoughts and feelings make me feel the way I do. Like most of us, I have an insatiable need for understanding.

In this instance, I think non-judgmental understanding toward yourself is the key.

I think we often forget that we are not here to please anyone else or to live for anyone else but ourselves. Easier said than done – I know – but the truth is you are deserving of love, care, understanding, and kindness just the way you are.

When we reach a place of self-acceptance it starts getting a little easier to take a step back and view the things that cause us to experience anxiety from a place of curiosity, rather than judging our perceived flaws that need fixing immediately.

Luckily, there are a number of calming strategies that can help calm down the ADHD brain.

Before we can even start considering how to contain our thoughts, we first need to make sure we're looking after ourselves in all other aspects. Having ADHD means having to deal with a whole host of symptoms that can make everyday life difficult. By implementing a strategy that you practice regularly, you can take a step towards taking back control of your overexcitable brain.

Here are a number of strategies for you to consider:

MAKE SURE YOU STAY ON TOP OF TAKING YOUR MEDS

There are more tools available to us today than ever before when it comes to treating symptoms of ADHD. Although pill shaming is a real thing a lot of people experience, you need to take advantage of all the tools available to you that can help make your life easier. There's no need to punish yourself for no reason. Or any reason for that matter.

When it comes to taking medication it is best to try and take it at the same time every day.[11] If you find it difficult to keep track of your medication, set yourself a reminder on your phone. A lot of people with ADHD don't like lists or reminders, in which case you can associate taking your medication with something you need to do every day. Like taking your meds with breakfast or dinner.

The important thing is to try to not skip out on meds and be consistent with when you take them. ADHD makes consistency tough, but not impossible.

GET ENOUGH SLEEP!

We all know sleep is important for you, but suffering from ADHD can mean that sleep often seems to elude you. Many children and adults who suffer from ADHD also suffer from sleep disorders. In fact, it's something that seems to go hand-in-hand with all neuroatypical-related disorders. Sleep disorders affect up to 4 out of 5 adults who suffer from ADHD.[12]

The average adult needs 7 – 9 hours of sleep a night. While the ideal amount of sleep can vary from one adult to the next, this is a good rule of thumb, according to the National Sleep Foundation.[13]

Sleep is essential in helping boost your immune system as well as flushing out the byproducts of the day's thinking from the brain with cerebro-spinal fluid. Not getting enough sleep can have a negative effect on our cognitive processes and ability to concentrate. This is already a challenge for people with ADHD, so you don't need the additional challenge.

Make sure you use your bedroom for sleep and sex only. Clear out all devices from your room to make sure it's free of distractions. It helps to follow a bedtime ritual. A good rule is to not eat anything within 3 hours of your bedtime. No fluids within 2 hours of your bedtime, and no screens within 1 hour of your bedtime. Except for a Kindle maybe. Just stay away from anything with a blue light. Make sure your bedroom is nice and cool; as it will help you fall and stay asleep.

In my personal experience, the number one rule that makes a big difference in my life is to make sure I wind down at least an hour before I go to bed by shutting off all screens and not eating or drinking anything. Then I read until I am ready to go to sleep. This works for me. That and making sure I take my medication at the prescribed time.

MOVE YOUR BODY

I am guilty when it comes to not moving my body around enough. I'm a writer, which means I sit at my laptop all day doing research and writing. Leading a sedentary lifestyle is bad for your health. We all know that, and I'm pretty sure you've heard the new saying that "sitting is the new smoking." That's not entirely accurate, but studies conducted by the Mayo Clinic have shown that people who sit for extended periods of time without moving are at as equal a risk of developing health risks as people who smoke or are obese.[14]

We all know exercise is good for both our bodies and our minds in so many aspects. Move your body at least once a day. It doesn't have to be a high-intensity CrossFit workout. It can be:

- Going for a walk.
- Some gentle yoga.
- Stretching exercises.
- Pilates.
- Cycling.

Or it can be a high-intensity CrossFit workout if that's your thing. I have this rule now where I get up from my desk every hour and walk up and down my garden for five minutes. I've set timers on my phone to remind me to get up and move. I also throw in drinking a glass of water whilst I'm at it.

GIVE YOUR BRAIN A BREAK FROM EXTERNAL STIMULI

I've only recently bought myself a set of noise-canceling headphones and it has changed my life! I wish I had known about these when I was a child growing up. Though back then they didn't have noise-canceling headphones or air pods. I had a Walkman (giving away my age here). That's about as close as I got.

Although sensory overload is usually more closely related to Autism, studies have shown that it can also go hand-in-hand with ADHD. [15] Many adults who suffer from ADHD struggle to focus when there is too much going on in their environments. I know my best friend who has ADHD (predominantly inattentive type) really struggles at work as people walk in and out of her office all day and it's very distracting. People with a neuroatypical brain also sometimes find it difficult to get back to what they were doing once they've been interrupted.

We all have our own unique sensory profiles. Some people are sensory sensitive to some stimuli, but sensory seeking to others. For instance, I am sensory sensitive to sound, light, and touch. This means I don't like loud noise, bright lights, or strangers touching me or standing too close to me. It freaks out my nervous system. I loved social distancing during the Covid-19 pandemic, to be honest. Though I am sensory seeking when it comes to movement and smell. I like to move my body and I love a person or a place that smells nice.

Because I know what my sensory profile looks like, I can set up my environment in such a way that it's more soothing to my nervous system. I have block-out curtains for example, and only use warm-white low-wattage light bulbs. I have a diffuser in my home with scents that I like, like lavender and vanilla. Now that I have a set of noise-canceling headphones, they are a part of me no matter where I go. As for personal space, I've figured out that if I place a shopping cart behind me in the grocery store instead of in front of me, I can control the distance of both the person in front of and behind me in proximity to where I'm standing. You're welcome.

When our nervous system is overwhelmed due to sensory overload it can be difficult to focus. You can fill out a free assessment online to get a rundown on your own personal sensory processing style by visiting the Sensory IntelligenceTM website.[16]

TAKE ACTION!

When we are stuck in that place of ruminating, it can lead to all sorts of negative byproducts such as procrastination, guilt, self-loathing, imposter syndrome, and depression. The best way to get out of your head is to take action. Do something. Anything! Even if you just go for a walk or wash the dishes or go visit a friend. Like James Redfield said: *"Where attention goes, energy flows.*

Taking action is the antidote to the poison that is overthinking. It's when we indulge in sitting in the puddle of rumination that things go awry. Often that also permeates throughout every aspect of our lives. It's like that meme of two individuals painting whilst sitting in the prison cell they share. The one paints that prison cell, because that's all he can see. The other focuses on what's beyond the cell and paints the beautiful landscape outside.

Ask yourself what it is you're indulging in focusing on? Because at the end of the day, it is a choice, and choice is our most powerful weapon.

Meditation and relaxation techniques for keeping calm

I personally have a number of friends who have ADHD, and I know from experience the moment I mention *meditation*, they immediately go *"nope, it doesn't work with an ADHD brain."*

I think a lot of ADHDers feel this way. I get it. It's hard enough to try to get your ducks in a row when you actually don't have any ducks but a bunch of squirrels at a rave instead. Nevermind trying to force yourself to sit still in one place for an extended period of time whilst trying to clear your mind. It's not easy. Not even for neurotypicals.

Meditation is a concept that has been a part of various religious and spiritual practices for thousands of years. Today it has religious ties with various cultures and religions around the world including Judaism,

Hinduism, Sikhism, and of course Buddhism. Archeology dates the origins of meditation back to as early as 5,000 BCE. [17]

There are teachers of meditation out there who suffer from ADHD themselves. As we've learned in previous chapters, the ADHD brain has this constant need to engage in pleasurable activities that will allow it to get its fix of dopamine. Forcing yourself to sit still and focus on just your breathing is a challenge for people with ADHD, but it can help teach you how to build up a tolerance by easing into the discomfort of not scrolling through your phone or doing a million things at once which can also drive anxiety. [18]

There are many potential benefits related to meditation like:

- Lowering your blood pressure.
- Improving your sleep.
- Increasing creativity.
- Helping you focus on, and live, in the here and now.
- Calming your nervous system.
- Build self-awareness.
- And many more.

The practice of meditation is more than just sitting in one spot and focusing on your breathing, and because it can be a challenge for ADHDers, here are some ADHD-specific tools you can try out to help you get into a meditation practice.

➊ Start by grounding yourself

Practicing various grounding techniques can really help *'ground' (hence the term)* you in the present moment. These techniques usually include practices that involve the senses and/or visualization. By connecting with your body and getting in touch with your senses you can effectively 'get out of your own head', which is great for combatting overthinking.

Use the senses: There is a great technique used in Cognitive Behavioral Therapy called the 5-4-3-2-1 technique. It is usually used in the event of a panic attack and helps one calm yourself down by focusing on your five senses to both distract you from the overwhelming symptoms you are experiencing, and ground you in the moment.

It goes like this: Find a quiet place where you can sit or lie down. (In reality, you can do this absolutely anywhere. I've practiced this technique in grocery stores, banks, at home, in the office, etc.) Next, focus on the following:

- **5 things** in your environment that you can **see**.
- **4 things** in your environment that you can **feel/touch** – like the texture of your clothes, stroking your cat, etc.
- **3 things** you can **hear** – like birds chirping outside, a printer going in the office, etc.
- **2 things** you can **smell** – like the smell of your hair (if you have long hair, otherwise it would be a bit of a struggle to smell your own hair), perfume, food, a beverage, your clothes, etc. (Maybe don't smell your colleagues. That would be weird.)
- **1 thing** you can **taste**.

❷ Just observe your thoughts

I think many people have this misconception that meditation is all about sitting in the lotus position and clearing your mind of any and all thoughts. If your primary focus is going to be on 'clearing your mind', I can almost guarantee that you will fail.

Meditation is more about *'observing'* **non-judgmentally** than it is about *'not thinking'*.

So try this instead: just observe your thoughts. No judgment. No need to try and control them. Just observe. Then every time you become cognizant of being distracted, just bring yourself back to observing your thoughts. Imagine your thoughts are clouds drifting in and out of your mind.

3. Do a body scan coupled with progressive muscle relaxation

This is my go-to technique when I cannot sleep. I always find that it relaxes me to a point where I can fall asleep. Though for this step we'll essentially be combining two different techniques.

The body scan is focused on 'scanning' your body from head to toe (or the other way around) and just focusing on each part of your body to notice how it feels. Do you notice any aches or pains? An area that needs stretching or a massage perhaps. Again, this helps to connect to your body and get you out of your head.

Then you are going to find a quiet place where you can either lie down or sit comfortably. Next, you're going to run the focus on different parts of your body again, either top-down or bottom-up. Focusing on your breathing, you want to contract the muscles in the area you're focusing on, on your in-breath – then relax on the out-breath.

E.g. Contracting all the muscles in your feet as you slowly breathe in through your nose, then relax as you slowly breathe out through your mouth. Then contract your calf muscles on the next in-breath, and relax as you breathe out, and so on, and so on.

4. Visual focus-point.

This is one I find especially useful for ADHDers. Because we neuroatypical folk have a dozen tabs open whilst working and having conversations and watching television at the same time, focusing on something with your eyes closed can feel like an impossible task.

Implementing a strategy that involves a single visual point to focus on can help you to build up a tolerance for forcing your brain to focus on *one thing* for more than a few seconds.

You can achieve this by either using a candle or finding a point on a wall to focus on. All you do is literally just look at that point on the wall or the flame of the candle and keep your focus there. Maybe you'll find that you're only able to focus on that point successfully for a minute, or thirty seconds even. That's okay. The next time you try to build it up to two minutes, then three minutes, etc.

As you can see now, there are various ways of practicing meditation. The key is to find what works best for you. Not all techniques work the same for everyone. We're all unique individuals with unique brains and nervous systems.

Lastly, be kind to yourself. Some days it will be easier than others and that's perfectly normal. Perfection is not the aim here. Practice is. The more you practice, the better you'll get at it. Like anything else in life.

CHAPTER 4.

IMPROVING FOCUS AND CONCENTRATION

Focus vs Concentration (Similarities and Differences)

Despite the fact that focus and concentration refer to separate aspects of your attention, they are sometimes used interchangeably. Concentration is the capacity to sustain one's attention on a particular item, task, or activity over an extended length of time. Focus, on the other hand, is where you choose to concentrate.

If I asked you to concentrate on a painting, you would probably shift your focus to different parts of the painting. Your concentration is taking in the entire painting, your focus is on the specific areas of the painting you are looking at and taking in.

Focusing your attention is an intentional and conscious action. It is the capacity to tune out outside noise and focus solely on one job. Focusing enables us to devote all of our mental resources and attention to the task at hand, which improves performance. For instance, when preparing for an exam, a student needs to concentrate on their notes and textbooks in order to absorb the material and recall it afterward.

Concentration involves both needing to focus on certain specifics and being able to do so for a certain period of time. As the mind has to continuously focus on the job at hand and ward off any distractions that may be present in your environment, it means that concentration involves mental effort. For instance, even when they are feeling tired and their mind is telling them to quit, long-distance runners must focus on keeping up their pace.

Although both focus and concentration are crucial for peak performance, they serve different purposes in the pursuit of success. The first step is focus, which enables you to direct your attention to the current work, and concentration, which enables you to sustain that focus for a prolonged period of time. You can work effectively and efficiently when you have both focus and concentration because you can direct your attention toward your activity and keep it there for a longer amount of time.

Both focus and concentration functions can be increased in a number of ways, including through meditation, physical exercise, and getting enough sleep at night. It is simpler to focus attention on a task when you are calmer and more aware of your surroundings. Physical activity on the other hand boosts blood flow to the brain and enhances its functionality, i.e. ability to focus and concentrate.[19]

Does ADHD Make it Hard to Focus?

One of the most common symptoms of ADHD is difficulties with focus and attention, leading some to question whether having ADHD makes it harder to focus.

The answer is yes, having ADHD can make it harder to focus. People with ADHD often have difficulty sustaining attention and filtering out distractions, which can make it difficult for them to focus on a task for an extended period of time. They may also experience what is known as "mind racing," in which their thoughts wander constantly and they are unable to concentrate on a single task. This can make it challenging for people with ADHD to complete tasks, follow instructions, and stay organized.

However, it is important to note that not all individuals with ADHD have difficulties with focus and attention, and the severity of these difficulties can vary widely from person to person. Some individuals with ADHD may have relatively mild difficulties with focus, while others may have severe difficulties that significantly impact their daily life.

Several factors can contribute to difficulties with focus in individuals with ADHD. These include an inability to regulate attention, difficulties with working memory, and an overactive reward system in the brain. For example, people with ADHD may have a low threshold for boredom, which can lead to difficulties sustaining attention. They may also be easily distracted by sights, sounds, and other stimuli, making it difficult for them to tune out distractions.

With strategies like the ones to follow, you can develop effective coping strategies to improve both your focus and concentration skills.

Strategies and Concentration – Building Techniques

Any challenge you experience in your life will need a strategy to overcome said challenge. Sometimes the first strategy you try might not be the one that helps you overcome the challenge you're experiencing. Or perhaps it just doesn't work for you. Other times you might need outside help to overcome a challenge in your life. This is the same for all of us – and challenges relating to ADHD are no different.

Here is a list of strategies you can try out to see which might help you overcome your own struggles with concentration:

1. **Structure your environment:** A structured environment can help reduce distractions and promote focus. This may involve creating a dedicated workspace, minimizing clutter, and setting aside specific times for work and relaxation.

2. **Make a to-do list:** This is one of those tools that people either love or hate. I myself love a to-do list. I make a list of tasks I need to achieve every day. It helps me to catch myself when I'm going off track and need reminding of what I'm supposed to be doing.

3. **Break tasks into smaller parts:** Breaking larger tasks into smaller, more manageable parts can assist you in maintaining focus and avoiding becoming overwhelmed. This can also help to prevent procrastination, which can further exacerbate symptoms of ADHD.

4. **Use images:** Visual aids, such as pictures, diagrams, or videos, can help individuals with ADHD to better understand and retain information. This can help to increase focus and reduce distractions. I know I am very much a visual learner.

5. **Establish routines:** Establishing routines can help individuals with ADHD to better manage their time and maintain focus. This may involve setting specific times for work, exercise, and relaxation. It has been found that individuals who prioritize doing their most difficult tasks first and leave the easier tasks for later in the day tend to be more productive and successful in their careers. Again, we're all different and you need to find what works best for you. [20]

6. **Limit distractions:** Minimizing distractions can help individuals with ADHD maintain focus. This may involve turning off notifications on your phone, using noise-canceling headphones, and avoiding social media and other time-wasting activities while working. These days you can set a time limit on certain apps that will lock you out during certain times of the day.

7. **Use memory games & techniques:** Memory techniques, such as mnemonics, can help individuals with ADHD to retain information and improve focus. These techniques work by associating new information with something you already know, making it easier to recall.

8. **Seek professional help:** If you've tried everything and you're still struggling, you may benefit from seeking professional help, such as therapy or medication. A mental health professional can help you to develop a personalized plan to manage symptoms and build better concentration skills.

Focus Exercises For People With ADHD

Several exercises can help individuals with ADHD improve their focus and attention. People with ADHD can take everyday tasks and turn them into brain games or mental activities that can help boost dopamine levels, and in turn, focus.

Here are a few exercises and strategies for you to try out:

1. **Avoid Multitasking:** If you don't know it yet, I'm sorry to have to inform you that multitasking is technically impossible. When we 'multitask' by focusing on different tasks at the 'same time' – what's actually happening is that your brain is switching focus between tasks at a rapid rate. This means your full attention is never on a single task.

   Staying focused on a single task for at least some time is necessary to complete any given task. [21]

2. **Try The Pomodoro Technique:** I've been implementing this specific tool to help with my own productivity and focus over the last year or so and can attest to its validity. It works a bit like 'time blocking' and involves breaking down work into short intervals (usually 25 minutes) with short breaks in between.

   You can download a Pomodoro app to your phone which will run the Pomodoro timing cycle of 4 x 25 minutes working cycles with 5-minute breaks in between. Then after you've completed the fourth 25-minute work stint you get to take a longer, 15-minute break. [22]

3. **Mind Mapping:** This is a visual tool for organizing and categorizing information, which can be helpful, especially for someone who struggles to organize their thoughts. As the name suggests, mind mapping involves 'mapping out' ideas or tasks to help you keep track of sequences and which tasks relate to which.

4. **Sensory Integration:** Engaging in activities that stimulate the senses, such as playing with playdough or jumping on a trampoline, can help individuals with ADHD improve their focus and attention. Standing desks can be useful for moving around whilst working.

5. **Become A Parrot:** I used to offer motorcycle training as an instructor and one of the things I'm really not good at is remembering names, especially when I have to remember fifteen new names all at once. I learned this technique which involves parroting back information as it's said. E.g. As we'd go around the room introducing ourselves I would repeat people's names in my head one by one. This helped me to be able to remember multiple people's names at a time.

   At work, you can repeat instructions back as they're given to you. This does two things: it shows the other person that you have listened to what they said, and it helps you to ensure you understand the instructions correctly as well as remember the details of the task.

6. **Use Visual Reminders:** We can so often forget about something that needs doing once it has been moved out of the 'do this now' folder and into the 'for later' folder. Which is why I love lists. If I can see it I can remind myself of what I've done and what still needs doing. Sticky notes work great for reminding yourself of certain tasks that need completing or deadlines, etc. We all know the saying: "out of sight, out of mind."

7. **Practice Self-Care:** Self-care is something that I believe to be so important, yet so few people really take the time to practice taking care of themselves. You need to look after yourself first before you can accomplish anything else. Although many think of self-care as only involving spa days and gourmet meals, it's so much more than that. Self-care involves also holding yourself accountable by doing the things you don't really want to; like eating healthy and working out. These things ultimately add to being able to better look after your body and maybe more importantly, your brain.

Does Medication Help To Improve Focus?

Although medication is not a cure for ADHD, it does help improve focus in individuals who suffer from ADHD. It's important to note that it does not work the same way on a neurotypical brain. In years past, many students have turned to drugs like Adderall or Ritalin to help them focus when they're studying. Although it might result in giving you a boost in energy, it doesn't necessarily help you focus better. Reason being that it was developed for the neuroatypical brain and not for someone with a 'normal' brain.

A study conducted at the UC Irvine Sleep and Cognition Lab at the University of California aimed to study whether taking a drug like Adderall would result in an increase in the ability to retain information as they're studying. [23]

The study ultimately showed that stimulants caused significant disruptions in nighttime sleep and had no effect on working memory.

The way that medication helps an ADHD brain focus is by balancing out certain chemicals so they can do their job better and pass the information along neural pathways in your brain in a better manner. Two of these chemicals involved in the process are dopamine and norepinephrine.

A friend of mine who is a brilliant psychiatrist once described it like this to a patient of hers: "the medication is like the scaffolding that helps keep things together whilst you're working on putting healthier coping mechanisms in place." Meaning it's not a cure, it's just there to help. And there is nothing wrong with using every tool available to you when you need help.

Just know that if you don't suffer from ADHD, the medication won't help. It might actually have the opposite effect. It's like taking heart medication to help heal your metaphorically broken heart. It's not going to help. It might just make things worse with unwanted side effects because the medication wasn't developed to heal metaphorically broken hearts, it was developed to heal physically broken hearts.

Guided Meditations To Help Improve Focus

Suffering from ADHD might make you feel like meditation is an impossible task. As we now know, medication plays an important role in helping alleviate symptoms in individuals with ADHD. We'll still explore different therapeutic models for the treatment of ADHD in the upcoming chapters, but in this section, we'll be focusing on guided meditation.

Research shows that adults who practice meditation report a decrease in impulsivity and distractibility, and 40% of those who practice it daily give it high ratings in helping to alleviate their symptoms. [24]

The ADHD brain is hooked on adrenaline because it helps wake up those sluggish frontal lobes of your brain. It seems pretty obvious to think that running on adrenaline on a regular basis might have negative effects in the long run. When I say adrenaline, I'm not just referring to jumping off airplanes or going on rollercoaster rides. Any kind of drama in our lives also causes a rise in adrenaline and cortisol, which is why so many people with ADHD become addicted to drama, even creating it to get that kick of adrenaline so their brain can work better. Although adrenaline boosts the immune system, the stress hormone, cortisol, that accompanies adrenaline can divert important chemical and protein resources away from your immune system, which ultimately causes illness. Just think about it, anyone who has ever run on stress for an extended period of time will eventually burn out and become physically ill.

So practicing meditation can help give your body, brain, and immune system a break from the adrenaline roller coaster so it can have access to the resources it needs to function optimally.

Before we get into what guided meditation is, here are a few tips to be aware of before you start:

MEDITATE AT THE SAME TIME EVERY DAY

I have tried meditating at different times of the day. Either first thing in the morning to help organize my thoughts and get ready for the day, or at night before I go to bed to help my brain settle down for a good night's sleep. For me, personally, first thing in the morning works best. I find it's when I'm most likely to get things done, so when I leave it for the evening chances are it might not happen.

Sitting down to meditate in the morning has helped me to make it part of my morning routine, so now I do it without needing to think about it. I think by meditating at the same time every day you're boosting your odds of successfully working it into your schedule and making a habit of it.

COMFORT IS EVERYTHING

I think the reason so many people are put off by meditation is that they perceive it as something really uncomfortable. I know that was my initial perception of the practice. Though in reality, you don't need to sit in a perfect lotus position to practice meditation. You don't even have to sit, you can lie down if that's more comfortable for you. The point is to find a position that feels most comfortable to you.

On the point of comfort, also make sure to wear comfortable clothes. Or no clothes if that's your thing. No judgment here; you do you. Wearing comfortable clothes will help keep you from getting distracted by scratchy labels or a certain piece of material cutting off the circulation in your legs.

GET RID OF ALL DISTRACTIONS

This point is pretty self-explanatory I think. Turn off your phone and any other devices that could potentially cause you to feel distracted. If you live with someone or have your family around, notify them that this is your 'me time' and ask that they do not disturb you.

FOCUS ON YOUR BREATHING

I personally find this very helpful. Mindfulness meditation is something I can practice anywhere at any time and I find it helps me to bring back my focus to the present moment, instead of my focus jumping around all over the place.

It's important to approach mindfulness meditation with an open and non-judgmental attitude. The goal is not to achieve a certain state of mind, but rather to simply be present and aware of your thoughts, feelings, and sensations in the moment. Start by just focusing on your breathing. You're not trying to breathe in and out a certain way. You're just noticing your breath. Do this for a minute and then turn your attention to the sensations you notice as you're breathing in and out. Does your belly rise? What happens to your rib cage? Etc.

If you get distracted and realize you've wandered off, just gently bring yourself back to focusing on your breath. There is no right or wrong way to meditate, so you literally cannot screw it up. Which ties in with our next point.

ALLOW YOUR MIND TO WANDER

It is only natural for your mind to wander. So many people think that meditation is all about being super strict with yourself and forcing your mind not to have any thoughts whilst sitting in the lotus position for hours on end. If this is your perception of meditation, you're setting yourself up for failure.

You're not a monk. You haven't lived all your life dedicating thousands of hours to the art of meditation, so you can't expect yourself to have monk-like focus when meditating. That's not the point of meditation anyway.

Your mind WILL wander. Allow it to. Then just gently guide it back to home base when you become aware that your mind has left the building.

SET REALISTIC, ACHIEVABLE GOALS FOR YOURSELF

If you've never meditated before and you leave the starting blocks with the aim of sitting still for half an hour whilst trying to force your mind to not have any thoughts, I can 100% guarantee you that you will fail. Success looks different to different people and it's important to be kind and gentle with yourself. If you learn nothing else from meditation other than how to practice kindness towards yourself, then I'd count that as a huge success.

There is no right or wrong when it comes to meditation, so you don't have to practice for a certain amount of time for it to 'count'. Maybe that means starting with just trying it out for 2 minutes a day and then slowly increasing it by thirty seconds at a time. That's perfectly fine. Find what works for you, set realistic goals, and be gentle with yourself.

USE SENSORY CUES TO HELP YOU MOVE FROM ONE STATE TO ANOTHER

This might seem silly but it really isn't. Using different sensory cues like wearing your 'meditation hat' or 'meditation pants' can help your transition from one state to another. It tells the brain that you're not moving from one activity to another. You might also have a specific meditation spot you sit in, or certain scented candles you burn when you meditate. All of these can help as cues to notify your brain that "we're going to meditate now."

USE MINDFULNESS AND GUIDED MEDITATIONS

These two forms of meditation work best when the aim is to cultivate kindness and understanding toward yourself. It allows you to move out of a position of judgment and into a place of non-judgmental observation.

Guided meditation is led by a teacher or an individual through a video or an audio clip that you listen to. It's usually accompanied by some soothing background music whilst the person talks you through the experience. This is definitely something I'd recommend to someone if they're just starting as it makes it a bit easier to be led by someone rather than just going at it on your own from the get-go. Though, even if you're an expert it is always very helpful. I don't consider myself an expert meditator at all but I do know that it's sometimes easier for me to listen to a guided meditation, especially if I'm tired or have been working very hard.

There are numerous tools available these days that will introduce you to guided meditations, like the well-known Headspace app for example. (*Headspace*, www.headspace.com) There are numerous other applications you can download onto your phone that offer daily guided meditations, as well as many videos dedicated to this topic on YouTube.

A guided meditation will give you instructions to follow like: "*breathe in slowly through your nose, noticing how your belly rises as you breathe in, then exhale slowly through your mouth, noticing how your chest falls as you breathe out."* It can be quite helpful to just follow along with instructions, so I really would suggest that you try it out.

Foods That Help Improve Focus

Food is one of our body's primary sources of energy, and what we eat greatly affects our capacity for concentration and focus. For optimum brain function and cognitive efficiency, a well-balanced diet full of nutrients, vitamins, and minerals is crucial. The following foods can improve concentration and brain function.

Foods rich in protein: like pork, lean beef, eggs, low-fat dairy products, and beans can help prevent surges in blood sugar that cause hyperactivity and impulsivity.

Blueberries: Blueberries are renowned for their high quantities of anti-inflammatory and antioxidant compounds that help shield the brain from oxidative stress and damage. Blueberries are a great dietary choice for people who need to focus for extended periods of time because they also contain components that enhance memory and learning ability.

Nuts: particularly almonds, walnuts, and hazelnuts, are a great source of protein, good fats, and protein that provide a constant supply of energy for the brain. Additionally, they are rich in vitamin E, which has been demonstrated to enhance memory and cognitive performance.

Avocados: These fruits are a great source of monounsaturated fats, which are vital for the health of the brain. Additionally, they are rich in potassium, which helps control blood flow to the brain and enhances cognitive function.

Omega-3 fatty acids, which have been demonstrated to enhance cognitive ability and brain function, are an excellent source of nutrition in salmon. Additionally, omega-3 fatty acids aid in lowering inflammation in the brain, which over time may result in a loss in cognitive function.

Green leafy veggies: Iron and B vitamins, which are critical for brain health, are abundant in green leafy vegetables like spinach and kale. Additionally, they are rich in antioxidants, which help shield the brain from oxidative stress and damage.

Whole grains: Whole grains are a great source of fiber, vitamins, and minerals. Examples of whole grains are oatmeal and brown rice. They give the brain slow-release energy, allowing it to maintain focus and concentration all day long.

Foods to avoid: This is not singular to ADHD but foods you should try to avoid are simple carbohydrates like pasta, white rice, or potatoes, as well as processed foods and too much sugar. The brain is a glucose-hungry organ that needs sugar to function [25] – this doesn't mean eating chocolate all day, it simply means that you might want to add some fruits to your diet on a daily basis.

Avoiding these foods and including the foods recommended above in your diet can help you be more focused and perform better mentally. To provide your brain with the energy and nutrition it requires to perform at its best, it's crucial to maintain a well-balanced diet and eat a range of nutrient-dense foods.

Hyperfocus In ADHD And How To Manage It

Hyperfocus is the term for an extended time of great concentration on one task or activity, frequently at the sacrifice of other very important duties and commitments. It is a typical sign of attention deficit hyperactivity disorder and, depending on the circumstance, it can be both helpful and disturbing. Hyperfocusing is when you concentrate on something so hard and so deeply that you lose track of everything else, e.g. time, eating and drinking, other tasks, appointments, etc.

While being overly focused might boost creativity and productivity, it can also result in poor time management, procrastination, and the neglect of other crucial activities. Hyperfocus can make it difficult to switch between tasks and pay attention for a long time, but it is also thought to be related to the brain's capacity to block out distractions and concentrate intensely on a job.

So as you can see it can be useful in the case of needing to dig in to a project that really needs all your attention, but can be less-than-useful when it causes friction at work because you keep missing deadlines on other projects.

Here are a few tips on how you can manage hyper focusing:

1. Make a list of things you tend to hyperfocus on so you are aware of them. Investigate what particularly it is that you like to hyperfocus on and why? This level of self-awareness will help you monitor when hyperfocus has taken over when you need to be completing a different task.
2. Don't start something you can easily hyperfocus on close to bedtime. Chances are you won't be getting much sleep that night which has a whole domino effect on symptoms you'll experience in days to come.
3. Use some of the mindfulness exercises you've learned to help ground you in the here and now so you aren't caught up in the hyperfocus state.
4. Use timers to help you with completing certain tasks and chores. If you do get distracted and hyperfocus on something else, an alarm will help pull you out of that state and reset your focus again.
5. Find yourself an accountability buddy who checks up on you or who you need to report to on your progress. It can help keep you on track.
6. Break tasks into smaller chunks and give yourself a mini high-five every time you complete a task.

Anyone can fall victim to hyper-focusing and it has its advantages. You just need to practice self-awareness so you can either redirect your focus to more important tasks or call on your hyperfocus superpowers when you need to finish an important project and work on a deadline.

Should I Consider Neurofeedback Therapy?

Neurofeedback therapy, commonly referred to as EEG biofeedback, is a type of therapy that teaches people how to self-regulate their brain function by using real-time displays of brain activity, frequently in the form of EEG waves.

By teaching patients to manage particular patterns of brain activity, neurofeedback therapy aims to assist patients in improving specific mental and physical ailments, such as anxiety, sadness, sleeplessness, and ADHD. The non-invasive therapy typically uses scalp-mounted sensors to record brain activity, which is then shown in real-time on a computer screen.

Some studies have shown promising results with neurofeedback therapy as a potential treatment for Attention Deficit Hyperactivity Disorder (ADHD). To compare neurofeedback's efficacy to other treatments, additional study is required as the evidence for it as a treatment for ADHD is still growing.

It is crucial to remember that evidence-based therapies for ADHD like medication and behavioral therapy should not be replaced by neurofeedback. The alternative is to combine it with other treatments as an adjuvant therapy. A mental health expert should be consulted before beginning any ADHD treatment program, as well.

That being said, neurofeedback therapy does hold a number of positives such as:

- It's natural. The efficacy relies on the brain's natural ability to learn a new behavior that can lead to long-lasting positive results. It doesn't rely on any substances or medications.

- It's efficient. Most patients report long-lasting positive results after completing a program that consists of 30 – 40 sessions, with sessions held at least twice a week.
- The scientific evidence gathered to date looks promising. I'm one of those individuals that will tell you from the get-go: "*show me the science.*" Even though more studies are needed, Neurofeedback therapy is based on scientifically proven protocols that show improvements in both impulsivity and inattention. [26]
- Improves sleep.
- It has no side effects.
- It's safe to use.

Seeing as it is a natural therapy with no negative side effects, I'd say it's definitely something worth trying out just to see if it works for you. If nothing else, it might be a good learning experience.

CHAPTER 5.

STRENGTHENING YOUR MEMORY

ADHD And Memory Issues

The cognitive system in charge of temporarily storing and rearranging information required for task completion is referred to as working memory. Working memory is a common problem for people with ADHD, and these people may have trouble remembering and applying information to immediate activities. This may lead to forgetfulness and a diminished capacity for handling difficult activities.

In those with ADHD, long-term memory, which involves storing and recalling prior events, is typically unaffected. However, due to issues with attention and working memory, people may still have trouble recalling and retrieving the knowledge they had previously stored. Particularly when asked to concentrate attention for an extended amount of time, like during lectures, people with ADHD may have trouble memorizing material.

It is crucial to remember that comorbid illnesses like anxiety and depression as well as the usage of specific drugs can make memory issues in people with ADHD worse. Additionally, people with ADHD may struggle with organization and time management, which can further hinder their memory capacity.

People with ADHD can employ a variety of tactics to enhance their memory, such as mindfulness and relaxation exercises, task-splitting techniques, the use of memory aides like flashcards or mnemonics, and a reduction in distractions. Additionally, ADHD medications and behavioral therapy can aid in enhancing focus and reducing impulsivity, which may enhance memory performance.

Memory issues are a prevalent concern in people with ADHD and can negatively affect their daily lives. However, there are a number of methods and therapies, such as medication, behavioral therapy, and lifestyle modifications, that can help enhance memory performance. To choose the best course of action, it is crucial to consult a mental health expert.

Does Mind Mapping Work?

Making a visual representation of concepts and data is part of the mind-mapping approach. It has been proposed as a viable method for helping people with attention deficit hyperactivity disorder organize their thoughts and memory (ADHD).

According to research, mind mapping can be a useful tool for people with ADHD because it enables them to connect information in a non-linear, visual way that may be simpler for them to absorb and remember than conventional linear note-taking techniques. Additionally, mind mapping can assist people with ADHD in identifying and prioritizing vital information as well as minimizing environmental distractions. [27]

It's crucial to remember that mind mapping does not treat ADHD, and each person will respond to the technique differently. While some ADHD sufferers might find mind mapping to be a valuable tool for enhancing memory and organization, others might not.

Mind mapping can be a helpful method for those with ADHD who have trouble remembering things and staying organized. To find what functions best for each person, it is crucial to experiment with various strategies and instruments. For a thorough assessment and treatment plan for ADHD, it is also crucial to seek the guidance of a mental health specialist.

Principles Of Mind Mapping

Making a visual representation of concepts and data is part of the mind-mapping approach. The foundation of mind mapping is the premise that organizing knowledge visually can aid in better understanding, memory, and organization. The following are some important mind mapping principles as per the inventor of mind map, Tony Buzan[28]:

1. A mind map, in its purest form, should be organic, with corresponding ideas branching out from the central idea. The lines for the branches start thick and narrow as they branch out.
2. Each branch should only have one word on it. This is important as it is almost like the root from which more ideas and associations will flow as you expand your map.
3. Your branch section should only be as long as your word on it. This helps with a visual queue associated with that word which makes it easier to remember.
4. Color is important as it stimulates creativity and makes concepts easier to remember when you associate certain ideas with certain colors.
5. Use images in your notes. These can be sketches and doodles that help you to better remember certain associations. I am a visual thinker and learner and use a lot of sketching and doodling in my notes.
6. Choose words that create an image for you in your mind. This makes the association stronger, which, again, makes it easier to remember.

7. Lastly, clarity is important when you structure your mind map. If you're writing by hand, make sure your handwriting is legible. In this instance, clarity also refers to the ideas you jot down. Be clear on what it is you want to include and omit from your mind map so it is easier to navigate and remember.

How To Apply Mind Mapping For ADHD

When it comes to creating your mind map, you have two options. You can either create it on a piece of paper, or you can use mind-mapping software. There are a number of options available for computer-based mind mapping these days. A simple Google search will help point you in the right direction.

Applying mind mapping for ADHD looks like this:

- **Start with a main concept or subject:** Pick a topic you wish to learn more about or a project you need to finish. Place this main notion in the page's center. Let's say you want to explore different types of workout genres in order to set up an exercise routine for yourself.
- **Create branches**: From the main idea, make branches that stand in for related themes, e.g. cardio, weight training, high-intensity interval training, yoga, etc.
- **Specify further:** Note important ideas, concepts, or points pertaining to each branch. To reduce space, use symbols, or abbreviations, but make sure they are clear. What exercises do you want to include under each type of exercise? E.g. under cardio you might have spinning, running, swimming, etc.
- **Utilize visual aids like pictures and color:** These can draw your attention and improve memory recall. You can maybe make each topic a different color with all the branches on that part of the map being the same color for easy reference.

- Reviewing your mind map on a regular basis might help you maintain focus and improve your recall.
- It's crucial to maintain your mind map and keep it tidy and structured since people with ADHD may find a disorganized mind map confusing.
- **Adapt to your needs:** Since mind mapping is a highly individualized tool, it's critical to customize it for your own requirements and learning preferences. Try out several formats, illustrations, and colors to see which suits you the best.
- **Use it as an organization tool:** Mind mapping is a useful tool if you might have trouble focusing and keeping organized since it can be used to arrange your thoughts, ideas, and projects.
- **Use it as a problem-solving tool:** Mind mapping can be used as a tool for problem-solving, enabling you to divide difficult issues into smaller, more manageable chunks and to visually arrange alternative solutions.

Executive Dysfunction And ADHD

Memory can be impacted in a variety of ways by executive functioning. Organizing the information that is kept in memory, aids in controlling how much memory is used. This enables you to obtain the information that is most pertinent to a given job. Executive functioning also has an impact on working memory, which is the short-term storage and processing of data required for ongoing tasks.

Executive dysfunction can also make it difficult to start and finish tasks, which interferes with the storage and recall of memories. Since executive functioning and memory are interdependent, a problem with one can have an impact on the other.

This group of mental abilities known as executive functions is in charge of organizing and controlling ideas, behaviors, and emotions. Working memory, inhibitory control, flexibility of thought, and planning are some of them. These are functions that people with ADHD frequently struggle with, which causes issues with organization, impulsivity, and attention.

Some of us who suffer from ADHD may exhibit executive dysfunction in a number of ways. For instance, you could struggle to prioritize chores, finish them quickly, or even begin projects at all. You might also have trouble controlling your impulses, which can cause impulsive actions or decisions.

You may struggle with working memory, which can affect your capacity to pay attention, remember information, and pick up new skills. You might also struggle with cognitive flexibility because of difficulty switching your attention from one task to another.

Additionally, issues in social and intellectual contexts might result from executive dysfunction. Maintaining connections, adhering to rules and social conventions like not interrupting someone when they speak, and finishing work on time can be difficult for you when you suffer from ADHD.

There are a number of methods that can help you manage your symptoms. These include prescription drugs, counseling, and lifestyle modifications like regular exercise, being present in the moment, and stress reduction. Furthermore, tools like mind maps and other organized techniques can assist with enhancing your executive function skills.

Core Executive Functions Skills That You Need

We can efficiently plan, organize, and complete tasks thanks to a set of mental capabilities called executive function skills. These abilities, which are essential for success in work, education, and daily life, can be grown and enhanced over time. Success depends on a number of fundamental executive function abilities, including:

1. **Attention and Concentration:** We need the ability to pay attention and concentrate so we can learn from

instructions given to us verbally or visually. We also need these skills to be able to complete tasks both at home and in the workplace.

2. **Working Memory:** This refers to all the information stored in our brain that we need to be able to access at any point in time, like phone numbers and remembering appointment dates, birthdays, etc.

3. **Inhibition:** The ability to suppress impulsive behaviors, resist temptation and delay gratification. This skill is particularly helpful in keeping you from eating an entire tub of ice cream in one sitting or buying a whole bunch of stuff you don't need on credit.

4. **Emotional Control:** Emotional control or emotional regulation is a very important skill and something we can keep developing throughout our lives if we dedicate some time and effort to it. The skill helps us bite our tongue instead of saying something hurtful to someone, or the ability to stay calm in stressful situations.

5. **Initiation:** This refers to the ability to start and complete tasks, set goals, and initiate projects. If we didn't have any initiation skills, nothing would ever get done.

6. **Flexibility:** This skill relates to the ability to adjust to changing situations, and switch between tasks, and problem-solving.

7. **Planning and Organization:** The ability to create a plan, prioritize tasks, and manage time effectively is something we need to engage in on a daily basis. You need to plan what groceries you need to buy. You need to prioritize and organize paying your bills on a monthly basis, etc.

It's crucial to work on improving each of these abilities because they are interconnected and have an effect on one another. Being organized can boost flexibility, and exercising excellent emotional control can aid with attention and working memory. There are many ways to improve executive function abilities, including mindfulness and meditation, physical activity, and cognitive training. Moreover, getting assistance from a therapist or counselor can aid in developing these abilities.

ADHD-Friendly Tips To Strengthen Your Memory

ADHD is often linked with memory challenges, making it important to implement strategies to strengthen it. Here are some ADHD-friendly tips for improving memory:

1. **Get organized:** Information that has a framework can help people with ADHD remember things better. This can entail making a to-do list, maintaining a planner, and breaking tasks down into more manageable chunks.
2. **Employ visual aids:** Flashcards, mind maps, and other visual aids can assist activate various brain regions and improve the likelihood that knowledge will be retained.
3. **Repeat information:** Improving memory requires repetition. To reinforce information, repeat it, in a variety of contexts, and different ways.
4. **Regular exercise:** It has been demonstrated that exercise enhances memory and cognitive performance. Regular exercise can help strengthen the brain and enhance memory.
5. **Get enough sleep:** Sleep is key for memory consolidation, thus getting enough sleep is necessary to enhance memory.
6. **Keep your attention on the task at hand:** Distractions can have a negative effect on memory recall, so it's critical to keep them to a minimum. You can make use of screen time-limiting apps etc.

7. **Practice mindfulness:** Investing time into a regular mindfulness practice can help improve memory by lowering stress and boosting focus. Deep breathing exercises and mindfulness meditations are examples of mindfulness practices that can aid in improving memory.

8. **Tell a story in your mind:** I often use this technique to help me remember important information. As the name suggests it involves linking information to a story that you visualize in your mind. E.g. if I told you to remember: a blue balloon, a green monkey, a candy cane, a pink cloud, a purple lizard, and a leprechaun...you'd probably have some difficulty doing that I'd imagine? But if I asked you to picture the route from your front gate to your bedroom and asked you to place these items along the way as you visualize it with a story attached, it would make it easier to remember.

These tips can help to improve your memory, but it's important to remember that everyone's brains are different and what works for another person might not work for you. Spend some time trying out different tools to find what works best for you.

Online Memory Tools That Work

Have you ever heard the saying that 'memory is a muscle' and that you 'need to exercise it regularly'? It's one of those clichés that is a simple truth. It's like learning a foreign language. You either use it or you lose it.

Here are a number of online tools you can use to help improve your own memory [29]:

- **Elevate Training App:** I personally use this app on a daily basis to exercise my brain. It has a number of different areas of focus it takes you through in a workout like memory exercises, mathematics, vocabulary, etc.

- **Cognifit Brain Training:** This is similar to Elevate and allows you to work on different areas such as reasoning, memory, and attention skills.
- **Lumosity Brain Training:** Another app I have used before. This app was designed by neuroscientists to help with improving one's cognitive skills by using games that focus on training different skills like focus and memory.
- **iThoughts For Mind Mapping:** We've covered mind mapping previously. This app is great for helping you virtually organize and share your thoughts and ideas. Or you can just use it for your own planning needs.
- **Stacking:** This is a video game available on online that requires you to solve different puzzles. It helps with improving working memory.
- **Sudoku:** My all-time favorite game to pass the time. I absolutely love Sudoku and have more puzzle books than I care to admit. There are a number of Sudoku apps available for download that can help improve your working memory and problem-solving skills.
- **Cogmed:** A research-based, scientifically proven computer program that improves memory through the implementation of targeted exercises. The program aims to improve visual, verbal, and spatial memory.
- **Dual-N Back Game:** Another game with solid research to back it up. The game displays a sequence of images and your task is to indicate an image that you've seen before in the sequence 'n' times ago. I personally haven't tried this one but am certainly going to do so now.

Science and research are constantly evolving and finding new ways in which we can profit from different tools and strategies to help improve ourselves on different levels. You just need to do a little research every now and again to find out what the newest tools on the market entail.

ADHD-Friendly Mental Exercises

Anyone who suffers from ADHD can turn everyday tasks into game-like or exercise activities that can boost Dopamine and help with attention and memory. Here are some exercises you can implement on a regular basis to help keep your brain happy and healthy:

- Move your body! Especially higher intensity exercises can help boost your mood and cognitive ability. [30]
- Take short 20-minute power naps. According to the sleep foundation, the optimum length for a nap for an adult is between 20 to 30 minutes, but no longer than 30 minutes, and not after 3 p.m. When we sleep cerebro-spinal fluid pumps through our brain to wash away residual protein build up from thought processes. So a little nap during the day can help with cognitive functioning. [31]
- Engage in something creative like drawing or adult coloring. Perhaps you enjoy painting or gardening. Engage in something you enjoy at least once a day to help feed your brain more of what it likes whilst stimulating creative juices.
- Deep breathing exercises are a great way to ground yourself in the here and now whilst stimulating relaxation. As we've discovered before, it's important to take breaks, and this is one of those useful activities you can engage in whilst taking a break.
- Dance it out. Put on your favorite song, turn up the volume, and just dance as if nobody's watching. This can help both energize you and give your mood a bit of a boost. Movement helps to get all those feel-good hormones going in our bodies.
- Do some journaling. It's like downloading your brain's RAM to make space for more memory. I try to journal every morning before I settle in to work. I admittedly don't always get it done but do engage in a little RAM download a few times a week.
- Engage in a little stretching, yoga, or Tai Chi. Maybe even get your coworkers to join. You could set up a yoga-Fridays stretchy pants day at work. Yoga helps

CHAPTER 6.

CURB OVERTHINKING

The Destructive Nature Of ADHD Overthinking

Although all of us can fall victim to overthinking, people who suffer from ADHD can have a harder time dealing with intrusive thoughts. Because the neurodivergent brain is so creative, restless, overactive, and works faster than a neurotypical brain, it's easy to see why we might struggle with it a bit more than the average person might.

Overthinking can have detrimental effects on your relationships, your capacity to function in daily life, and your mental and emotional health. Overthinking, for instance, can result in hesitation, procrastination, and avoidance of particular people or activities, all of which can have a detrimental effect on your relationships at home and work.

A lot of your overthinking may be based on past events. Something you said that you now think may have been received the wrong way. It's easy for something as small as one line you said weeks ago to plant the seed for overthinking. It can lead to your mind getting stuck in a loop of: *"maybe they're angry with me," "I've screwed up, I'm such an idiot," "WHY did I say that?," "what if I...,"* and so on and so forth.

It is not only exhausting, but it can lead to being harmful in the way of dragging down your self-esteem to the point where you beat yourself up over the smallest things. You start to believe you can't do anything right or even that you don't deserve anything good, including love.

This in turn can lead to you experiencing symptoms of anxiety, depression, or even suicidality.

What might start out as a small seed of doubt can soon grow into a strong weed of self-loathing.

It's critical for you to understand how detrimental overthinking can be and to take action to control it. This may entail talking to a mental health professional for assistance, employing breathing exercises and mindfulness practices, moving around, and cognitive behavioral therapy to confront and reframe negative thoughts.

The first step is to make yourself aware of when you are overthinking and what the root cause of that overthinking is.[32]

Identifying Your Overthinking Triggers

Finding the causes of your overthinking is a crucial first step in reducing it. Events, thoughts, or experiences are known as triggers when they cause excessive rumination and negative mental patterns. You can take action to prevent or lessen the effects of your overthinking by becoming aware of what sets it off.

Here are a few typical triggers/causes of overthinking:

Anxiety and stress: Excessive worrying and negative thoughts can be brought on by stressful situations and events, such as work deadlines, money worries, or relationship issues.

Negative self-talk: Self-criticism, perfectionism, and self-doubt are examples of negative self-talk that can lead to overthinking. Although it may be difficult to challenge and reframe these deeply embedded thoughts and attitudes, facing them can lead to an extremely fulfilling experience of self-discovery and understanding.

Social comparison can result in overthinking, feelings of uneasiness, inadequacy, and self-doubt. This can happen when you compare yourself to others in person or on social media. These days we are bombarded with images of what 'happy', 'successful', and 'beauty' looks like. We can so easily fall victim to believing we are 'lesser than' if we do not live up to perceived societal expectations.

Uncertainty and ambiguity: Uncertain or ambiguous circumstances, including not knowing what the future holds or not having a clear plan can cause stress, which in turn causes overthinking, which can result in indecision and avoidance, possibly leading to anxiety and depression.

Physical symptoms: Physical symptoms like a stabbing pain in your side, exhaustion, headaches, or muscle aches or pains can cause overthinking and result in feeling anxious or stressed because you immediately go to the worst-case scenario. This is called *catastrophizing* and is something that often relates to overthinking.

It's crucial to keep in mind that triggers might differ from person to person and can evolve over time. So it's important to regularly reflect on and become aware of your overthinking patterns in order to recognize your unique triggers and gain a better understanding of what causes your overthinking.

Keep a 'worry journal' and note it down whenever you are feeling stressed or notice that you are overthinking something. Write down as many details as you can about what you're thinking and feeling, what the preceding event was, who was involved, etc. After about a week or two read through your worry journal and see if you can identify some commonalities and specific triggers you need to be more aware of going forward.

Strategies For Overcoming Overthinking

Your mental and emotional health, relationships, and day-to-day functioning can all be negatively impacted by overthinking, which can be a difficult and crippling experience. There are, however, a number of techniques that can assist in combating overthinking and lessen its effects.

Here are some suggestions for avoiding overthinking:[33]

- **Be present in the now** and pay attention to your thoughts, feelings, and bodily sensations by practicing mindfulness. I have found that employing my senses is the easiest way for me to be present in the here and now. E.g., using my sense of touch, I will touch my clothing and a few items around me whilst just focusing on describing to myself what it feels like. I.e. my jeans feel rough in texture, my knitted pullover feels fuzzy, etc.

The idea is to really just place your attention on what you are feeling with your hands. This is what mindfulness is. Using mindfulness in this way can help lessen and lower anxious thoughts and negative thinking, which in turn can aid in reducing overthinking.

- **Participate in physical activity:** Stress and worry can lead to overthinking and if you don't have a way of releasing that buildup it can really have a negative effect on your overall health. Physical exercise helps boost levels of those all-important feel-good neurotransmitters called Endorphins. Endorphins play a big role in helping to reduce stress, relieve pain, and improve your sense of wellbeing. It doesn't necessarily have to entail high-intensity levels of exercise and can be any type of exercise, even if you just go for a brisk walk for 5 minutes.

As a result, getting in some regular physical exercise can enhance mood and build self-confidence, reducing the detrimental effects of negative thinking.

- Reduce exposure to triggers: Now that we've done the exercise on how to identify our triggers above, reducing exposure to those triggers can help reduce the negative effects of overthinking. Let's say, for example, that you have noticed that ambiguity can be a trigger for you that leads to overthinking. This makes sense as a lack of clarity leaves the door open for all sorts of interpretations.

Now let's say that one of your direct line managers is someone who communicates ambiguously. Let's call him Steve. To reduce your exposure to Steve's ambiguous communication style you might ask that you report to a different manager.

Now, let's say there's a certain friend in your life who you find particularly triggering. You know, one of those people who just knows how to push all your buttons. For the sake of your own well-being, it might be a good idea to cut ties with this individual. If they're not positively contributing to your life, there's no sense to keep them in your life.

- **Negative thoughts** should be reframed since they might cause rumination and worry by encouraging overthinking. Reframing unfavorable beliefs is one strategy used in cognitive behavioral therapy that might help lessen their influence.

Let's say for example, that you have this recurring thought that you are incapable. Where did this thought come from? There must've been an event that led to your brain coming up with this thought/belief. Do you really believe yourself to be incapable? Or is it an overreaction to a small mistake you made eons ago? The first step is to become aware of the negative thoughts. Next, challenge that thought and ask yourself whether it is factually correct? Is it really a fact that you're incapable? I highly doubt it.

Lastly, let's reframe that wrongful negative thought by rather repeating to ourselves that: "*I am a highly capable individual who is allowed to make mistakes so I can learn and grow as an individual.*" Now, whenever you become aware of that particular negative thought, I want you to reframe it like we just did.

- **Seek support:** Getting help from a mental health professional or talking to a trusted friend or family member can help lessen overthinking and enhance mental and emotional wellbeing. Others can help provide a different way of looking at something that you might be stuck on. Professionally trained individuals such as counselors, psychologists, and psychiatrists can help you to both identify negative thoughts, and work with you to come up with a strategy on how to best overcome this challenge.

Friends can also make excellent sounding boards and they can help by simply just listening as we unpack our struggle with a negative thought for ourselves. Just because you are capable of doing something on your own doesn't mean that you should have to. Never feel like you shouldn't ask for help. If you put yourself in the shoes of someone you care for, you would want them to come to you for help if they needed it.

- **Set boundaries for yourself:** Spending a lot of time on activities like scrolling through social media for a hit of dopamine can have a negative effect on our thinking patterns as it portrays an image of what society *'thinks'* is happiness and success.

Photos of people you went to college with showing off their luxury holiday in the Bahamas might make you feel like you're behind in life because you're not where your peers are, for example. Instead, spend some time writing about the things you have accomplished in your life. List things you've done that you're proud of. No matter how small. Another example of setting boundaries for yourself is doing the things you don't want to do, but you know you should do because it's good for you. Like eating healthy, moving your body, taking care of your personal hygiene, etc. This is a form of self-care. It's in the name really – self-care = take care of self. Before an activity, like doing the dishes, it feels really cumbersome and annoying to have to wash the dishes. But once you've done and packed it all away, you get to feel good because you can *see* your accomplishment (i.e. the empty sink) which makes you feel good about yourself.

- **Journal:** This is an excellent way to take the thoughts swirling around in your head and on to paper. Sometimes just having an outlet like writing can help you gain a more objective perspective on your overthinking tendencies. You can look up some journaling prompts and use one of those to get you started. E.g. "*what makes me feel happy right now...*," or "*what are the main things I'm struggling with right now*"?

Sometimes, writing can help us come up with our own answers. It helps us to get out of our own heads by dumping it all on paper so we can see it, instead of it being this '*thing*' floating around in our heads.

- **Take action:** No matter how small. If you're worried about something you said to someone, ask them for some time to talk it over. If you're worried about your health, join a gym and set some achievable goals like going three times a week on specific days, etc. Action begets motivation. It may sound strange but, when you do something, a result follows, and when you can see a result you feel more motivated. People often think you need to have motivation first to do something, but it is taking action first that creates motivation.

Doing something about your negative thoughts or worries like coming up with a plan of action for working out so you can lose those few pounds you're worried about, can help curb your negative thoughts and overthinking tendencies. Because you're doing something about it and making progress.

It is important to remember that everyone's journey is different and that overcoming overthinking might take some time and effort. It's also critical to practice self-compassion, be patient with yourself, and ask for help when you need it. Remember, Rome wasn't built in a day.

As we've now discovered in previous sections, overthinking can be both challenging and detrimental to our health. Though with the right strategies you can challenge and combat your own tendencies to get stuck in the loop of overthinking. Here are a few strategies to get you started:[34]

- **Plan dedicated overthinking time:** As you probably know, what makes overthinking such a problem is that it can be extremely difficult to stop. Trying to force ourselves to stop doing something that has become somewhat of a habit also brings with it, its own set of challenges. To work towards spending less time ruminating/overthinking, plan some dedicated time for ruminating on a daily basis. That's your time to overthink as much as you want. Set yourself a timer for 5 or 10 minutes and spend that time focusing on ruminating. Literally force yourself to overthink, (e.g. saying to yourself: "Sally didn't text me back, she always texts me back, that must mean I've done something wrong") and when that timer goes off you get up and go do something different.

Go for a run, go see a movie, or meet a friend for coffee. That way your mind will be occupied with the activity and your dedicated overthinking time won't spill over into the rest of your day.

- **Write it out:** As you may have noticed by now, journaling is one of my go-to tools for many different things concerning mental health. It's also an excellent tool for self-discovery, solution-seeking, planning, etc. So spend some dedicated time either in the morning or in the evening before you go to bed and just write it out. Get it out of your head so it can't get stuck living there anymore. Use some writing prompts to get you going if you find yourself just staring at a blank page, not knowing what to write.

Here are a few prompts to get you started: 'what's keeping you from living your dream life'? 'what do you wish you could do more of'? 'what beliefs are you holding onto that are holding you back'? 'What are the aspects of yourself that you like'?

- **Phone a friend:** Sometimes all we need is just a good sounding board. Hash it out with your bestie. Give them a call and tell them you need their expert input on an overthinking matter. Give them as much detail as possible and then listen to their feedback. They might just be able to offer you a completely different point of view and something you hadn't thought of before.

- **Distract yourself:** This may sound a little counterintuitive, but not all distractions are bad. If we're trying to distract ourselves from something that can have a negative impact on our lives, that makes distraction a good thing in this scenario. Go out for lunch with your friends, take your dog for a walk, or go see a movie. Just do something different to take your mind off the overthinking.
- **Seek professional help:** Make an appointment with your therapist. Don't have a therapist? Get one. Therapists are worth their weight in gold and are trained to help people with issues like overthinking. Seeing a therapist on a regular basis can be extremely helpful in keeping you on track and accountable to someone who is going to check in on your progress.

Mindfulness Meditation For Overthinking

A study conducted by the Journal of Attention Disorders[35] has found that mindfulness meditation can have a positive impact on individuals who suffer from ADHD. People who suffer from ADHD, and stick to a regular mindfulness meditation practice report experiencing positive results in helping calm their thoughts and thwart overthinking tendencies.

I'll share my favorite mindfulness meditation practice with you. I'm hoping it might help you build this into your daily routine so you can make it a habit.

1. First, find a quiet place to make your dedicated meditation spot at home. Preferably a room where you won't be disturbed or distracted by other inhabitants of your home.

2. Next, I want you to set an intention for your meditation session, e.g. you want to spend the next 5 minutes just focusing on your breath and set yourself a timer.

3. You can practice meditation in any position you find most comfortable. You can sit on the floor with your legs crossed, or on a chair, or you can lie down on your back with a pillow beneath your head and knees for oomfort. Just find what is most comfortable for you.

4. Now start focusing on your breathing. You're not trying to breathe a certain way, you're just noticing your breathing. Do this for 10 counts – one in and out breath is one count.

5. After you've done ten breathing cycles, I want you to start focusing on *how* you are breathing. Focus on breathing slowly and deeply in through your nose all the way into your belly. Then slowly breathe out of your mouth. Keep your focus on your breath until the timer goes off.

6. Your mind will wander and that's perfectly fine. When you notice your mind has wandered off and away from your breathing, just gently bring yourself back to focusing on your breath. No judgment. No beating yourself up. There is no wrong or right.

There you have it. My favorite mindfulness meditation routine. I hope you might find it helpful in building up your own practice. Just always remind yourself to be kind and gentle with yourself.

CHAPTER 7.

MIND DECLUTTER GUIDE

Can I Be Organized Despite My ADHD?

Despite having ADHD you can be organized. It might be a bit more of a challenge than for people with a neurotypical brain, but that doesn't mean it's impossible. You just need to find the tools and strategies that work best for you to help you stay organized. For me, the most important thing, which I hope I've also relayed throughout this book, is that you need to be kind, gentle, and understanding of yourself. Nobody is perfect and you will have your off days where things go all haywire. That's okay. Just regroup and fall back on your tools and strategies.

I can be exceptionally hard on myself, and have a sneaky suspicion that you can probably relate, right? I've spent a lot of time in my life pondering why that is, and for me, it comes down to always having been told what I do wrong since I was a child. E.g., my father forever told me to stop fidgeting with a stern face. Or a teacher shouting at me for getting distracted. Or supposed friends judging me because my home environment is in – what they define as – disarray.

When the focus is so often placed on pointing out what you are doing wrong, you start to think that you can't do anything right. You start believing that you can't do certain things because of your ADHD. Like being organized – which is something you've always struggled with – and now believe to be impossible.

Logically we have to admit that it's not impossible though. I don't like to prescribe to the notion of impossibility. I also don't like when people assume to know what I may or may not be capable of.

There are many people out there who suffer from ADHD can organize their lives. I can now call myself one of them, thanks to the tools I'm about to share with you.

Here's a comprehensive list for you to work through and explore to find what works for you. [36]

You will note that the list is broken up into three sections, or three areas of focus.

ORGANIZATION STARTS WITH SELF-AWARENESS AND BOUNDARIES:

- **Know your triggers:** learn to identify the things that distract you. Perhaps it's when people walk past your door or when you can hear talking in the background. Maybe the lights in your office are too bright and distracting. Come up with a way to combat these distractions, e.g. close your door, get yourself a set of headphones to drown out background noise, close your window, or dim the lights.
- **Learn to say no:** I've only recently learned how to set healthy boundaries, with others and with myself. All I can say is that it has been truly life-changing. Before I would be a complete people pleaser who allowed people to walk right over me. This caused me to focus on things that were not mine in the first place which would lead to not achieving what I needed to achieve for myself. This just turns into resentment, which can sully any relationship. Learn how to say no and stop picking up other people's stuff.

- **Learn to ask for help:** This is the last one I'll leave you with. I know we'd love to think of ourselves as being super independent people who don't need anyone else. You're just human, it's okay to ask for help when you need it. Sometimes life gets overwhelming and you might find yourself with more on your plate than you can handle. Ask for help. You would jump in when one of your people expresses that they need help, I promise you they want to do the same for you.

ORGANIZATION AND PRODUCTIVITY HACKS:

- **Set SMART goals:** If you haven't heard of SMART goals before, it's a mnemonic for Specific, Measurable, Attainable, Relevant, and Time-bound. Set small, SMART goals for yourself. This can help ensure that you achieve more of your goals, which in turn helps boost your confidence and motivation.
- **Focus on one task at a time:** Seems easy enough, but as we know, it's not always that straightforward. For this one, you need to set a boundary and be strict with yourself. It's so easy for us to get distracted. I know for myself I might be busy with a task and then read something interesting whilst doing research, then that piece of information leads me down a different research rabbit hole, and before I know it, I'm watching YouTube videos on how to groom a giraffe. It's a bit like mindfulness meditation. When you notice that you've strayed from the task you're supposed to be focusing on, just gently lead yourself back to it. Just one, not multiple tasks at once.
- **Place, retrieve, return:** I was taught this simple yet powerful tool as a child. Dr. Tracy Marks[37], a YouTube psychiatrist also suggests this to her viewers as a strategy for staying organized. It's simple; everything needs to have a place. My medications all live in the same place. All my important bills and mail live in the same place in a box on my coffee table. All my keys go onto a hook on my wall. When I need something I retrieve it, and once

done with it, I return it to its rightful place. This means I always know where everything is and never lose anything.

ORGANIZATION TOOLS:

- **Lists:** I know this one is not everyone's cup of tea, but I LOVE lists. I have lists for everything. A daily to-do list to help me stay on top of tasks, a shopping list for my weekly grocery shop that I update on a daily basis, etc.
- **Use reminders:** I have dozens of reminders set on my phone and laptop. Reminders for when I'm supposed to be working and when I'm supposed to take a break. Reminders for when I'm supposed to eat. Reminders for when I'm supposed to be studying. Reminders for when I have appointments, etc. It might sound silly to neurotypicals that one needs a reminder to eat, but I know you know what I'm talking about. Reminders are your friend, utilize them.
- **Use visual reminders:** It's easy to lose track of certain tasks you were supposed to pay attention to, especially when we go into hyperfocus drive. Use visual reminders like sticky notes on your desk, wall, or computer to remind you of tasks you need to complete today. Don't leave them up there. Once the day is done take them down, then you can put back up what still needs completing tomorrow.
- **Organizational apps:** There are a number of apps available that are aimed at helping people with ADHD be more organized like Evernote, Todoist, or Brain Focus. You can look them up in your app or play store, along with many others. These can help you keep track of events, tasks, to-do lists, etc.

Why Is Decluttering Difficult For Me?

Decluttering is another one of those things that are not necessarily singular to people with ADHD, but again, suffering from ADHD can make it harder for us to declutter. There are a few reasons for this:[38]

- **Keeping things for 'just in case':** It's like finding a piece of a screw on the floor, not being able to figure out where it came from, so you put it in your desk drawer 'just in case'. That piece of screw will die in that drawer. I have a simple rule: If I haven't used something for a year, it gets thrown out.
- **Scarcity mentality:** Some people feel safer when they have lots of stuff around them, because having only the bare minimum can make them feel like they don't have enough to survive, which causes anxiety. This can cause us to hold on to things we don't actually need, very much like the 'just in case' items. The reality is that you don't need two of everything.
- **Emotional attachment:** I don't have that much of a problem on this front because I'm not a sentimental individual. Though I do understand that it can be difficult to let go of something a loved one gave you. It holds emotional value.
- **Sensory overload:** I know that I experience high levels of anxiety when I walk into a cluttered space. A lot of people feel overwhelmed by the same thing and they would rather just ignore it. Though sometimes we need to sit with discomfort so we can achieve what we need to.
- **Decisions are tough:** It might feel like you're afraid of making the wrong decision by throwing out something that you could need soon. This can lead to being overwhelmed and ultimately indecision and giving up.
- **Not knowing where to start:** Because we tend to be less organized, it can be challenging to figure out where to start and how. Though now that I've shared those organizational tools with you earlier, you have the power to overcome this.

- **Distractibility:** Have you ever seen that photo on the internet where a girl is sitting on a couch with a mask, an old PlayStation, and a neck pillow with the tagline: *"When you're cleaning out your room but get distracted by all the nifty things you find?"* This can easily happen to me. Or maybe keep getting distracted by message notifications on your phone.

All of the above can make decluttering a challenge, for sure, but as we know by now, there are always ways to overcome these challenges.

The Mindblowing Benefits Of Decluttering One's Mind

Beyond just having a clean and ordered environment, there are many advantages to decluttering one's thinking. Our mental and emotional health can be harmed by the constant clutter of bad ideas, concerns, and tension in our heads. The following are some of the main advantages of clearing your mind:

- **Increased concentration and focus:** Cleaning up your mental space makes it easier to block out distractions and maintain your attention on the task at hand. As a result, production and efficiency increase.
- **Reduced anxiety and stress:** You can free up mental space, lower your stress levels, and enhance your mood by letting go of worries, pessimistic ideas, and stress.
- **More restful nights:** A crowded mind might result in racing thoughts that can induce insomnia. You can relax and sleep better after decluttering, which can enhance both your physical and emotional health.
- **Enhanced creativity and clarity:** When you clear your thoughts, you make room for fresh, original ideas to emerge. Increased creativity and mental clarity may result from this.

- **Decluttering can help you focus more clearly** and minimize distractions, which will help you think more clearly and make better judgments.
- **A clean space is a happy space:** I know that for me personally when I've cleaned my home I feel so much happier. It's like when you get into a freshly made clean bed, it's just the best feeling in the world.

The bottom line is that decluttering is important for both your physical space and your mental space, and brings with it a whole host of benefits.[39]

How To Declutter With My ADHD Brain

Keeping our homes and working spaces free from clutter can be a real challenge, but with the following steps in this guide, you will be well on your way to spring cleaning your life. The task of decluttering may seem daunting to you, or even insurmountable. Though you just need to remind yourself to take it one step, one small task at a time to not overwhelm yourself even more.

If you do get overwhelmed or experience high levels of anxiety, practice those sensory grounding skills I shared with you previously to help calm down your nervous system.

Here we go:[41]

- **Keep a 'donate' box in the laundry room:** Every time clothes come through that don't fit your children anymore, they go straight into the donate box. The same goes for any and all other items in the house that haven't been used in a long time. Even if you paid good money for it. There's no use holding on to something you don't use or need that could be of use to someone else.
- **Start small:** It's easy to get overwhelmed. Remind yourself to focus on one task, and one item at a time. If you look at an

entire room that needs decluttering it will cause anxiety and a need to day-drink.

- **Get yourself a 'body double':** A body double is someone who is there to help you complete difficult or annoying tasks. They don't actually do anything. They're just 'there', which for many people with ADHD is all they need to get things done. It makes you feel like you have someone keeping you accountable and this motivates you to get stuck in. A supportive presence also adds motivation.[40]
- **Label everything:** Having clearly labeled baskets, boxes, storage containers, cupboards, and shelves can help keep your environment more organized. Have teenagers who leave their shoes all over the house? Have a basket at the front door labeled 'shoes' for everyone's shoes. This way it can't go missing or create clutter. Have a container for all-important documents. A basket or key holder for everyone's keys, etc.
- **Do a 10-minute tidy-up on a daily basis:** As the saying goes: *"prevention is better than cure."* You can get ahead of clutter by setting aside just 10 minutes a day and going around the house picking up some clutter and moving items to their relative holders/boxes/baskets.
- **Doom bags/baskets/boxes:** Anything that doesn't have a home goes into the general doom box, which gets sorted through once a month.
- **Touch once:** If you pick up and open a bill that needs paying, pay it, and file it or throw it away. Don't open it and then set it down to pay it later. It won't get done.
- **Hire a professional organizer:** There's absolutely no shame in calling in backup. Sometimes we need professional help. So if you find that you're just not managing, get in a professional helper.
- **Recycle/repurpose/reuse:** Sometimes items we buy can later be repurposed for something else. A cutlery organizer can be repurposed as a stationery organizer for example. That

basket you no longer use for laundry can become a basket for tv blankets, etc. First, think about how you can repurpose something before you go out and buy something else that will take up even more space.

- **Get your friends or family involved:** If you're struggling to decide whether you should keep something or get rid of it, ask your friends or family. Make a game of it where you need to tell your jury where the item comes from, what it is used for, when you last used it, and what you will use it for next. They then have the final say on whether to toss or keep it.
- **Reframe 'obligations' as 'self-care':** Because it is actually self-care. We often think of self-care as only being about spa days and massages, when it is actually also about doing the things we need to do for ourselves and are good for us, but don't want to for whatever reason. Start seeing it as something you're doing to take care of yourself.

CHAPTER 8.

SIMPLE EXERCISES AND MINDFULNESS TECHNIQUES

Take Things One Day At A Time

Life is challenging with many obstacles and ups and downs. You won't get it right all the time. Sometimes you'll fail, and that's okay too. What's important is that you start fostering a more curious and kind attitude toward yourself. The aim in life isn't to never make mistakes. It's about learning from our mistakes so we can grow as individuals and move forward in life.

If you're not moving forward as fast as you'd like to, you must practice kindness and self-love. We are taught to go-go-go from the time we can walk and talk. Go to school, go to university, get a job, have a family, accumulate wealth and 'stuff', retire rich, die. There's so much more to life. Learn to drink in the small blessings on a daily basis.

I have always felt like I'm behind in life due to a combination of my neurodivergence and traumatic upbringing. I spent decades trying to figure out what it is I'm 'supposed' to do with my life. My purpose. My Ikigai (Japanese for 'purpose in life'). The Japanese believe that one's purpose in life lies at the intersection of four circles: what you love doing, what you are good at, what you are paid to do, and what the world needs.

I always, and have always felt extremely rushed. I have to achieve things. Otherwise, I feel like a failure. My friends often refer to me as an overachiever. I have this driving force at the center of my being that keeps pushing me to do more, do better, and achieve more.

I remember when I decided to pursue my lifelong dream of becoming a doctor. A psychiatrist to be exact. At age 40! Once I was accepted, registered, and paid for my first year's studies, it all became extremely overwhelming. I mean I had to catch up on and refresh my memory on mathematical concepts and biology I hadn't even looked at it for the last 20-odd years. I got so overwhelmed that I couldn't see my path ahead anymore. I was planning a million things in a million different ways and it all just got to be too much.

Then my psychiatrist, bless her soul, reminded me to implement all the tools and strategies I already know. Because I had gotten so caught up in the overwhelm of it all, I completely forgot that I actually know what needs to be done.

Take things one day at a time!

Here are some pointers that have helped me cope better with my ADHD on a daily basis:

- **Activities planner:** Get yourself a daily planner. It can be either a big physical planner you can stick or hang on your wall, a physical daily planner in book form, or a daily planner in digital form in the way of an app on your phone/tablet/desktop. Fill out and color code your daily activities like work time, sleep time, meals, gym, etc. Mark important events like birthdays and anniversaries. This way you'll have a clear indication of free time available so you can plan what to do during those times. Again – remember to make time for resting as well.
- **Important items near the door:** So often I'm on my way out but can't find my sunglasses or my keys and then I have to spend time looking for them when I'm already late. The easy fix is to keep important items in a container of sorts near the door. Or at least just in the same spot. Items like your house keys, car

keys, wallet, sunglasses, jackets, purses, etc. This way you can just grab and go.

- **Break it up:** We've covered this before as well. Break up large tasks into smaller tasks that are easier to achieve. This will help increase your success rate and boost your motivation in turn.
- **There's no such thing as perfect:** Perfect is a subjective and very dangerous term. If you're always aiming for perfection you are setting yourself up for failure and quite possibly overcomplicating things. Don't needlessly add steps to processes that needn't be there. Keep it simple.
- **Separate your spaces:** Your bedroom is for sleeping and sex only. Your office space is for work only. Your living room is for leisure time only. We can often make the mistake of thinking I'll just work in bed today because it's more comfortable. What this causes is blurred lines in your brain. No, it's not sure when it's supposed to focus and when it's supposed to relax. Keeping your spaces separate and what each is meant for can help you be productive when it's time for work, and wind down and relax when it's time for bed.
- **Prepare ahead of time:** Mornings can be chaotic when you're dealing with a neurodivergent brain. Firstly, it takes a while to get going, then once you do get going you have a power hour within which you need to achieve everything otherwise that window closes and all is lost. Not quite, but I'm sure some of you can relate. The solution to this is to prepare ahead of time. Set out your clothes for the next day in the evening. Have your lunch packed before you go to bed. Preparation can save you a lot of headaches.
- **Time blindness:** A very common and distressing element of ADHD is 'time blindness'. Someone with ADHD often has a weaker sense of time and might get lost in doing something without realizing how much time has passed. Before you know it you've been scrolling on Instagram for an hour and now missed your lunch appointment. Alarms and timers are a great solution to this problem. Allow yourself to scroll or do whatever it is you

wanted to, but set an alarm so you don't get lost in time and miss appointments or times at which you need to be taking care of yourself, like eating or taking a shower.[42]

- **Set aside time for self-care:** It's important, and as I've mentioned before, it's not just about doing self-indulgent things, but also about doing the things that you need to and are good for you, like that annual doctor's checkup you've been dodging. Going to the gym or doing a workout when you don't feel like it is also self-care. Self-indulgence for self-care is also perfectly okay, don't get me wrong. Just try to maintain a balance between the two. Remember the saying: *"if you don't make time for your health, illness will do it for you."*

  A reminder on this point is that getting enough sleep and making time to see your therapist are also forms of self-care.

- **Don't beat yourself up when you mess up:** You will mess up. We all do at one point or another. It's inevitable. Though rather frame it in a way that it's a lesson to learn. Making mistakes is good in that way. As long as we learn from them and don't do it again. Like Einstein said: *"insanity is doing the same thing over and over again and expecting a different result."*
- **Make use of technology:** There are so many useful apps and websites you can make use of to help make your life easier. Planners, timers, reminders, trackers. These are all things you can utilize on a daily basis to help you stay on top of your ADHD symptoms.

Now you have a whole bunch of resources[43] to tap into on a daily basis. I sincerely hope you find these pointers helpful, what is most important to remember is that you need to practice these on a regular basis. Like anything, the more you do it, the easier it gets. It doesn't help just reading over these tools, you have to physically participate and practice for it to have any effect.

With a bit of dedication, I do not doubt that you will be able to find what works for you and implement it into your life on a daily basis.

How To Make Your ADHD Work For You

Yes, ADHD comes with its own host of challenges. Though – when managed properly – ADHD could give you an edge. We've learned that we can hyperfocus, which means we pay excellent attention to detail. We have a very creative mind, which allows us to think differently, come up with alternative solutions, and create amazing work.

Now let's look at things you can do to make your ADHD work for you on a daily basis[44]:

- **Get treatment for your symptoms:** I'm not only referring to medication here. Treatment is an umbrella term that includes medication, talk therapy, art therapy, occupational therapy, coaching, and more. You must work with professionals who can help guide you along your way and give you expert advice when you need help. On the point of medication, there is absolutely no shame in taking them. Pill shaming is a horrible thing people do, but in the end, you need to do what works for you and use all the tools available to you. If medication works for you, go for it.
- **Take regular breaks:** We've covered this point before, but it's an important one. Because we have such busy brains, we tend to get lost in time and before we know it we're knocking on burnout's door. This should make up part of your self-care routine on a daily basis. And yes, you should be practicing self-care on a daily basis. Meditation, personal hygiene, feeding yourself, exercising, and taking your medication – these activities all fall under self-care.
- **Do something relaxing or fun first thing:** Because your mind never stops and it's already going at 100 miles per hour as you roll out of bed, it can cause you to feel anxious about your day before you've even started. Already thinking about everything you need to do during the day can make it seem like a mountain that needs climbing. One way to combat this is to start your day off by doing something relaxing or enjoyable. Like going

for a nice relaxed breakfast before work. Participating in some mindfulness meditation first thing in the morning. This helps set the tone for your day.

- **Make sure your first task is an easy one:** Again, this is the kind of thing that can help set the tone for the rest of your day. Pick something that you need to do that you have a 100% chance of succeeding at first thing, when you get to the office. Now you've already achieved something, you're feeling motivated, and you can tackle the more difficult tasks you have ahead of you.
- **Give yourself more time than you need:** Because we tend to get easily distracted and have to deal with time blindness, setting aside more time than you need can help act as a buffer in case you lose track or get distracted. If you think something might take you an hour, set aside two hours for it. If you think it will take you half an hour to get ready in the morning, put an hour aside. Then also set yourself an alarm so you aren't caught out when hyper-focusing or time-blindness kicks in.
- **Find a way to make things fun:** This circles back to using things like visual cues. Find ways of making boring tasks novel and fun by using creative ways of approaching said tasks. Use colorful markers, sticky notes, images, and a whiteboard for notes perhaps. Anything that adds a little color and fun to your day.
- **Avoid multitasking:** We've covered this point as well. It doesn't work. As tempting as it may be, it's not useful or productive. Stick to working on one task at a time.
- **Focus on your strengths:** We all have our own strengths. When you grow up with ADHD you often feel like there's something 'missing' within you as people treat you like there's something wrong with you. Because of a diagnosis. There's nothing wrong with you. In fact, as you might have discovered in this book; you have your own superpowers to explore. Instead of naturally swinging towards beating on yourself, start making a concerted

effort to acknowledge your own strengths. This helps increase self-awareness, self-worth, motivation, empathy, etc.

Fun Exercises For People With ADHD

We know that physical exercise is good for us. Exercise is a fantastic approach to controlling ADHD symptoms and boosting energy, focus, and attention. But for those with ADHD, conventional workouts like treadmill running can be tedious and uninteresting. Here are some enjoyable workouts to get you moving and maintain your concentration:

1. **Rock climbing:** a strenuous activity that demands both mental and physical focus and coordination. It's a terrific technique to increase focus and lessen ADHD symptoms because it requires both physical and mental work.

2. **Parkour:** In a park or urban setting, parkour involves jumping, climbing, and vaulting over barriers. This physically and mentally demanding activity is perfect for those with ADHD who want a fast-paced, high-intensity workout.

3. **Dance:** is a fun and energizing technique to increase focus and lessen ADHD symptoms. Dancing is a fantastic way to raise your heart rate and keep active, whether you love hip-hop, salsa, or ballroom.

4. **Martial arts:** Focus and concentration are necessary for martial arts like karate, taekwondo, and jiu-jitsu. Martial arts are a fantastic technique to increase concentration and control the symptoms of ADHD due to the physical and mental work involved.

5. **Trampoline parks:** Getting moving and sharpening your attention can be fun and interesting at trampoline parks. Trampoline jumping is an excellent technique to increase balance and coordination and can help with ADHD symptoms.

6. **Obstacle course competitions:** Obstacle course competitions, including Tough Mudder and Spartan events, are a cognitively and physically taxing technique to increase focus and lessen symptoms of ADHD. Obstacle course races are an excellent technique to increase concentration and manage symptoms of ADHD because they combine physical effort and mental focus.

7. **Swimming:** Another excellent example of a moderate aerobic activity that has been connected to a boost in executive function is swimming.

To accompany your fun exercise regimen, here are some fitness tips to consider:[45]

1. **Get a fitness/accountability buddy:** I know I am personally far more likely to show up if I am accountable to someone else. Plus, it's more fun having someone who can work out with you rather than having to do it on your own.

2. Avoid all-or-nothing: Another one of those fun ADHD symptoms is the tendency to engage in all-or-nothing behavior. A surefire way to crash and burn. Moderation is key here. Instead of aiming to work out every single day straight out of the gate, rather make it your goal to go 3 times a week. Remember SMART goals.

3. Get yourself a fitness tracker/watch: We love info and statistics and a fitness watch can make exercise activities fun as it gives you a visual representation of what you're achieving, which helps boost motivation.

4. Set yourself up for success: Along with setting SMART goals for yourself, take some time to consider what the minimum acceptable goal would be for you. Maybe it's working out for 15 minutes twice a week. That's an easily attainable goal. Next, set a maximum goal for yourself, e.g. working out for 20 minutes, 3 times a week. This way you are pretty much assured that you'll accomplish your minimum

goal, which boosts your sense of accomplishment and in turn, motivation.

Mindfulness Worksheets

Mindfulness is a powerful tool that can help manage symptoms of ADHD and improve focus, attention, physical, and mental well-being. Here are some tips for practicing mindfulness for people with ADHD:[46]

YOGA

A practice that is all about observing, being aware, and being in touch with your own body. Yoga is an excellent mindfulness exercise that holds a number of health benefits. An 8-week study that followed a group of children diagnosed with ADHD, looked at the benefits of a regular yoga practice. The study showed that yoga had a positive effect on the children's inattentiveness and impulse control. I'd bet the same goes for adults.[47]

1. When do you plan to spend time on this activity? Which days of the week and at what time? E.g., I usually schedule this for myself on Sunday afternoons when I can just relax and spend some time being creative.

____

____

____

2. Where will you participate in this activity? E.g. a physical art class, a pottery class, an online class, or maybe just coloring by yourself at home?

____

____

____

3. What medium do you prefer to focus on? Pottery? Oil painting? Coloring with pencils? Sketching with charcoal?

4. What do you hope to achieve from this activity?

5. Rate your experience on a scale from 1 to 10 after the activity. 1 = did not enjoy it at all, 10 = it was excellent!

6. What are some of the sensory details you noticed whilst engaged in this activity? E.g. the texture of the paper you were coloring on, the smell of the clay in your pottery class, etc.

7. How do you think this activity has helped you in dealing with your own symptoms of ADHD?

GARDENING

I recently decided that I want to grow my own vegetables. I didn't expect that it would be such a soothing and fulfilling experience. I find working in the garden a great way to practice using my senses to ground myself in the present moment. My veggies have just started maturing and getting to the point where they're ready to be harvested.

I cannot tell you how fulfilling it is to cut up tomatoes I grew in my own garden. It's wonderful. If you don't have a garden, you can use pots or containers.

1. When do you plan to practice this activity? Which days of the week and at what time of the day? E.g., I do my gardening on the weekends around 5 p.m. when it's cooler outside.

   ____

   ____

   ____

2. Which plants do you plan on planting in your garden? E.g., if it's veggies, which veggies? If it's flowers, which flowers?

   ____

   ____

   ____

3. Do you plan on using seeds, or buying seedlings from a nursery?

   ____

   ____

   ____

4. Rate your experience after the activity on a scale from 1 to 10. 1 = I hated this activity, 10 = I absolutely love gardening!

   ____

   ____

   ____

5. What are some of the sensations you noticed whilst engaged in this activity? E.g., the smell of the soil? The texture of the soil, etc.

   ____

   ____

   ____

6. How do you think this may have helped you to cope with some of your symptoms of ADHD?

   ____

   ____

   ____

In reality, mindfulness is something you can practice anywhere at any time. Like anything else, the more you practice, the easier it gets. When I just started out I struggled to remember the 5-4-3-2-1 technique, but now I don't even need to think about it anymore. When I feel emotional or overwhelmed, I automatically revert to a breathing or sensory observation exercise.

The more you practice, the easier it gets to automatically fall back on these coping strategies.

Simple Visual Exercises For People With ADHD

For those of us who have ADHD, visual exercises can be a useful tool since they can boost concentration, focus, and general well-being. If you are diagnosed with ADHD as a child, you'll find that your symptoms will change over time as your brain develops fully into your mid-twenties. The idea that our brains stop developing altogether at some point is a misnomer. As we've learned in more recent years, a process called neuroplasticity allows new neural pathways to be formed when we perform new activities on a regular basis.

This is a natural process. It happens with anyone who practices something on a daily basis. The more you do something, the stronger those connections become and the better you become at that activity. Practicing visual exercises can help strengthen certain connections in the brain to help with focus.[48]

Here are a few quick visual exercises you can practice at home or work:

- **Visual scanning** is a basic activity that requires concentrating on and closely examining objects in your environment. Start by focusing on one thing, then shift your attention to another, and so forth. Pay close attention to the objects' hues, forms, and textures.

- **Visual tracking** is an exercise that includes using your eyes to track a moving object. You can use a tiny ball, a pen, or any other slow-moving object. Keep your eyes on the target and move along with it as it moves.
- **Visual memory:** This practice involves briefly studying a scene or an object and then trying to remember as many specifics as you can about it. Try to recall the hues, contours, and textures of the items you observed.
- **Visualization:** Imagining something in your mind is a mental practice called visualization. Close your eyes and visualize a serene setting, such as a beach or a forest. Pay close attention to the scene's hues, noises, and sensations.
- **Color therapy** is a visual activity that involves concentrating on various colors. Choose a color, like blue or green, and concentrate on it for a while. Pay attention to the feelings and ideas that the hue arouses in you.
- **Mandalas** are complicated geometric patterns that can be drawn visually by physically drawing the pattern or coloring an already-drawn pattern. You can find patterns online or buy mandala coloring books in bookstores. Coloring these patterns can really aid with concentration and anxiety reduction.

CONCLUSION

There you have it. We have explored a great deal of information, tips, tools, strategies, and techniques in this book. I sincerely hope that you have found the content shared with you in this book to be both helpful and useful.

Living with ADHD in a predominantly neurotypical world can be challenging and daunting. Having to fit in with norms and abide by rules set by brains that do not have an understanding of what it is to struggle with things like distractibility, overthinking, rejection sensitivity, time blindness, and all the other challenges that ADHD brings with it can be extremely difficult and exhausting.

Though, as medicine and scientific research progress, we are constantly gaining new insights into the condition that gives us a deeper understanding of how to best help ourselves.

I think the greatest lesson I've had to learn is that having been born with a neuroatypical/neurodivergent brain doesn't make me any lesser of a person. If anything, it makes me a unique individual with my own set of strengths and the ability to see things differently.

I've learned to embrace my difference and love who I am. I hope that you might have gained new insights into what makes you, you reading this book. I hope that it serves as a resource that you can always revert to when you need a reminder of how special you are.

My aim with this book is for it to serve as a manual for you that you can come back to when you need to refresh yourself on the many different tools you can implement to help you manage your symptoms and improve your concentration. Because as we have learned on this journey, it is absolutely possible to live with ADHD and be able to master concentration.

At the back, there is an extensive list of resources you can visit to further your own research on the various topics discussed in this book.

You are worthy in your own right and deserve love, understanding, and support.

I want you to remind yourself of this on a daily basis and every time you come back to these exercises. Remember that you are unique in your own right and have far more to offer than this world, or even you know.

Tap into those superpowers of yours. Practice the tools I've given you on a regular basis. Make time for reflection and curious questioning to discover the things you hope to improve on.

Above all else, learn to love your beautiful, unique, neurodivergent brain.

SOURCES:

[1] Arnsten, A. F., PhD (2009). The Emerging Neurobiology of Attention Deficit Hyperactivity Disorder: The Key Role of the Prefrontal Association Cortex. *National Library of Medicine.* https://doi.org/10.1016/j.jpeds.2009.01.018

[2] Slocombe, A. (2022, March 3). *Was Einstein Autistic, Dyslexic, Dyspraxic, or Did He Have ADHD?* Exceptional Individuals. Retrieved February 6, 2023, from https://exceptionalindividuals.com/about-us/blog/did-einstein-have-dyslexia-dyspraxia-autism-and-adhd/

[3] Massuti, R., Moreiro-Maia, C. R., Campani, F., Sônego, M., Amaro, J., Akutagava-Martins, G. C., Tessari, L., Polanczyk, G. V., Cortese, S., & Rohde, L. A. (2021). Assessing undertreatment and overtreatment/misuse of ADHD medications in children and adolescents across continents: A systematic review and meta-analysis. *Neuroscience & Behavioral Reviews, 128,* 64-73. https://doi.org/10.1016/j.neubiorev.2021.06.001

[4] (2013). *Diagnostic and Statistical Manual of Mental Disorders – Fifth Edition* (5th ed., pp. 59-60). American Psychiatric Association.

[5] Qasim, T. B., Sahar, A., Nihal, T., & Bashir, A. (2022). *Review of Applied Management & Social Sciences, 5,* 255-262. https://doi.org/10.47067/ramss.v5i2.233

[6]Schmerler, J. (2015, May 28). *Don't Overthink It, Less Is More When It Comes to Creativity.* Scientific American. Retrieved February 7, 2023, from https://www.scientificamerican.com/article/don-t-overthink-it-less-is-more-when-it-comes-to-creativity/

[7] – LaChance, N. (2017, May 1). Overthinking: When your mind won't turn off. Institute for Educational Advancement. Retrieved January 31, 2023, from https://educationaladvancement.org/blog-overthinking-mind-wont-turn-off/#:~:text=It%20can%20also%20lead%20to

[8] Abramovich, A., & Schweiger, A. (2009). Unwanted intrusive and worrisome thoughts in adults with Attention Deficit\Hyperactivity Disorder. *National Library of Medicine.* https://doi.org/10.1016/j.psychres.2008.06.004

[9] Pattillo, A. (2022, February 1). *HOW TO SHUT OFF YOUR BRAIN: 4 SCIENCE-BACKED TIPS TO STOP THINKING AND RELAX.* Inverse. Retrieved January 31, 2023, from https://www.inverse.com/mind-body/how-to-shut-off-your-brain

[10] Jacobs Hendel, H. (2018, July 12). *Why Can't I Shut Off My Mind?* Psychology Today. Retrieved January 31, 2023, from https://www.psychologytoday.com/intl/blog/emotion-information/201807/why-cant-i-shut-my-mind?amp

[11] Charach, A., & Fernandez, R. (2013). Enhancing ADHD Medication Adherence: Challenges and Opportunities. *National Library of Medicine.* https://doi.org/10.1007/s11920-013-0371-6

[12] CHADD (n.d.). *ADHD and Sleep Disorders.* Retrieved January 31, 2023, from https://chadd.org/about-adhd/adhd-and-sleep-disorders/#:~:text=Many%20children%20and%20adults%20who,have%20significant%20long%2Dterm%20effects.

[13] Suni, E. (2022, August 29). *How Much Sleep Do We Really Need?* Retrieved January 31, 2023, from https://www.sleepfoundation.org/how-sleep-works/how-much-sleep-do-we-really-need#:~:text=National%20Sleep%20Foundation%20guidelines,to%208%20hours%20per%20night.

[14] Laskowski, E. R., MD (2022, July 13). What are the risks of sitting too much? Mayo Clinic. Retrieved February 2, 2023, from https://www.mayoclinic.org/healthy-lifestyle/adult-health/expert-answers/sitting/faq-20058005

[15] Burch, K. (2022, January 12). *Sensory Overload and ADHD: What to Know.* Verywell Health. Retrieved February 2, 2023, from https://www.verywellhealth.com/sensory-overload-and-adhd-5209861

[16] Sensory IntelligenceTM Sensory Quiz https://sensoryintelligence.com/self-assessments/sensory-quiz/

[17] Ross, A. (2016, March 9). *How Meditation Went Mainstream.* Time. Retrieved February 2, 2023, from https://time.com/4246928/meditation-history-buddhism/

[18] Sosnoski, K., PhD (2022, March 21). *The Best Meditation Strategies for ADHD.* Psych Central. Retrieved February 2, 2023, from https://psychcentral.com/adhd/adhd-meditation

[19] Cooper, S. (2021, January 7). *Physical activity is good for your concentration – here's why.* The Conversation. Retrieved February 2, 2023, from https://theconversation.com/physical-activity-is-good-for-your-concentration-heres-why-151143 (n.d.). *How Meditation Can Improve Your Concentration.* Opt Health. Retrieved February 2, 2023, from https://getopt.com/2022/01/14/meditation-to-concentrate/ (2014, March 1). *Sharpen thinking skills with a better night's sleep.* Harvard Health. Retrieved February 2, 2023, from https://www.health.harvard.edu/mind-and-mood/sharpen-thinking-skills-with-a-better-nights-sleep

[20] Singh, D., Staats, B. R., Kouchaki, M., & Gino, F. (2017). Task Selection and Workload: A Focus on Completing Easy Tasks Hurts Performance. *Social Science Research Network.* https://doi.org/http://dx.doi.org/10.2139/ssrn.2992588

[21] (2006, March 20). *Multitasking: Switching Costs.* American Psychological Association. Retrieved February 3, 2023, from https://www.apa.org/topics/research/multitasking

[22] Drake, K. (2021, September 1). *Pomodoro Technique May Aid Folks with ADHD.* Psych Central. Retrieved February 3, 2023, from https://psychcentral.com/adhd/how-to-adapt-the-pomodoro-technique-adhd

[23] Tselha, T., Whitehurst, L. N., Yettin, B. D., Vo, T. T., & Mednick, S. C. (2019). Morning stimulant administration reduces sleep and overnight working memory improvement. *Science Direct.* https://doi.org/10.1016/j.bbr.2019.111940

[24] Levine, H. (2022, January 17). *Meditation and Yoga for ADHD.* Web MD. Retrieved February 5, 2023, from https://www.webmd.com/add-adhd/adhd-mindfulness-meditation-yoga

[25] Rittler, S. (2021, June 14). *Monitoring and Maintenance of Brain Glucose Supply.* National Library of Medicine. Retrieved February 5, 2023, from https://www.ncbi.nlm.nih.gov/books/NBK453140/#:~:text=Glucose%20is%20the%20essential%20metabolic,rapidly%20corrected%2C%20can%20be%20lethal.

[26] Vallines, Z. (2018, October 9). *Is neurofeedback effective for treating ADHD?* Medical News Today. Retrieved February 5, 2023, from https://www.medicalnewstoday.com/articles/315261

[27] Kajka, N., & Kulik, A. (2021, February 18). *The Influence of Metacognitive Strategies on the Improvement of Reaction Inhibition Processes in Children with ADHD.* National Library of Medicine. Retrieved February 5, 2023, from https://www.ncbi.nlm.nih.gov/pmc/articles/PMC7908166/

[28] (n.d.). *Mind Map principles will provide clarity.* Using Mind Maps. Retrieved February 6, 2023, from https://www.usingmindmaps.com/mind-map-principles.html

[29] Kulman, R., PhD (2022, March 26). *8 Apps and Tools That Build Better Retention.* ADDitude Magazine. Retrieved February 6, 2023, from https://www.additudemag.com/adhd-apps-tools-games-build-memory-retention/amp/

(2023, January 30). *Like a Personal Trainer for Your Brain.* ADDitude Magazine. Retrieved February 6, 2023, from https://www.additudemag.com/slideshows/brain-training-apps-like-lumosity/ https://www.cognifit.com/ADHD-adults

[30] (2021, May 21). *Physical Activity Boosts Brain Health.* Center for Disease Control and Prevention. Retrieved February 6, 2023, from https://www.

cdc.gov/nccdphp/dnpao/features/physical-activity-brain-health/index.html#:~:text=Physical%20activity%20can%20improve%20your,of%20physical%20activity%20can%20help.

[31] Summer, J. (2022, November 3). *Napping: Benefits and Tips.* Sleep Foundation. Retrieved February 6, 2023, from https://www.sleepfoundation.org/sleep-hygiene/napping#:~:text=Naps%20can%20deliver%20a%20number,be%20alert%20at%20irregular%20times.

[32]Sinfield, J. (2020, September 14). *How to Stop Overthinking When You Have ADHD.* Verywell Mind. Retrieved February 7, 2023, from https://www.verywellmind.com/how-to-stop-over-thinking-3868209

[33] Maynard, S. (2021, March 24). *How to Stop Overthinking Things: A User's Manual for Your ADHD Brain.* ADDitude Magazine. Retrieved February 7, 2023, from https://www.additudemag.com/how-to-stop-overthinking-adhd-brain/amp/

Dempsey, K. (n.d.). *Seven Strategies To Stop Overthinking.* The Awareness Center. Retrieved February 7, 2023, from https://theawarenesscentre.com/seven-strategies-to-stop-overthinking/

[34] Gordon, K. (2019, May 5). *9 Strategies for Overcoming Overthinking.* Psychology Today. Retrieved February 7, 2023, from https://www.psychologytoday.com/us/blog/out-the-ivory-tower/201905/9-strategies-overcoming-overthinking?amp

Lamothe, C. (2022, June 7). *14 Ways to Stop Overthinking.* Healthline. Retrieved February 7, 2023, from https://www.healthline.com/health/how-to-stop-overthinking

[35] Zylowska, L., Ackerman, D. L., Yang, M. H., Hale, S. T., Pataki, C., & Smalley, S. L. (2008). Mindfulness Meditation Training in Adults and Adolescents With ADHD: A Feasibility Study. *Journal of Attention Disorders, 11*(6). https://doi.org/10.1177/1087054707308502

[36] Gillette, H. (2021, July 7). *32 of the Best Ways to Get Organized When You Have ADHD.* Psych Central. Retrieved February 7, 2023, from https://psychcentral.com/adhd/the-best-ways-to-get-organized-when-you-have-adhd#32-tips

[37] Dr. Tracey Marks. (2020, August 19). *3 Easy Steps for ADHD Organization | ADHD Skills Part 3* [Video]. YouTube. https://www.youtube.com/watch?v=_uXOKGY-tQU

Hatfield, H. (2018, January 8). *Get Organized With Adult ADHD.* Web MD. Retrieved February 7, 2023, from https://www.webmd.com/add-adhd/features/got-adult-adhd-get-organized_

[38] Russel, M. (2021, September 24). *13 Reasons You Struggle to Declutter & How to Overcome Them.* Simple Lionheart Life. Retrieved February 7, 2023, from https://simplelionheartlife.com/struggle-to-declutter/#:~:text=Sometimes%20you%20struggle%20to%20declutter%20because%20having%20a%20lot%20of,t%20use%20or%20love%20them.

[39] (n.d.). *Spring Cleaning and Mental Health: Why Decluttering is Good for your Body, Mind and Soul.* Everwell Counselling. Retrieved February 7, 2023, from https://everwellcounselling.ca/blog-counselling-psychotherapy-mental-health/spring-cleaning-and-mental-health

(2022, September 20). *Why Decluttering Is Important For Your Wellbeing And How To Do It.* Onya Magazine. Retrieved February 7, 2023, from https://www.onyamagazine.com/australian-affairs/why-decluttering-is-important-for-your-wellbeing-and-how-to-do-it/

[40] (2022, October 24). *The Body Double: A Unique Tool for Getting Things Done.* ADD.org. Retrieved February 7, 2023, from https://add.org/the-body-double/#:~:text=ADHD%20body%20doubling%20is%20a,hand%20to%20reduce%20potential%20distractions.

[41] (2022, April 7). *10 Decluttering Hacks Designed by and for ADHD Brains.* ADDitude Magazine. Retrieved February 7, 2023, from https://www.additudemag.com/decluttering-tips-adhd-brains/amp/

Roggli, L. (2021, September 16). *How to Declutter with an ADHD Brain: Organization Solutions for Real Life.* ADDitude Magazine. Retrieved February 7, 2023, from https://www.additudemag.com/slideshows/how-to-declutter-adhd/

Long, A. (2021, October 31). *How to get organized at home when you have ADHD or mental health issues.* The Washington Post. Retrieved February 7, 2023, from https://www.washingtonpost.com/home/2021/10/31/adhd-home-organization-tips/

[42]Green, R. (2023, February 1). *ADHD Symptom Spotlight: Time Blindness.* Verywell Mind. Retrieved February 7, 2023, from https://www.verywellmind.com/causes-and-symptoms-of-time-blindness-in-adhd-5216523

[43]Bettino, K. (2021, April 24). *9 Tips for Creating a Routine for Adults with ADHD.* Psych Central. Retrieved February 7, 2023, from https://psychcentral.com/adhd/9-tips-for-creating-a-routine-for-adults-with-adhd#schedule-ahead

Low, K. (2020, November 3). *Time Management Tips for Adults With ADHD.* Verywell Mind. Retrieved February 7, 2023, from https://www.verywellmind.com/time-management-tips-20409

McCabe, J. (2019, April 18). *A Day In the Life with ADHD: The Ups and Downs.* Healthline. Retrieved February 7, 2023, from https://www.healthline.com/health/adhd/adult-adhd/a-day-in-the-life

Segal, R., M.A., & Smith, M., M.A. (2022, December 30). *Tips for Managing Adult ADHD.* HelpGuide. Retrieved February 7, 2023, from https://www.helpguide.org/articles/add-adhd/managing-adult-adhd-attention-deficit-disorder.htm

[44] Lebow, H. I. (2021, June 24). *How to Stay Productive with ADHD.* Psych Central. Retrieved February 7, 2023, from https://psychcentral.com/adhd/adhd-productivity-strategies-for-getting-things-done#tips

O'Carroll, I. (2020, March 18). *I Have ADHD. Here Are 9 Productivity Tips That Really Help Me.* Self. Retrieved February 7, 2023, from https://www.self.com/story/adhd-productivity-hacks/amp

Wilding, M. (2018, April 19). *How To Use ADHD To Your Advantage, According To A Psychologist.* Forbes. Retrieved February 7, 2023, from https://www.forbes.com/sites/melodywilding/2018/04/19/how-to-use-adhd-to-your-advantage/?sh=6f5554e87b5d

[45] Ratey, N., ED.M. (2021, December 30). *6 ADD-Friendly Tips for Starting and Maintaining an Exercise Program.* ADDitude Magazine. Retrieved February 7, 2023, from https://www.additudemag.com/exercise-fitness-tips-adult-adhd/amp/

Garza, E. (2021, May 10). *8 Best Workouts For Women With ADHD.* Discover Brillia. Retrieved February 7, 2023, from https://discoverbrillia.com/blogs/articles/8-best-workouts-for-adhd-women

[46] Harveston, K. (2019, December 9). *7 ADHD Mindfulness Exercises for Kids, Teens and Adults.* The Mindful World. Retrieved February 7, 2023, from https://www.themindfulword.org/2019/mindfulness-exercises-adhd/

[47] Chou, C. C., & Huang, C. J. (2017). Effects of an 8-week yoga program on sustained attention and discrimination function in children with attention deficit hyperactivity disorder. *National Library of Medicine.* https://doi.org/10.7717/peerj.2883

[48] Moore, D. T., Ph.D. (n.d.). *EYE EXERCISES TO INCREASE ATTENTION AND REDUCE IMPULSIVITY.* Your Family Clinic. Retrieved February 7, 2023, from https://www.yourfamilyclinic.com/adhd/vision.html

Bandhari, S., Dr (2022, August 25). *A Brief History of ADHD.* WebMD. Retrieved January 10, 2023, from https://www.webmd.com/add-adhd/adhd-history#:~:text=In%201798%2C%20a%20Scottish%20doctor,deficit%20hyperactivity%20disorder%20(ADHD).

A. (2020, January 29). *A brief history of ADHD.* APSARD. Retrieved January 10, 2023, from https://apsard.org/a-brief-history-of-adhd/

Barkley, R. A., & Peters, H. (2012, November 1). *The earliest reference to ADHD in medical literature.* PubMed. Retrieved January 10, 2023, from https://pubmed.ncbi.nlm.nih.gov/22323122/

Sun, H., Chen, Y., Huang, Q., Huang, X., Shi, Y., Xu, X., Sweeney, J. A., & Gong, Q. (2017, November 22). *Psychoradiologic Utility of MR Imaging for Diagnosis of Attention Deficit Hyperactivity Disorder: A Radiomics Analysis.* RSNA. Retrieved January 10, 2023, from https://pubs.rsna.org/doi/10.1148/radiol.2017170226

Joszt, L. (2017, November 30). *Brain MRIs Can Identify ADHD and Distinguish Among Subtypes.* AJMC. Retrieved January 10, 2023, from https://pubs.rsna.org/doi/10.1148/radiol.2017170226

Johnson, S. (2019, June 18). *Is there a link between ADHD and dopamine?* Medical News Today. Retrieved January 11, 2023, from https://www.medicalnewstoday.com/articles/325499

Faraone, S. V., Banaschewski, T., Coghill, D., Zheng, Y., Biederman, J., Bellgrove, M. A., . Wang, Y. (2021). The World Federation of ADHD International Consensus Statement: 208 evidence-based conclusions about the disorder. Neuroscience & Biobehavioral Reviews. doi:10.1016/j.neubiorev.2021.01.022

U. *ADHD Myths & Misunderstandings.* CHADD – Children With ADD. Retrieved January 11, 2023, from https://chadd.org/about-adhd/myths-and-misunderstandings/

How to ADHD. (2016, October 31). *10 ADHD Myths That Just Won't Die* [Video]. YouTube. https://www.youtube.com/watch?v=V5tLi1bYilA

Epstein, J. N., & Loren, R. E. (2013, October 31). *Changes in the Definition of ADHD in DSM-5: Subtle but Important.* National Library of Medicine. Retrieved January 14, 2023, from https://www.ncbi.nlm.nih.gov/pmc/articles/PMC3955126/

U. *What are the different types of ADHD?* John Hopkins Medicine. Retrieved January 14, 2023, from https://www.hopkinsmedicine.org/health/conditions-and-diseases/adhdadd

U. *Attention deficit hyperactivity disorder (ADHD).* NHS. Retrieved January 15, 2023, from https://www.nhs.uk/conditions/attention-deficit-hyperactivity-disorder-adhd/symptoms/

Sachdev, P. (2022, June 26). *Beyond Inattention: How ADHD May Be Affecting Your Life.* WebMD. Retrieved January 15, 2023, from https://www.webmd.com/add-adhd/ss/slideshow-adhd-life#:~:text=ADHD%20can%20make%20you%20forgetful,%2C%20school%2C%20and%20personal%20projects.

U. *ADHD Causes & Effects.* Piney Ridge Treatment Center. Retrieved January 15, 2023, from https://www.pineyridge.net/adhd/causes-effects-symptoms/

Editors, A. (2022, July 22). *Talking about ADHD – What I Would Never Trade Away.* ADDitude Magazine. Retrieved January 15, 2023, from https://www.additudemag.com/slideshows/positives-of-adhd/

Elmaghraby, R., & Garayalde, S. (2022, June 1). *What is ADHD?* Psychiatry.org. Retrieved January 15, 2023, from https://www.psychiatry.org/patients-families/adhd/what-is-adhd

U. (2021, December 24). *Attention deficit hyperactivity disorder (ADHD).* NHS UK. Retrieved January 15, 2023, from https://www.nhs.uk/conditions/attention-deficit-hyperactivity-disorder-adhd/treatment/

U. (2019, June 25). *Attention Deficit/Hyperactivity Disorder – Treatment.* Mayo Clinic. Retrieved January 15, 2023, from https://www.nhs.uk/conditions/attention-deficit-hyperactivity-disorder-adhd/treatment/

Clarke, D. A. (2020, January 18). *Are You an Overthinker?* Psychology Today. Retrieved January 17, 2023, from https://www.psychologytoday.com/intl/blog/the-runaway-mind/202001/are-you-overthinker?amp

Morin, A. (2019, January 7). *10 Signs You're An Overthinker.* Inc Magazine. Retrieved January 17, 2023, from https://www.inc.com/amy-morin/10-signs-you-think-too-much-and-what-you-can-do-about-it.html

Taylor, L. (2021, July 26). *Are you an overthinker? Psychologists explain how to get out of your head.* Independent Publications. Retrieved January 17, 2023, from https://www.independent.co.uk/life-style/health-and-families/mindfulness-b1890380.html?amp

Morin, A. (2022, October 5). *How to Stop Overthinking.* Verywell Mind. Retrieved January 17, 2023, from https://www.verywellmind.com/how-to-know-when-youre-overthinking-5077069

U. (2022, May 17). *Overthinking Disorder: Is It a Mental Illness?* Cleveland Clinic. Retrieved January 17, 2023, from https://health.clevelandclinic.org/is-overthinking-a-mental-illness/#:~:text=Overthinking%20is%20 commonly%20associated%20with,GAD%20due%20to%20their%20genes.

Grinspoon, P., MD (2022, May 4). *How to recognize and tame your cognitive distortions.* Harvard Health. Retrieved January 17, 2023, from https://www.health.harvard.edu/blog/how-to-recognize-and-tame-your-cognitive-distortions-202205042738

Sinfield, J. (n.d.). *ADHD and Overthinking.* Untapped Brilliance. Retrieved January 21, 2023, from https://untappedbrilliance.com/adhd-and-overthinking/

Roberts, W. (2021, April 5). *THE LINK BETWEEN ADHD AND OVERTHINKING: THREE WAYS TO TAME YOUR BRAIN.* Focused Mind ADHD Counseling. Retrieved January 21, 2023, from https://focusedmindadhdcounseling.com/the-link0between-adhd-and-overthinking/

Metrinki, L. (2020, July 30). *7 Dangerous Effects of Overthinking.* Psych 2 Go. Retrieved January 21, 2023, from https://psych2go.net/7-dangerous-effects-of-overthinking/

(n.d.). *7 Dangerous Effects of Overthinking.* GoodReads. Retrieved January 21, 2023, from https://www.goodreads.com/quotes/816367-where-attention-goes-energy-flows-where-intention-goes-energy-flows#:~:text=Quote%20by%20James%20Redfield%3A%20%E2%80%9CWhere,%3B%20Where%20Intent...%E2%80%9D

Ciotti, G. (2015, March 11). *How Over-Thinking Kills Your Performance.* Psychology Today. Retrieved January 21, 2023, from https://www.psychologytoday.com/us/blog/habits-not-hacks/201503/how-over-thinking-kills-your-performance#:~:text=It%20makes%20you%20question%20your,from%20the%20same%20seed%3A%20overthinking.

(2020, August 12). *ADHD Superpowers.* Minnesota Neuropsychology. Retrieved January 21, 2023, from https://www.mnneuropsychology.com/articles/ADHD_Superpowers.html

Sedgwick, J. A., Merwood, A., & Asherson, P. (2018). The positive aspects of attention deficit hyperactivity disorder: A qualitative investigation of successful adults with ADHD. *Springer Link*. https://doi.org/10.1007/s12402-018-0277-6

Gehricke, J. G., Kruggel, F., Thampipop, T., Alejo, S. D., Tatos, E., Fallon, J., & Muftuler, L. T. (2017). The brain anatomy of attention-deficit/hyperactivity disorder in young adults – a magnetic resonance imaging study. *National Library of Medicine*. https://doi.org/10.1371/journal.pone.0175433

Del-Ponte, B., Quinte, G. C., Cruz, S., Grellert, M., & Santos, I. S. (2019). Dietary patterns and attention deficit/hyperactivity disorder (ADHD): A systematic review and meta-analysis. *PubMed*. https://doi.org/10.1016/j.jad.2019.04.061

Orenstein, B. W. (2014, February 13). *Can't Focus? Try These 7 Simple ADHD Concentration Tips*. Everyday Health. Retrieved February 3, 2023, from https://www.everydayhealth.com/adhd-pictures/cant-focus-try-these-simple-adhd-concentration-tips.aspx

Low, K. (2022, September 12). *How to Focus With ADHD*. Verywell Mind. Retrieved February 3, 2023, from https://www.verywellmind.com/work-tips-from-adults-with-add-20396

(2022, June 10). *ADHD Medication*. Cleveland Clinic. Retrieved February 5, 2023, from https://my.clevelandclinic.org/health/treatments/11766-adhd-medication

Kelly, K., & Ramundo, P. (2022, July 13). *Forget the Lotus Position: How to Meditate — ADHD Style*. Web MD. Retrieved February 5, 2023, from https://www.additudemag.com/how-to-meditate-for-adhd-symptoms/

Saunders, M. S. (2022, September 12). *Guided Meditations for Working with ADHD and Anxiety*. Mindful. Retrieved February 5, 2023, from https://www.mindful.org/guided-meditations-for-working-with-adhd-and-anxiety/

Whelan, C. (2021, April 12). *8 Tips for ADHD Meditation*. Healthline. Retrieved February 5, 2023, from https://www.healthline.com/health/adhd/adhd-meditation

(2023, January 21). *Why Sugar is Kryptonite: ADHD Diet Truths.* ADDitutde. Retrieved February 5, 2023, from https://www.additudemag.com/adhd-diet-nutrition-sugar/#:~:text=Foods%20rich%20in%20protein%20%E2%80%94%20lean

Roybal, B. (2021, June 14). *ADHD Diet and Nutrition: Foods To Eat & Foods to Avoid.* Web MD. Retrieved February 5, 2023, from https://www.webmd.com/add-adhd/adhd-diets

Langmaid, S. (2022, August 25). *Hyperfocus.* WebMD. Retrieved February 5, 2023, from https://www.webmd.com/add-adhd/hyperfocus-flow

Barrell, A. (2019, July 18). *What to know about ADHD and hyperfocus.* Medical News Today. Retrieved February 5, 2023, from https://www.medicalnewstoday.com/articles/325681

(n.d.). *ADHD Hyperfocus: How to manage this double-edged sword for your health and productivity.* Dr. Sharon Saline. Retrieved February 5, 2023, from https://drsharonsaline.com/2022/01/26/adhd-hyperfocus-how-to-manage-this-double-edged-sword-for-your-health-and-productivity/

Rabiner, D., Ph.D., & Hamlin, E. D., Ph.D. (2020, September 3). *Can Neurofeedback Effectively Treat ADHD?* ADDitude Mag. Retrieved February 5, 2023, from https://www.additudemag.com/neurofeedback-therapy-treat-adhd/amp/

Heyl, J. C. (2022, June 2). *Neurofeedback Treatment: Can It Help Treat ADHD?* Verywell Mind. Retrieved February 5, 2023, from https://www.verywellmind.com/neurofeedback-treatment-for-adhd-5271502#:~:text=Neurofeedback%20is%20a%20promising%20treatment

(n.d.). *HOW TO MAKE A MIND MAP IN 8 STEPS.* IMind Q. Retrieved February 6, 2023, from https://www.imindq.com/how-to-make-a-mind-map/#:~:text=Mind%20maps%20work%20on%20the

Abramovich, A., & Schweiger, A. (2009). Unwanted intrusive and worrisome thoughts in adults with Attention Deficit\Hyperactivity Disorder. *Psychiatry Research, 168*(3), 230-233. https://doi.org/10.1016/j.psychres.2008.06.004

(2021, August 24). *10 Executive Functioning Skills: The Ultimate Guide*. The Pathway 2 Success. Retrieved February 6, 2023, from https://www.thepathway2success.com/10-executive-functioning-skills-the-ultimate-guide/

BOOK 2.

ADHD Organization and Cleaning

Simple Solutions To Quickly Get Organized, Stay Organized Long Term, and Make Cleaning With ADHD Easier

---

PART 1.

Making Organization and Cleaning Easy – Even With ADHD

INTRODUCTION

Growing up, I always kept my bedroom door shut. If people came over, I imagined them asking, "How can you live like that?". I was embarrassed.

I didn't want to draw the looks or comments from my parents, who had long given up on telling me to clean my room.

I took my first crack at home organization when I was 6. "Clean your room," they said. "We want everything off the floor."

I was proud of my out-of-the-box thinking when I announced I was done.

"It's just a blanket on the floor. I like it there". It certainly looked like an improvement to me.

No toys or clothes were in sight, but that blanket was pretty lumpy.

That's part of it for us, though. Out of sight, out of mind. Because if there is too much in sight, we have no idea where to start, mental overload, and we go find something else to work on.

I wouldn't recognize that I had ADHD for another 20 years. Despite the books and papers embarrassingly falling out of my school locker every time I opened it, constantly forgetting things I needed, teachers calling home because I was 'zoning out' in class, and setting the kitchen toaster on fire twice – we only got the pop-up ones after that. The ones that stayed on until you decided your food was done were a hazard in our house. I'd forget I had food in there at all.

These were just deemed character flaws. That's just the way he is. That kind of thinking had me trying all of the typical suggestions. Just put it back when you're done using it. Make yourself a list. Clean your room once a day, and then you can keep up with it. I did want to live in an organized space. I liked seeing others' homes or rooms all put together. But these basic suggestions never worked for me, and I was sure I was the problem.

Fast forward to my twenties. I had found my passion in mental and behavioral health. I became a coach and worked with people from all walks of life. I loved learning strategies that worked and being able to help others through their struggles. But like the mechanic who never fixes his own car in his downtime, my apartment and car were still a mess.

One day, the director at the organization I worked for pulled me aside and asked if I wanted to manage one of their recovery homes. I had a strong reputation at that organization. This position meant that I would be responsible for running a household where 12 residents lived. A 4000 sq. ft, 5 bedroom, 2 bathroom house meant to be a clean, healthy, structured living space for residents working on their recovery. Ensuring they made their beds, kept their rooms clean, and stuck to a regular chore schedule that contributed to the home they lived in was all part of it. Our organization had a strong 'practice what you preach' culture. Not a job I should take at this point, right?

I was in my late twenties, facing a mountain of student debt, working two jobs to keep up, and this offer came with my own separate sunny one-bedroom apartment attached to the main house. Rent-free. I said yes almost immediately.

I had no idea how I would do it, but I had to make it work. I wanted to be the person that could do well at this job for the residents' sake and for my own as well. Because this entire property belonged to the organization, we were subject to regular inspections on short notice, if any notice at all. So there was no faking it.

At this stage, I had several advantages beyond the average person with ADHD looking to get organized. First, I was freshly moving into this space, so I was mindful of what I brought with me and what got tossed. I also had time to pick the brain of the director who had managed that house for several years before me. Finally, I did a deep dive into the research to learn what made my brain different and what might help me in this scenario. Then, I started applying what I was learning and building systems and habits. Ultimately my mindset and perspective on my ability to keep things organized began to shift drastically.

Soon enough, my success at running this house was being echoed back to me at the most unexpected times. I would hear comments from residents that they were glad they were in this house compared to others. Staff would say things like, "I heard you run a tight ship over there." or, "I hear you've got a solid house."

I cannot describe how proud I was of myself. I had beyond surpassed my goal of just wanting a friend to be able to drop in for coffee unannounced. I had actually changed the way I was living. I was organized, and I was keeping it that way. I was keeping the whole house organized with 12 other people in it as well, all while still working a full-time job outside of that home.

Years after leaving that house, I still have the same systems in place. Schedules and family life have changed, but the habits I developed were both flexible and structured enough to keep me organized and proud of my home. That's my hope for you. I want you to be able to understand how ADHD impacts you and leverage the way that your brain works. I want you to establish systems and habits that make it almost effortless and help you have a home you can be proud of.

Bins, lists, and timers are all great, but I'm here to bring you the systems that work. The perspectives and habits you can put in place to start changing your life. By breaking down the science of ADHD and organization skills, sharing the stories that matter, and giving you actionable steps you can use immediately, this book is the guide you haven't seen before because it's made for you. Specifically for the person with ADHD, for you as an individual to take these strategies and make them your own.

I've spent the last several years teaching effective ADHD strategies and systems to others. In working with other adults who have ADHD, I've come to realize a few things. Many don't have a clear concept of what ADHD really is and how it's impacting them. They rarely come to therapy seeking treatment for it. It is a common misperception that the only way to address ADHD symptoms is through medication. So it can be surprising when they learn there are habits and behavioral techniques that will help.

People with ADHD often come to therapy to work on things like stress related to their home life, work performance, and academic achievement. They are coming in to talk about their anxiety and hopelessness because they can never figure out how to keep up. They explain how they struggle with laziness and want to learn how to have stronger discipline and willpower to do what they need to do.

People come in very aware that something is wrong. They can describe the impacts of their struggles in detail, and they outline their goals to be more consistent, motivated, productive, less emotionally reactive, and generally feel more in control of their lives.

At the point when they hear about ADHD, they imagine the little boy in class that can't sit still, climbs on everything, and is always disruptive. That boy was in my class too. But I sat a few rows away with symptoms that looked quite different from his.

Sometimes people will disagree that ADHD is what is going on, which often has to do with the stereotypes and stigma they perceive. Other times they remember something about having ADHD in their childhood but figured they grew out of it, and then there are the people who have a lightbulb moment, where so many things across years of time finally make sense.

It starts to click for many as they go through the diagnostic criteria. I find that the clients who do best in really changing their lives and their homes are the ones who acknowledge the problem at hand. Then they open up to genuinely learn about their brain and functioning.

Understanding the ADHD brain is key because we need a shift in our perspective and overall mindset about ourselves, our needs, and our abilities. I needed to understand that it's not just a matter of trying harder or doing the things that work for others who don't have ADHD. It's a matter of really grasping the roles of executive function and the dopamine reward pathway so that we can use strategies tailored to address these issues.

Over time I have witnessed people change their lives completely. We really underestimate the power that our home environment plays in our lives. The impact is huge! It influences the mood we wake up in, how smoothly our morning runs, and whether we leave the house feeling calm, in control, and looking forward to our day.

The habits we have at home often play out in our workspaces as well. I often see the insights and behaviors that I teach, which are aimed at the home, become generalized to other spaces that my clients spend time in, like their office or car. This is a true indicator of skill building. In these scenarios, the person is not just following and repeating instructions. They are mastering concepts and adapting them in unique ways to other situations that work.

By now, I hope it's clear that If you really want to change what is going on in your life and get your home under control, you'll need a solid understanding of what is really going on so that you can fully take in the concepts that can help. I spent a long time trying to work on my issues the wrong way. By that, I mean I had temporary success, but it never lasted.

These were like behavioral crash diets. And we know how well those work – until they don't. I could send you a beautiful picture of the room I just reorganized, but undoubtedly it would soon be back to normal. I'd be stepping over things, losing items I needed, leaving the house late because I had spent 30 minutes trying to find my keys, and losing money of all things. I would feel frustrated and ashamed. It wasn't until I learned how my brain worked and the reasons that I struggled so much that I was able to transform them into solutions that stuck.

So I'm going to walk you through that process to help you develop your own systems and solutions that stick. Once you've completed this book, you'll better understand your patterns and behavior. You'll understand how to leverage your ADHD brain and make it work for you, and you'll learn to accommodate your needs to turn your home into the stable, clean, peaceful sanctuary you deserve.

How to use this book and what you'll learn

I've broken this book down into two parts. In the first part, you'll learn about what ADHD is, how it impacts the brain's functioning, and why it can be so damn difficult to stay organized or to motivate yourself to clean when you don't feel like it. Next, we'll cover the various practical techniques and strategies that will address ADHD issues with motivation and procrastination so that you can actually get started!

We'll have a full chapter on your step-by-step process for decluttering and staying decluttered. Clutter is a huge issue when you have ADHD. It comes back to your executive functioning. The idea of decluttering can often feel just as daunting as getting organized. By the end of that chapter, you'll have what you need to get rid of the clutter and prevent it from building back up. Then we're ready to get organized!

I'll walk you through how to establish a home organization system that works for you and that you can sustain long-term. This chapter is one of the most comprehensive in the book and guides you through how to establish a simple yet powerful organizational system based on your individual needs. You'll find that once you have developed a simple system made up of small habits, staying organized becomes automatic and easy.

Now that you've decluttered and organized, we need to keep your place clean. Cleaning is different from organizing and decluttering. This involves ongoing maintenance of your home once it's organized. People with ADHD often struggle to clean consistently and efficiently, making mistakes that waste valuable time and energy. I'm all about simplicity because I know that if it's not served up simply, it's much less likely to happen.

In the last section of Part 1, we'll talk about sustaining long-term habits. Believe it or not, there is a science to building habits! I'll tell you what you need to know about the science of building habits for people with ADHD and how you can make your new organizational system stick for good.

I encourage you to fully read Part 1 in order. I would also suggest you start practicing the concepts and strategies you are reading about and really put them into action in your own life. Try them on, see how they feel, and stick with them. I often point out to my clients that our session typically takes up about 1 hr of their week. There are 167 more hours in your week! If you only spend 1 hour reading or thinking about improvements and the other 167 practicing and reinforcing habits and behaviors that don't work for you, you are unlikely to change.

Use the key takeaways and suggestions at the end of each chapter to start making changes immediately. Don't expect perfection. Habits that stick around are built in small steps over time. We're looking for incremental tiny changes one day and one moment at a time.

In the second part of this book, I'll guide you through each room individually. You'll see short chapters for every room in your house, from the living room, bathroom, kitchen, bedrooms, etc. Each room differs in how you use it, the traffic it gets, and the best ways to get it organized and keep it that way. So we'll do a deep dive into each space, leaving no bill, pillowcase, or coffee filter unturned.

Whereas the first part of this book should definitely be read in order, in the second part of the book, you might choose to jump around depending on what suits your needs or what area of the house you want to focus on first. For example, if you don't have a home office, feel free to skip that section! But even if you have rooms in your house that are doing pretty well, I would still suggest reviewing the chapters pertaining to those rooms – you might pick up some tips you hadn't thought of!

By the time you finish this book, you'll be an expert on how ADHD affects you and your home. You'll have a strategic plan of attack to deal with it and know how to motivate yourself to action. You'll feel confident using solid approaches tailored to your ADHD brain so that you can declutter and get organized. Finally, you'll have an exact blueprint of the best strategies for each room and how to keep it all going.

CHAPTER 1.

ADHD – ACCORDING TO SCIENCE

"Adults don't really have ADHD...."

I actually worked with a psychiatrist who had been in the field for at least two decades and said this. So I'll just say that if it's possible for some mental health professionals to feed into the stigma, stereotypes, and general misinformation about ADHD, you could have been misinformed at some point as well. So let's get aligned about what ADHD is, how it affects the brain, and what the impacts are.

For a long time, ADHD was widely thought to only affect children. The American Psychological Association defines ADHD as a neurodevelopmental disorder that can be both chronic and debilitating. It doesn't come and go, it won't disappear if we work hard enough, and although the severity and presentation of symptoms can change over time, we generally take it with us into adulthood.

Another common misconception is that males are more likely to have ADHD than females. This is based on common differences in how the symptoms present. Males are more often observed to have hyperactive, more outwardly disruptive symptoms, while females more frequently experience inattention, which can be harder to see, resulting in underdiagnosis.

People who are undiagnosed or diagnosed later in life, or even those who get diagnosed early but are given no understanding of what to expect as an adult, will struggle more with their symptoms of ADHD. We may go years feeling like we just don't measure up and wondering what is wrong with us. We might come to view ourselves as uniquely flawed in some way. But this is very much not the case.

A person with ADHD has physical differences in how their brain develops and functions. In fact, MRIs have shown consistent differences in several parts of the brain when comparing people who have ADHD and those who do not. One of the most noteworthy structures that are impacted by ADHD is the frontal lobe which is why we have significant impairments in executive functioning (Khadka et al., 2016). The executive function system generally refers to a group of mental skills we use to set goals, make plans, and accomplish things.

Additionally, we generally have less dopamine available than people who don't have ADHD (Volkow et al., 2009). This impacts our memory, motivation, mood, and feelings of satisfaction. This is why we often find ourselves chasing quick hits of dopamine by opting for fast rewards rather than being able to wait or spend time working for bigger rewards. We have a strong aversion to delaying gratification. Rewards are typically tied to motivation, and with ADHD, we frequently have a reward-motivation deficit (Volkow et al., 2009). We want the reward right now, and our preference for immediate gratification naturally makes tasks that require time and effort more difficult.

As a side note, our reduced levels of dopamine are why some people find medication helpful. The medications prescribed for ADHD tend to increase our available dopamine, thereby helping to address some of the related struggles. Though these medications do not solve our problems completely, and many people choose not to go the medication route for one reason or another. This book is both relevant and necessary whether you've chosen to use medications or not. As you've learned by now, dopamine is only one piece of the puzzle.

Knowing these differences in how our brain works and viewing our behavior through this lens can help us understand why "just try harder" and " I just need to focus" simply won't work for us. When we fully grasp the reasons behind our struggles, we can start looking toward solutions that accommodate our differences and still find ways to reach our goals.

Why ADHD Makes Cleaning and Organizing So Difficult

So what does any of this have to do with home organization? We tend to put things down everywhere, we forget them if they're not directly in our line of sight, we stop seeing things when they sit in our line of sight for too long, and we can be impossible to motivate to action when there is no direct pressure, urgency, or reward attached to it. That's not to say that we don't want our homes to be more clean and organized, but it can feel impossible to cross the bridge from desire and intention to effective action.

When it comes to changing our behavior, knowledge is power. Knowledge builds the foundation for the strategies we need to put into practice. ADHD often makes us feel out of control, especially when it comes to simple things that we feel we should be able to do. The more we understand ourselves, the more equipped we'll be to make the changes we want to see in our lives.

So far, we've addressed common misconceptions about ADHD and explored important biological differences. Now we'll look at the behavioral patterns and challenges that stem from these biological differences and contribute to making cleaning and organizing feel like such a hopeless endeavor.

People who have ADHD typically struggle with persistent patterns of inattention or hyperactive/impulsive behaviors. They can also have a combination of both.

Inattention generally shows up as:

- overlooking details
- struggling to stay on task

- getting easily distracted or sidetracked
- having difficulty organizing tasks that involve multiple steps
- losing necessary items
- forgetting daily activities

While symptoms of hyperactivity/impulsivity include:

- fidgeting or difficulty remaining in one place
- frequent restlessness
- talking excessively
- difficulty waiting for one's turn
- interrupting or intruding upon others.

As I've mentioned, we struggle with executive dysfunction because of deficits in our pre-frontal cortex. Our executive function system is basically our brain's manager. The part that is supposed to take charge, delegate, and run the ship. Often it can feel like our manager is out to lunch. So we end up winging it and struggling to prioritize tasks effectively, identify how to approach a problem or task and decide how much time and attention we should give to things. This is why we consistently struggle with organizing, planning, managing our time, regulating emotions, and why we can often make impulsive decisions.

Working memory is a key area of the executive function system that greatly impacts our ability to maintain a clean and organized environment. Working memory is the ability to take in information and hold onto it long enough to use it. Imagine the server who takes your order without writing it down and still gets it correct. He used working memory to do that.

A working memory deficit is why I can go to the mailbox, take a look at my mail, understand quickly what needs to be addressed, decide that I'm going to address it when I get inside the house, then put it down somewhere and forget it ever existed. Even for that simple task, I easily determined the steps in my head but couldn't hold onto them long enough to follow through. In this way, working memory creates clutter and can make large tasks with multiple steps feel overwhelming and overly complicated.

Researchers also suspect our working memory impairments create the experience of time blindness (Zheng et al., 2022). Many people with ADHD do not assess time accurately. We don't correctly judge how long a task will take us, and we don't tend to accurately track how much time has passed. This, combined with difficulty focusing and a tendency to get sidetracked, lead to poor time management.

Now take that large task with multiple steps that have started to feel a bit overwhelming and combine that with our time blindness and tendency toward immediate gratification. Multiple studies have highlighted that people with ADHD struggle with delay aversion (Sjowall et al., 2013). In other words, we don't do well with delayed rewards. In fact, we avoid them. Combined, you can start to get a full picture of why we procrastinate, struggle with motivation, get easily overwhelmed, and just avoid a task altogether.

When I was younger, my stepfather could not understand why I couldn't get organized and keep things that way. He would try to incentivize me by saying, "It will just take you 2 hours, but once you're done, that's it! You'll feel so good about it and won't have to think about it anymore." Nope. First off, it would take me way longer, and I knew that. Second, delay aversion was at play. That kind of incentive made no sense to my brain because it skipped over all the misery of actually doing the organizing. I had zero capacity to think about feeling good *after* the misery was over.

Now that I've painted the picture of how entrenched our struggles are, I want to remind you that I don't struggle to keep my home organized anymore. I still have a poor working memory, I absolutely experience time blindness and delay aversion, and I experience almost every symptom of inattention and a few of the hyperactive/impulsive behaviors as well. So this is not about a magic cure-all that makes our symptoms go away. But my house is in good shape. It stays that way, and I feel good about it. The two are not mutually exclusive. We can have ADHD and still have homes we're proud of.

You Can Have ADHD and an Organized Home

I used to say I had a butterfly brain. If you've ever watched butterflies, they seem to flutter from one flower to the next with no apparent strategy or sense of purpose, just fluttering around. You know there is a point to what they're doing ultimately, but how they go about it just looks random and like they probably could get a bit dizzy along the way. This resonated with me because it felt like my brain was constantly fluttering from one thing to the next with not much structure or purpose. I just kind of had to hope that it wanted to land on the right thing. Because when it did, I could be insanely productive.

People who have ADHD have the capacity to be highly creative because when we brainstorm, we can think of a bunch of different angles very quickly. The same mental process that makes a large task super overwhelming because of all of its daunting pieces is also the process that allows us to come up with lots of creative ideas very quickly.

The same brain that avoids tasks we might not find enjoyable and avoids working toward rewards that seem too far off will hyperfocus with intensity and precision when we find something that engages, interests, or otherwise rewards us. You've undoubtedly experienced this hyperfocus at various times. It's those moments that have you saying, "wow if I could always do this, I would get so much done!".

It really is about creating the right circumstances. So, while many components of cleaning and organizing a home seem difficult or nearly impossible for someone with ADHD, that may have more to do with the fact that we've been looking at the process through a neurotypical lens. We've been trying to make it work using the advice and suggestions of people who don't have ADHD.

When we start using strategies that target our struggles, we can accommodate our needs more effectively. This means addressing the limits of our working memory before we lose important information, tapping into our need for dopamine by creating a more rewarding process, and using specific strategies to reduce getting sidetracked and distracted. Developing this skill set will help you to see how a disorganized home is a side effect of not knowing how to manage certain symptoms. ADHD does not mean you inherently can't have an organized home. You just didn't have the right tools until now.

Progress, Not Perfection – The Importance of Self-Compassion

It's common among people with ADHD to struggle with perfectionism. When combined with our challenges regulating emotions, this can quickly lead to a spiral. If left unchecked, we can go from fine to doomed in 60 seconds. Knowing this, I am very deliberate about not beating myself up. I work on the same concept with my clients. There is no benefit to holding yourself to a standard of perfection and making yourself feel shame and guilt every time you don't measure up. It still won't make you perfect. But it will make it harder for you to move forward.

Self-compassion is extremely important throughout this process. This involves acknowledging where you're at, giving yourself credit for your efforts, and accepting that you will not be perfect and that you'll likely mess up along the way. That is okay, and it's all part of the process. You can still learn from your mistakes and encourage yourself to do better as you go.

Self-compassion sounds the way you might talk to a younger sibling, a close friend, or a loved one who is going through the exact difficult moment you are having. What might you say to them, and what's the tone you would use when you say it? That's how you need to talk to yourself. We naturally have a tendency to be much harder on ourselves. Thinking that we can handle it or that it will motivate us to do better. But the truth is having ADHD has likely led to years of self-criticism and struggles with self-worth. Be mindful of the impact that being harsh on yourself will have. I want you to succeed with this. Triggering an emotional spiral by beating yourself up has the potential to stop you right in your tracks from making any progress and is simply not worth it.

I worked with a client who would regularly struggle with cleaning. Part of it was that if she thought about picking up one thing, it would spiral into thoughts about what else needed to be done in that room. Before you knew it, she created an expectation that was way beyond what she could handle at that moment. So instead of picking up one thing, which she definitely could have handled, she wouldn't do anything. She would avoid it entirely. Because in her mind, picking up one thing meant she should pick up all the things. Don't do that. Set realistic expectations. Be gentle with yourself.

I have heard many of my clients with ADHD repeatedly refer to themselves as lazy, careless, lacking willpower, etc. I assure you, these things are not the case. Ultimately, they just lacked a clear understanding of how their brain functions and responds in scenarios where people who don't have ADHD might typically be successful. When a person with ADHD tries to force those same circumstances to work by trying harder, it's not effective. This then leads to feelings of failure and self-condemnation. Once clients better understand and accept what is going on for them, they establish ways to successfully work toward their goals.

The same goes for you. It's all about realistic expectations and one small step at a time. The ultimate goal is progress, not perfection.

Key Takeaways

- ADHD is a neurodevelopmental disorder. Symptoms persist over time and can affect all areas of a person's life.
- Understanding your symptoms helps you identify the exact strategies you'll need to reach your goal of having an organized home.
- You may have symptoms of inattention, hyperactivity/impulsivity, or both.
- Having less available dopamine impacts your mood, motivation, memory, and feelings of satisfaction. It's also why you struggle with delayed gratification.
- Executive dysfunction, caused by deficits in the pre-frontal cortex, impairs your ability to organize, plan, manage time, and regulate emotions.
- Self-compassion is extremely important throughout this process.
- We never inherently had a problem with an organized home. We just didn't have the right tools until now.

CHAPTER 2.

GETTING STARTED
OVERCOMING COMMON ADHD CHALLENGES

By now, you understand that my goal is to teach you how to use specific strategies and build habits and systems that address the ways ADHD impacts you in order to help you get and stay organized. While many books about organization will overlook the unique way a brain with ADHD functions, this book will demonstrate the importance and efficacy of working *with* your unique brain.

It all goes back to knowing how ADHD impacts you, understanding the executive function deficits and your internal reward system, and understanding that your dopamine reward system may not act the same as it would in a person who does not have ADHD. Using that lens – you can identify what about a situation is not working for you and why the thing isn't working, whether it's your working memory, motivation, difficulty organizing the task in your mind, time blindness, lack of sustained focus, etc. Once you can identify which thing it is, you can use the right accommodation to address it.

In this chapter, you'll learn simple things that can make ADHD symptoms worse, practical strategies to address common challenges, and ADHD-specific tips to get motivated, stay motivated, and beat procrastination.

Let's Start By Not Making Your Symptoms Worse

You may have noticed you are sometimes especially distractible, unfocused, or irritable. Whereas you can go days feeling like your ADHD isn't so bad, other times, your symptoms can feel much more intense. A simple task you handled well enough yesterday just doesn't seem to be happening for you today, making you wonder what's changed.

It's essential to understand the triggers that can make ADHD even worse. Some of them you've heard before, but what can be surprising is the exact way these triggers impact your ADHD symptoms. Once we recognize the habits and circumstances that make our symptoms especially hard to manage, we can make small but necessary changes to set ourselves up for success.

REDUCE OVERSTIMULATION

Most people who have ADHD struggle with sensory processing to some degree. Meaning that we might be easily overstimulated by sensory experiences such as bright light, loud noises, and certain textures, odors, or tastes. These things can bother us to a higher degree than people who do not have ADHD and can lead to overstimulation which can leave you feeling incredibly stressed out and unable to function.

It's important to accommodate yourself. Have a set of earplugs if needed, or don't be afraid to ask a loved one to turn the volume down if it's set too high for you. Get yourself some rubber kitchen gloves if that gross texture at the bottom of the sink keeps you from going near it. If overstimulation is getting to you, don't be afraid to step away and take a breather. This is about learning to nurture yourself and the way your brain functions. In order to learn and implement some new behaviors, you can't afford to be overstimulated at the same time. Try to manage it where you can.

DOPAMINE

The Link Between Exercise, Sleep, and Your Ability to Get Organized

Having ADHD means that we are already lower in dopamine than the average person. So, it makes sense that being mindful of things that impact our dopamine levels is important because we can be even more affected. That means not taking good care of our bodies can make it harder to function through seemingly simple tasks like decluttering the kitchen counter or putting away the laundry.

We already know that stimulant medications are among the most common treatments for ADHD. Their efficacy is due to increasing the availability of both dopamine and norepinephrine in the body. Research has clearly demonstrated that aerobic exercise also increases the availability of dopamine and norepinephrine (Mehren et al., 2020). Research also shows that the effects of exercise can be immediate. While there are many more positive long-term effects of exercise on both the brain and body, a 20-30 minute session of moderate intensity can offer immediate improvements in both cognitive and behavioral functioning for people with ADHD (Mehren et al., 2020).

Another aspect of taking care of your body is sleep. Lack of sleep will make managing your mood, focus, and working memory even worse. If you have ADHD, chances are you also have some sleep issues (Hvolby, 2015). Addressing these issues and trying to get enough sleep is super important. While the Society for Neuroscience (2008) highlights a temporary increase in dopamine following a night of sleep deprivation, they found that this is our body's attempt to compensate, and it comes with reduced cognitive functioning. So while you may still feel somewhat alert after a night of poor sleep, ongoing sleep disturbances are unsustainable for someone with ADHD and will throw you off more in the grand scheme.

This doesn't mean you have to run out and get a sleep aid. There are many other places to start. Check your sleeping environment. Consider weighted blankets, sound machines, or sleep apps. Watch your carb, sugar, and caffeine intake in the evening. Give yourself 1-2 hours away from screens before bed. There are often small changes like this that we can make to improve our sleep. And it's easy to disregard these small shifts when we underestimate the impact of meeting this basic need.

A WORD ABOUT STRESS

Comprehensively addressing the topic of stress management is outside the scope of this book. But it is vital to consider whether you might have consistently high stress levels that are making your ADHD worse. Ongoing exposure to high levels of stress can further weaken the functioning of the pre-frontal cortex (Arnsten, 2015). Further impairing this part of the brain is something that people with ADHD would do well to avoid. High stress will directly impact your critical thinking abilities and can trigger your emotional dysregulation, leading to intense frustration that can be hard to calm down from. Stress will make it even harder to focus, problem solve, and organize your thoughts.

If you think you are experiencing chronic high stress, my first suggestion is to consider speaking with a mental health professional. Even if it is short-term to address the nature and cause of your current stress so that you can learn some individualized strategies. A quick search for therapists online will point you in the direction of therapists that you could speak with in person or via online therapy platforms. Therapists are more accessible now than they have ever been before, and they can help.

If therapy is not an option at this time or if you prefer to find other ways to manage your stress on your own, there are other options. The American Institute of Stress is a non-profit organization that maintains updated information on all things related to stress and managing it. They have reviewed several of the top stress management apps based on user experience and credibility. Some of their top suggestions are Headspace, Happify: For Stress and Worry, Pacifica, and ReachOut Breathe. These apps are grounded in evidence-based techniques to help you manage stress symptoms and may be useful as you continue making positive changes in your life.

Identifying Practical Strategies that Work with Your Brain

As we move toward developing your decluttering, organizing, and cleaning systems, it is important to build the foundation you'll need to be successful in implementing those systems. Here I have identified 5 specific foundational skills that will lay the groundwork for the rest of your success throughout this book.

These skills involve developing a deeper awareness of your own behaviors to start addressing the patterns that are not working for you. You'll learn how to manage time blindness, eliminate distractions, and navigate challenges in your working memory. Finally, you'll learn the importance of assigning a specific place for important items and how to choose the right spot so that you always know where to find them.

RECOGNIZE YOUR PATTERNS

Pay attention to the things you repeatedly do and say that cause trouble when it comes to trying to maintain a clean and organized space. This involves getting really honest with yourself about the things you are doing that are not working for you. If you can identify the ADHD challenge at hand, you can come up with more effective strategies to address it and get yourself moving in the right direction.

- Do you feel like you've been busy all day, doing things that had to get done, but you still haven't accomplished the one task you knew was important?
    - This is productive procrastination – you'll benefit from breaking up tasks, time blocking, and using anchor tasks

- Do you tend to sit there immobilized and binge-watching shows on Netflix or scrolling on social media because the idea of jumping into your task is just not something you want to do right now?

- Your dopamine reward system would prefer to watch those shows or scroll, so you'll need to find other ways to tap into your reward system

- Do you just keep forgetting?
    - Accommodate your working memory
- Do you really want to get it done but find that you keep putting it off because you don't really know where to start or how to proceed?
    - Motivation strategies and breaking down the task into smaller pieces will help
- Do you tend to put things down in the wrong place and lack routine and structure in areas where you feel you need some?
    - This is where assigning a home for important items and using strategies to accommodate your working memory can help
- Do you tend to say unhelpful things to yourself?
    - "I'll do it in 5 minutes." – That's just a rationalization to keep doing what you are doing right now. You won't want to do it in 5 minutes, either.
    - "This is going to take forever!" – You would benefit from using strategies that target time blindness.
    - "I'll remember because this is really important." – You know your limits with working memory. If it's really important, why risk it? Write it down.
    - "I'll just write it on this scrap of paper. At least it's written, and I can add it to my planner later." – That's not going to work. You'll lose it or forget to look at it. This is a working memory issue – we have better places that are just as easy to write this down.
    - "I'll get the bedroom done tomorrow afternoon." – That's a good goal, but time blindness can make it difficult for

us to accurately judge how long a task will take. Make sure you are truly giving yourself enough time.

Take a moment and think about your patterns. The moments and decisions that cause the biggest issues for you. What do they look like? What do you say to yourself? What can you do instead? This is how you recognize and address your problematic patterns.

MANAGING TIME BLINDNESS

Time blindness can affect anyone but is particularly common among people with ADHD (Weissenberger et al., 2021). It goes back to our executive dysfunction issues. If you have ADHD, chances are you tend to struggle with estimating how much time a task will take you and how much time has passed once you're involved in doing the task. You'll know this is a struggle for you if you often miss deadlines, misjudge how long things will take you, or you unintentionally tend to show up too late or too early for appointments.

While time blindness does not impact every single person with ADHD, if you consider it a problem that could get in the way of getting organized or moving through tasks in your home effectively, there are several ways to start managing it.

- Add more time, even if you don't think it will take that long.
- Shut down hyperfocus when it kicks in for anything but the task at hand
- Use visual timers
- Use TV shows or music playlists as a timer
- Make the most out of small amounts of extra time in your day. An extra 5 minutes can be enough for simple tasks like checking your calendar or picking up the clutter in one room

A common mistake I see with time blindness is continuing to try the same approach and hoping it will work the next time. If you have tried a particular approach to manage your timing but find that you're continuously not meeting deadlines, taking much longer than expected, or losing track of time altogether, try one of the strategies listed above. Any strategy that helps you to be more aware of the time that is passing will help, as we can be especially present-focused when experiencing time blindness.

ELIMINATE DISTRACTIONS

With ADHD, both internal and external distractions can pose a problem. When it comes to internal distractions, this might involve getting lost in your thoughts or daydreaming. This is a common challenge. If you are trying to listen to a lecture or meeting, you might try taking notes on what is being said. This can help keep your focus on what the speaker is saying. But when it comes to home organization, the goal is to keep your attention on the task you are engaging in.

If internal distractions are getting in your way, music can help. Research has demonstrated that our dopamine levels increase when we listen to music we like. This is why attention and focus can improve while we are listening to pleasurable music (Zhao & Toichi, 2020). There are different types of focus music; you'll have to try them out to see what works best for you. You can find them on youtube, Spotify, or focus apps. Some are just a specific type of steady sound that plays in the background of whatever you are doing. Other types of music that can help include instrumental music to help calm you or songs with lyrics. Different things work for different people, but if you find your mind wandering off too much when you are working in silence, try adding some focus music to the mix.

When it comes to external distractions, preplanning is key. Before you start working on a task, consider the potential external distractions that could come up. Phones are a common distraction, as are people around you who may not know that you need to be undisturbed. Planning ahead to prevent distractions before they occur is crucial because we may struggle to appropriately choose where our focus should be going in the moment.

For example, if you've decided to organize your closet, but your phone alerts you that an email just came through. Now you might stop organizing altogether and intensely focus on responding to that email. So it may not be that you can't focus, but more so that your focus is great – it's just not on the right thing at the right time.

We live in a time where we are used to being extremely accessible and have to handle multiple requests for our immediate attention. However, most things can wait an hour at least. Use the focus mode on your phone so that you can silence all but the most important apps for the duration of your task. For me, that looks like silencing everything but incoming phone calls for an hour at a time. If there's an emergency, I'll get a call. Anything else can wait an hour.

If others are in your house, tell them you will be busy for the next hour. Your partner might be able to help you by leaving you alone if they know you are unavailable for the next hour. If you have kids, you might set them up with a task for the next hour or ask them to help with something in particular. You could also plan certain tasks for when you know they will be otherwise occupied. This way, you have one less distraction.

ACCOMMODATE THE LIMITS OF YOUR WORKING MEMORY

Some things can help address working memory deficits in the long term. Daily meditation has been shown to thicken the prefrontal cortex, which could help improve your working memory (Lazar et al., 2005). But in the meantime, acknowledge that it's an issue and make accommodations for yourself.

I've grown to expect that I will forget it and that it won't happen unless it is written down somewhere that I am definitely going to look at or unless some kind of alarm accompanies it. I actually use a few types of calendars because I want to leave myself with as little ability as possible to forget to do the things that I know are important.

It can be so much extra work to remember things that, for many people, it creates more anxiety to keep reminding ourselves of important things. Knowing that you have a place to keep those things stored can be such a relief. In that way, I don't see my planner as work but as a huge help.

I don't feel any pressure to try to remember something as long as I know I've written it down. The thing you do have to worry about is looking at it. I keep mine open and on the kitchen counter. I also use a Google calendar on my phone that will sound an alarm both 30 minutes and 10 minutes before I have to do something. Ideally, I like my written planner and Google calendar to match, but at the very least, the most important tasks I cannot forget make it into both.

I also have catchall lists. These are the lists you have running for when you don't have time or when it's not readily accessible to put the information in the ideal place, such as your calendar, planner, phone, etc. I have a whiteboard on my fridge and in my bedroom. I also use the notepad on my phone. This may sound like many lists, but they all have one function. They are a catchall for things that need to be addressed. The reason they are in 3 different places goes back to the reward system. I won't do it if it's too hard with too little reward. That includes going to another room to write something down. With this system, things always get written down.

Setting a habit of checking your lists in the morning and at night also means you won't miss anything. Don't worry if this sounds overwhelming. I've introduced the concept of habit stacking, which you can start trying and practicing now. You can check your lists in the morning by attaching them to your coffee or breakfast routine. You can also check your lists in the evening by connecting this to a specific part of your nighttime routine. We'll also do a deep dive into the science of building habits later in chapter 6.

Starting these habits of writing things down and checking them is the first step to setting up your own systems for keeping your house in shape. When you start deciding to complete certain tasks, you'll need somewhere to commit that block of time so that you don't forget. You'll need to be in the habit of checking those lists to make sure you didn't miss anything. You'll be surprised at how much less stress and pressure you feel when you realize there is no need to try remembering the next thing. I've had multiple clients tell me they didn't realize they would feel that relieved at just being able to rely on writing things down.

To make this system work for yourself, you'll need:

- A calendar app for your phone (make sure it has the ability to set alerts, such as Google Calendar).
- A planner (I prefer one that has a weekly view with hourly timeslots on each day. when it lays open, you can see one entire week)
- 2 simple whiteboards (small ones are fine)
- A notepad app in your phone (your phone likely came with one. Simple is fine)

STEP 1:
LET'S WORK ON YOUR PLANNER.

- I try to have it filled at least 2 weeks out. But if I know of other things in advance, they also get written down. Every weekend I fill in another week so that I can always see at least 2 weeks out.
- Fill in all of the appointments, meetings, events, and commitments that you currently have scheduled. (block out time needed for travel/commuting)
- Now that the MUSTs are in there, you should have a clear view of what time is available.
- Now, you'll see the available space where you can write down things you want to accomplish, like decluttering the kitchen counter.

STEP 2:
SET UP YOUR PHONE CALENDAR.

- Take everything you put into the two weeks on your planner and enter it into your phone calendar.
- NOTE – if there are things that repeat, you should be able to choose to make them automatically repeat on this calendar on a daily, weekly, biweekly, monthly, or custom cadence. This means you won't have to manually enter it again.
- Now set up your notifications/alerts. This should be in the settings section of your calendar. I recommend at least 2 alerts for each task – one that tells you it's coming up soon and one that tells you it's almost starting. I use a 30-minute and 10-minute reminder. My phone will sound or vibrate (depending on whether I have the sound on). You might start with these alerts, try them out, and decide if you think they need to change. I would give it 2 weeks before you decide they are too much. Initially, I felt the 10-minute reminder was pointless and irritating. When I shut it off and ended up missing a meeting despite the reminder I had received 30 minutes prior, I turned it back on, and it's been that way since.

STEP 3:
YOUR WHITEBOARDS AND PHONE NOTEPAD

- Remember, they are catchalls. Essentially backups for when your phone calendar or planner is less convenient. Or for when you want more of a visual.
- Post one on your fridge, one in your bedroom or living room (where ever you think makes the most sense. My home office is on one side of my bedroom, so the whiteboard is in there)
- The phone notepad – this may initially sound like it doesn't make sense in light of the phone calendar – but you will have moments where you want to do something but don't have

the time or mental capacity to figure out when to schedule it. Rather than not saving it at all, that is when it goes on the notepad.

- The biggest thing about the catchall lists is checking them. Morning and night to see what you can move from the lists directly into your planner/phone calendar.

Perspective is huge. People often talk about writing lists and using planners. For many, this has been unsuccessful. Part of this is based on your perspective about it. I see these things as a tool to address my working memory deficit. There is definitely a deficit here with ADHD. I'm not going to remember because I want to or because it's important. So writing it down and having it attached to automatic alarms that I don't have to set are the tools that step in where my working memory stops. This also means it has to get written right away as soon as the commitment or plan is made. Use this strategy for appointments and tasks, such as a bill that's due or when you need to set aside time to work on something, like organizing your home office.

Find a home for important items

I know I lose things, so they need a permanent spot where they always go right back. If I don't know where to put something while I'm cleaning up, that means I haven't given it a home yet, and it's not my laziness and forgetfulness that is the issue. I just haven't given it a space to go, and I know that my mind is not great at organizing on the fly.

As you consider where to create permanent spots for things in your home, you will need to acknowledge when something is not working. This is always better than trying to force it to work. Building a habit is one thing, but if it genuinely feels like it's not going to work, you might need a different system.

My keys are a great example. They've had a few different homes, but only one has worked. I tried keeping them in my briefcase, which seemed to make sense. I figured as long as they were in there, I would always have them when leaving the house. This didn't stick because they would fall to the bottom, and I would have to find them, which would take a couple of minutes. Ultimately I would get annoyed and stop throwing them in my briefcase because I didn't want to have to deal with digging them out again. Next, I tried to give them a home in a basket on the kitchen counter with other miscellaneous items. The same problem again was that other things went in this basket, the keys weren't visible, and I stopped using the system without even thinking about it. What finally worked? Key hooks. Visible, easy to find, and easy to hang there when I get home. Perfect spot, and it stuck. The point is, don't be afraid to make tweaks to your system. Just because the first home you find for something doesn't work, that does not mean you can't follow a system. It means that a particular system does not work for you. It's a combination of building the habit and choosing the right strategy.

Be flexible with yourself. I have never thought of myself as a structured person. In fact, being structured seems daunting to me. But I genuinely appreciate the hooks for my keys. I love the file holder for my papers that need to be addressed and the fact that I have a routine for when and how I go through that file because it makes my life easier. These are accommodations that work for me. As you start using the strategies I've introduced, and as we continue deeper into this book, you learn to create the accommodations that work for you.

Get Motivated – Let's Talk About Your Why

Discovering your ultimate reason why is huge. For me, my initial reason why tapped directly into my reward system. If I kept things clean and organized, I could keep my apartment. I also had a fear of embarrassment. Knowing this wasn't a situation where I could get away with just not inviting people over, I had no choice but to accept that people might see my apartment from time to time and that I had to be prepared for that to happen on short notice. Aside from that, I very much wanted to practice what I preached. I knew I was in a position to help others, and I owed it to them to hold myself to the same standards. I did not feel good about telling the clients in that house to live one way if I was living another way. So that was my initial reason why, and it was strong enough to work.

After that, my reason became being able to enjoy when others could come over on short notice for dinner or coffee. The feeling that I got when I could just say yes or invite them felt great to be able to do something so "normal" and not to feel like I had to hide or like having friends over was off limits for me as it had been for so long before that. Nowadays, my why is my daughter. She deserves an organized space to live in rather than a chaotic one. She's more likely to run, jump, and dance around the living room when there is ample clear space for her to do so. She's more likely to play with her toys when they are clearly organized so that she knows where she can find things, and I love being able to provide that for her.

We will talk about day-to-day motivation, but I urge you to explore your bigger-picture motivation outside of that. We want an overarching motivator. Something that encompasses why you even picked up this book to begin with. Why does keeping your home and space organized matter to you? What is your bigger picture goal, the thing that drives you, the thing that you look forward to or feel proud of? That is your why.

Tap into Your Reward System

We need to make the process of cleaning or organizing extremely quick, easy, and instantly rewarding. It needs to be fun. Research shows that behaviors are more sustainable when they are enjoyable *during* the process, not just for the reward afterward. This is something that is especially true for people with ADHD when the concept of a reward after is usually not enough to get us going anyway. We have to find reasons to like it during the process. This may involve exploring a few different ideas that feel rewarding to you.

Put on a playlist that you enjoy. Play one of the 20 podcasts or e-courses that are currently in your queue to listen to. Or video a friend while you're cleaning and organizing. I almost always call a friend while I'm doing my dishes. I do this because I can prop my phone up on the windowsill above my sink, and staying in the conversation makes the dishes go by faster and keeps me standing near the phone. It's a running joke with my friend that I only call her when I'm doing the dishes – but it works for me, and it's become so automatic that when I start to do the dishes, I then remember to call her.

It really is all about accommodating yourself.

Once you know to pay attention to your own rewards, it won't be hard to come up with ideas. There are things that naturally boost our dopamine. Sweets, for example. So you might try a healthier sweets option to munch on while you are going through storage cabinets. Upbeat music is another mood booster. Or music from your past is another often-overlooked mood booster that can immediately energize you. I will often play the 80s or 90s music while I'm cleaning.

Mirroring is another strategy that works for people who have ADHD. If you have a friend or family member who has been wanting to get their place in order, you might try scheduling with them to do it simultaneously. Then you can have them on video. Seeing them working in their own space will make it easier for you to move forward with your own task at the same time.

The Pomodoro technique is another productivity strategy that can help us make up for low motivation. It also works by breaking down a larger task into smaller pieces which feels less daunting for us. This strategy works by setting a timer for 25 minutes where you just focus on doing that one task while minimizing other distractions. Once you hit 25 minutes, you can take a 5-minute break to do whatever you want. Ideally, you should do 3-4 pomodoros, and then you can take a half-hour break.

The main takeaway from these strategies is that they aim to be simple and practical. They are also individualized. You can easily tie each of them to the challenges and struggles outlined in the first chapter, but it is up to you to identify which struggles are the biggest barriers for you and, therefore, which strategies will be your go-to. When you consider your needs through the lens of how your brain is working, figure out which things you need to make accommodations for.

If the task is too overwhelming, then break it down by writing the steps in order, then practice mono-tasking – which means one task at a time. Your only job and your only concern at that moment is the one small task rather than the whole larger job. If you're not motivated because it's too boring and tortuous, then figure out what other thing you have been wanting to do that you could combine with this task to keep you entertained and rewarded. Another example of a reward in this scenario could be that you haven't gotten to read for fun in a while. So you download an audiobook that you only play while you are doing the tasks you need to do. This adds motivation and reward to the task because you want to see what happens next in the book.

It comes back to mindset. You are not forcing yourself to suddenly become an organized person who loves structure and cleaning. You are using what you know about how you function and how your brain operates so that you can leverage those things to meet the goals that you have.

Stay Motivated – Even When You Don't Feel Like It

Try not to get lost in the details. ADHD doesn't mean we simply can't or don't pay attention. Our difficulty is regulating which things we give attention to and how much attention we give those things. This explains why we can get quickly overwhelmed and demotivated when we consider a task that someone else might consider simple.

It is crucial to understand the kinds of things that can kill your motivation when you have ADHD. Things like a task feeling too overwhelming, lacking any immediate reward, and chasing perfection commonly lead to demotivation with ADHD. Here we'll talk about strategies that address these specific areas of motivation to help you keep the motivation going even when you don't feel like it.

Onions have layers, and so should your cleaning habits. One of your general rules should be to keep your floors and surfaces clear. Your surfaces are any other flat surfaces in the room where you might otherwise have a tendency to put things. This can include tables, counters, tv stands, couches, chairs, etc. Floors get prioritized above surfaces, but surfaces are super important as well. This way – you can walk without tripping, and it makes the whole room appear less overwhelming.

Remember, if something looks too big to address, we shut down. So keeping things off the floor and keeping your surfaces clear, even if that means your drawers or baskets are not organized, is okay. That's better than the alternative of leaving everything out everywhere until you have the time or motivation to actually organize it, which will never come if you take that approach.

So, think of it in layers. Your first layer is just getting things off the floor. Next, get the things off the surfaces. Having clear floors and clear surfaces feels better. It can be counterintuitive to just move it so that it looks cleaner even if it's not fully organized, but we already know that when you feel better, you feel naturally more motivated. This automatically triggers your reward system, making you feel a sense of accomplishment.

Then the next layer is to choose a drawer or a bin to go through. One at a time. But at least your room looks and feels better and is ready to go. As long as your most important items have homes – such as your keys, wallet, phone, checkbook, etc. These things need forever homes. Once those spots are established, you clean in layers so that you can keep moving forward without being overwhelmed. You're not losing important things you need, your home feels better, and the concept of organizing feels like something you can actually do because when you look around, it looks and feels clean!

BEAT PROCRASTINATION

We procrastinate on things when we really don't want to do them. A couple of reasons could be at play here. One is that you might not have tapped into your reward system. So the task itself doesn't feel incentivizing, and even if you know rewards will come, that's still not strong enough to get you moving. The other possibility is maybe you want to do it but feel like you have no idea where to start because the task itself feels too big and overwhelming. Let's talk about breaking things down.

EXTREMELY SMALL STEPS

When you are struggling to organize the steps in a way that makes sense to get the thing done, this is an executive function issue. While this book will break down many tasks for you by giving you step-by-step and room-by-room instructions to declutter and get organized, it's an important skill to develop for anyone with ADHD to be able to break things down to make them more achievable.

When approaching a larger task involving multiple steps, you want to break it into extremely small parts. At any given time, you are just doing that one small thing rather than the whole big thing.

For example, if you need to change the sheets and make the bed:

- Find and grab a fitted sheet, flat sheet, and pillowcases
- Bring them to the bedroom
- Strip everything off the bed until you get to the mattress
    - Put the clean blankets/pillows on a chair, top of a dresser, end table, etc.
- Put the fitted sheet on the bed
- Pull off the old pillowcases
- Put on new pillowcases
- Put the pillows on the bed

- Flat sheet on the bed
- Blanket(s) on the bed
- The bed is done!
- Everything that's left over goes into the laundry basket

For each step, you're just focused on that one small thing while reminding yourself that it's just going to take a few seconds or minutes.

The more you normalize how small the steps are and how fast they will go, the less daunting this task is, and the less you are likely to procrastinate doing it. When you break things down like this, you are just committing to the next small step. You are avoiding feeling overwhelmed by having tunnel vision on only that one small thing. Then you move on to the next thing.

USING AN ANCHOR TASK TO BEAT PRODUCTIVE PROCRASTINATION

Productive procrastination is when we do beneficial things that need to get done while putting off the more important task that we really should be doing at that time (Steel, 2011). Having an anchor task can help with this. You might be more likely to use productive procrastination while attempting to clean or organize a particular room. Choose an anchor task for that moment knowing and expecting that you might get sidetracked. If it's identified as your anchor task, you always return to it. It's your anchor.

So if you want to clean the kitchen, part of that is doing the dishes. If you're unloading and loading the dishwasher, you might get sidetracked several times – "Oh, I just thought of this – let me do that real quick – or let me write this down." A family member might come in and wants help with something, or perhaps your phone rings or an email comes through. Whatever the sidetracking things are, remember that while you expect a certain amount of distractions will happen, the dishwasher at that moment is your anchor, so you come back to that.

Using an anchor task means it's okay if your attention and focus are not naturally sustained, and you allow the tiny breaks as long as you return. Anything larger that takes more than 2-3 min is something you can write down quickly and come back to complete after the anchor task is done. Once that anchor task is finished, you can choose the next anchor.

COMMITTING TO SMALL BLOCKS OF TIME

When you're really struggling with procrastination, it helps to commit to an extremely small amount of time. With this strategy, you're not committing to an entire task or even a portion of a task. Rather, you're saying, "I'll give this 5 minutes."

When you commit to doing a tiny amount of time, that at least gets the ball rolling. We struggle with time blindness, so we don't accurately judge how long things will take us. You might think, "I could get this done in 2 hrs." Yet after 2hrs have gone by, you might still not be at the halfway point. Likewise, you could feel like something will take forever. Meanwhile, it could get done in 20 minutes.

So when you are struggling with motivation and telling yourself, "This could take forever.", commit to doing it for 5, 10, or 15 minutes. Whatever *small* chunk of time will get you moving. Set your timer and do the thing for that amount of time with maximum effort. When the timer goes off, ask yourself:

"How do I feel about what I just got done"

"Can I do that again?"

If so, give it the same amount of time with another short burst of focus. This works for a few reasons. We have taken away the daunting element of it taking forever and only committed to a time that we were okay with. We also trigger your reward response when we ask how you feel about what you just got done. This involves taking a little step back, assessing your progress, and triggering that sense of a reward and that dopamine hit, which will help you be more likely to say yes, I'll go for another chunk of time.

Now it's important to realize that you are not committing to a full hour or to completing the entire task. Rather you are just committing to that tiny amount of time, and you still have the full right to say, "no thanks, I'm done.". Decide when you might ask yourself again to do another 5-10 min. Maybe again that night, or maybe try again at the same time the next day? This is a great strategy for chipping away at an otherwise large task that might have never gotten done.

Struggles with motivation, time blindness, procrastination, focus, working memory, etc., are common challenges with ADHD. You may find that some of these challenges play more of a role than others or that the primary challenge differs depending on the type of task you need to do. Having an awareness of your core struggle at that moment will help you better identify which practical strategy will be most useful so that you can ultimately succeed in maintaining a clean and organized home.

Key Takeaways

- Drops in dopamine have a strong impact on your symptoms and your ability to function
- Minding your exercise, sleep, stress, and overstimulation will help you to stay functioning at your best
- It is crucial to recognize your patterns and how they contribute to the problem
- Time blindness is a common challenge with ADHD, but there are practical ways to manage it.
- Eliminating distractions is difficult but necessary
- Mitigate both internal and external distractions to keep your focus
- A simple system involving a planner, calendar app, whiteboards, and alarms combined with habitual checking of these lists and calendars can help make up for working memory deficits
- Important items need to be assigned specific and consistent places in your home
- Motivation starts with identifying your 'Why'
- Motivation continues by tapping into your rewards system, accommodating yourself, and breaking things up into small manageable pieces.
- Anchor tasks, time blocking, breaking things down into extremely small steps, and tapping into your sense of accomplishment can help beat procrastination.

CHAPTER 3.

HABIT BUILDING FOR PEOPLE WITH ADHD

Building habits is hard for us. People with ADHD are generally inconsistent and struggle with sticking to routines (Carr-Fanning, 2020). By nature we tend to have a low tolerance for boredom, we crave novelty, we are driven by immediate rewards and have lower than average impulse control. Not to mention, we can be a bit forgetful. So, while we know that routine and structure are good for us, they are also something we have likely never been naturally good at.

While you know building habits may not be automatic for you, it will be a necessary skill as you work to clean up, get organized, and keep things that way. After all, you've likely been able to get things looking neat and organized once or twice before, but your difficulty keeping it that way is one of the reasons you're reading this book now.

Choosing the Right Strategies for You

There are many strategies out there that promote habit formation and that are designed to help people create a routine and stick with it. Some of them are more ADHD friendly than others. One of the books that you will see ADHD coaches refer to across the board is *Atomic Habits* by James Clear (2018). His strategies are ADHD friendly because they hone in on some of the biggest struggles we have with habit building.

Clear points out that if you are having difficulty building a habit, it is likely your system that needs work and not some inherent flaw in your character. He emphasizes the importance of the reward system, not only after the task is completed but throughout the entire process. Additionally, he acknowledges and even frames in a positive light the concept that we typically lean toward the path of least resistance, and that this is an evolutionary strength.

If you're new to *Atomic Habits* this chapter offers a great introduction to some of the main components in Clear's framework, while delivering additional strategies developed with an ADHD brain in mind.

The most important thing when adopting strategies to build habits is to choose the ones that work for you. Have a sense of what your biggest downfalls are when you've tried to build habits before, and pick techniques that address these issues. Try things out and don't be afraid to adjust until you create a system that suits your individual needs. While having ADHD means we are likely to have common struggles and similar responses to certain sets of circumstances, we are still individuals and our presentations of ADHD symptoms will differ.

Understand your Goals

This is where the rewards process begins. Does "I want to clean my kitchen regularly" sound like a rewarding goal to you? When it comes to ADHD we are highly motivated by immediate rewards. We are also easily shut down by things that sound mundane or that don't entice us enough.

How about "I want to start my morning strong, feeling confident and in control of my day". That sounds like something you might actually want right? Tap into what your real goal is. You can get there by taking your boring goal and asking "Why?" or "What will it do for me?". If I were to ask you "Why do you want to clean your kitchen regularly?" or "What is a clean kitchen going to do for you?" This is how we got to the idea of starting strong and feeling confident and in control of your day.

Clear (2018) points out that our primary rewards are things like food, water, and sex. Secondary rewards are also powerful motivators. These can include things like money, power, praise, approval, status, personal satisfaction, friendships, and love. If you consider the goal above, it taps into the rewards of power, personal satisfaction, and if I want to be perceived as this person who is strong, confident, and in control, I also tap into the need for approval and potentially praise from others. It's very likely that if you have goals you really want to accomplish, they are linked to these primary or secondary rewards. Dig until you find that connection. That reward is the foundation of your ultimate goal, your hook, the initial piece of motivation that will move you to take action.

Be Specific

Now that you've identified your goal, you need to be specific about the action you want to take. This will ultimately lead into the habit you want to establish. If I want my mornings to start off strong so that I'm feeling confident and in control of my day, being able to make and enjoy my morning coffee is a big part of that.

I don't want there to be any friction in that part of my morning. I want it to run smoothly so that I barely have to think and I can move through the motions fluidly to the point where I can stare out my window drinking that hot cup without feeling pressured, or stressed in the process.

I could go in a few different directions with actions that would be conducive to this. One thing I know I'll need is to have the coffee area in my kitchen to be organized, clean, and ready to go without having to rummage around for the sugar or clean out the coffee filter. Everything should be ready.

So my specific action could be taking 5 minutes to quickly clean and prep my coffee station before I close down the kitchen each night. To make it even more clear, this includes wiping down the area, making sure coffee mugs are clean and available, and making sure there is no clutter in my way. The coffee scoop is where it needs to be on the side of the machine, the sugar and coffee are in the cabinet nearest to the machine, the coffee filter is clean, the water tank is filled.

This prep takes all 5 minutes at most. The next part of creating a clear and specific task is to decide when it will be done. This depends on what works best for you. You might want to set a specific time to wrap up the kitchen and prep your coffee station, meaning that an alarm goes off at 8pm to signal you to complete this task. Or perhaps an alarm goes off that signals you to do a few things that help you shut down your home for the night. Another method to decide when to complete this task is habit stacking.

Habit Stacking

There are already things that you do on a daily basis. Simple habits that you have as part of your normal activities of daily life. Habit stacking is when you associate the new habit you want to create with things you already do regularly.

These things include:

- brushing your teeth
- taking a shower
- getting dressed and undressed
- having lunch
- ending the work day
- walking into a room for the first time that day
- walking out of a room for the last time that day
- turning off the lights

This is a good moment to take note of the things you do daily. There are likely more things you can add to the list above. Any of these daily habits you already have can be used to habit stack.

For example, if every evening you check the door to make sure it's locked before you turn off the lights, this could be where you add the habit of your 5 minute coffee area prep. By making sure your door is locked and turning off the lights, you are signaling to yourself that your use of the kitchen is done for the night. So this time might make sense to ensure you are ready for the morning and the next that you will be doing in that room. Which will be to enter the kitchen and start making your morning coffee.

When it comes to establishing new habit stacks, write them out for yourself. Clearly. Include what you will do and when you will do it. Then when you completed it, take a brief step back, look at your work, and check it off your to do list. Accomplishing something you set out to do and acknowledging that by assessing the good job you did is also inherently rewarding. You want to keep the reward system engaged.

Start Small and Build from There

I'm sure you noticed the task that I chose to create for building our new habit was pretty small. This is another aspect of Clear's framework that makes it so ADHD friendly. We are unlikely to engage in something if it feels too big or overwhelming. If you recall the strategies to beat procrastination, one of them was breaking things down into very small parts. The same applies when you are building a habit.

If you recall the goal of starting the morning strong, so that I feel confident and in control of my day, this is not something that is solely associated with my morning coffee moment. When you hear that goal, and try to picture it, you likely see an entire kitchen. It looks nice, smells nice, it's bright, devoid of clutter, and everything is in its place. That makes sense!

But here is where I caution you to start small. You don't want to set a task that you are likely to feel overwhelmed by or procrastinate on. So if your mind jumps to a beautiful, perfectly organized kitchen, this is where you break it down. I chose one small yet important moment of my morning that takes place in the kitchen and created the task based on that.

Once the task you have set out to do starts to feel simple and easy, you build on it. So in a week or two if the task I chose has started to feel easy and automatic, that's when I might add scanning for any clutter that needs to be put away or wiping down all the kitchen counters and table.

Make it Work for *You*

Routines and habits should work for you based on your specific lifestyle, preferences, and what you find to be rewarding and motivating. Don't choose routines or habits solely because it feels like what you should be doing. That is a fast track to habit failure. The habit you develop needs to resonate and make sense for you.

If you're a night owl and you like the idea of an 11pm session of sweeping and mopping your kitchen floor while listening to an audio book you've been wanting to check out, that's great! If you tend to go to bed early but you like the idea of waking up early to listen to music and set your mood for the day while going through each room decluttering from the night before, that works too!

Your routine doesn't have to make sense to anyone else. It just has to work for you and your household.

Listen to yourself. Make space for what you like and what you don't like. Acknowledge that certain times of the day are more productive for you. Be okay with trying out the new routine or habit and be open to shifting it if it feels like it's not working.

Be Flexible

One of the quickest ways to fall off your newfound habit is to have rigid expectations. Be willing to adjust if needed. If you find that a habit is just not working, don't use that as a reason to beat yourself up. Rather use it as information. It signals that something isn't working here and we need to consider a different approach.

Watch out for perfectionism, find ways to make the task more fun and enjoyable, and give yourself positive feedback and grace during this process. If this was something that came easy to you, you would have done it a long time ago. You are working on figuring out the system that works best and sometimes, that is not readily obvious.

You also don't have to accomplish the task every day for it to be successful. You can aim for daily, but know that you are still making progress even if you fell off for a few days that week. Try to set a rule for yourself, such as 3 strikes and you're out. Aim to check it off daily. Ultimately, if you only completed the task 2-3 days that week, that's way more than before you tried to establish the routine at all! Aim to build the frequency as you go, but if you hit 3 days where you have not been able to complete the task, then consider what you can change to make it work better for you.

CHANGE IT UP

Another component of adding flexibility is that maybe your routine does work in the beginning. Maybe you notice that you tend to do great with the routines and habits you are establishing for 2 weeks or a month, and then it starts to fall off. Does this mean it didn't work?

It's likely that if you started strong with a routine and you were able to stick to it for a few weeks before you started falling off track, the habit started to become boring. We crave novelty and spontaneity. This is an excellent place to allow for flexibility rather than trying to force it to stick. It's pretty common that we'll love something initially and then quickly become bored and done with it.

You can still accomplish the tasks that need to get done without having to commit to one schedule forever. The house I ran had a weekly rotation of household chores. We met on a weekly basis, and in the last 10-15 min, everyone looked forward to changing up the routine. If one person did the kitchen this week, maybe she chose the living room the following week, and so on. This concept of novelty exists in various areas of our lives, and we can leverage it when it comes to our household tasks. If you follow sports, it's exciting when a new season comes up. If it were basketball all year, you'd probably get bored. It's more exciting when you can go from basketball to baseball to football. Or if you've gone to college, you know it can be exciting when a new semester starts. Still the same task of going to class, doing homework, and taking midterms, but the change can be initially invigorating.

When it comes to applying this kind of flexibility in your household tasks, it is essential to strike a balance between structure and flexibility. For example, you wouldn't start keeping your keys in a different location once you've found a spot that works. That will just make you more likely to start losing them again. The combination of effort, time, and boredom puts us in the danger zone.

To address your need for spontaneity, you'll change those tasks that require some of your time and attention but no longer feel interesting in the way you are doing them. So instead of doing the laundry every morning, you might decide to do it right after work every day. Instead of going through your paperwork on Sunday mornings with your coffee, you might decide it feels nicer to let yourself have that morning coffee to just relax and reflect. So, you'll do the paperwork while having a smoothie and listening to music on Wednesdays during your lunch break. Same task but a very different vibe.

You might thrive on changing up aspects of your routine on a weekly, biweekly, or monthly basis. Or you can challenge yourself to see how long it works before you start missing days and then use that as your signal to come up with a new one. Building habits doesn't have to mean extreme rigidity. The more flexible you can be with yourself, the easier it will be to stick to your decluttering, organizing, and cleaning systems.

Make it Rewarding All the Way Through

Remember the importance of establishing a system that is rewarding. You learned about the role of the dopamine reward system in previous chapters, and we touched on the role of rewards in the habit building process earlier in this chapter.

Your ultimate goal is based on a primary or secondary reward that triggers your motivation to act. While you are completing the action, you can make that process enjoyable and rewarding as well. This is where music, podcasts, phone calls with friends, audio books, your favorite cup of tea, etc. come in. Finding ways that you can incorporate other things you really like at the same time as your task to build an association between the two will make you less likely to avoid doing the task.

Assessing the outcomes of your work is another way to reward yourself, as well as using positive self talk along the way. Being gentle with yourself and giving yourself credit for the progress you are making even if it's not perfect end goals. It's all about making progress one small step at a time.

Finally, find a way to reward yourself after you've completed the task. You don't have to do this for every task, but if you have one that you think might require a bit of an extra incentive then this is where the reward comes in to acknowledge your completion of the task.

Consider things that you personally find rewarding. Maybe a full week of completing the habit means you can order in from your favorite restaurant. Perhaps a month of daily completion means you can grab yourself tickets to a basketball game. You can even consider paying yourself for your hard work. Maybe each day that you accomplish this task means $5 or $10 more in your recreation/entertainment budget for the month. Consider what you really like or want and find ways to use them to reward yourself.

Each time you have completed a task, don't forget to check it off. If on your calendar or in your planner, you can start to see a string of completions indicated by little green check marks, or whatever symbol you'd like, that feels like success! Clear supports this concept as well. Seeing those little checks can be an intrinsic reward as you start to feel proud of yourself for consistently accomplishing what you set out to do.

The Only Failure is When You Stop Trying Altogether

You will fall off track. But this doesn't mean the habit is dead. Try not to beat yourself up. A quick way to kill a habit before you've even gotten a chance to establish it is to associate it with lots of guilt and shame. That's essentially what you are doing if you beat yourself up every time you fall short.

We are immediate gratification driven, we can be impulsive, and we tend to struggle with regulating our emotions. Recognize that you are trying and that this is a work in progress. If you make this something extra unenjoyable because it makes you feel bad about yourself, you'll be more likely to toss it out the window, never to be attempted again.

Rather, give yourself credit for the strides you make. Be gentle with yourself. And if it is repeatedly not working, be willing to see what you can do differently, bringing back our concept of being flexible.

Apply What You've Learned

Remember what you know about how ADHD works. It is highly unlikely that everyone will be successful the first time around with these strategies. There is nuance to them. There are ways that you need to individualize them for yourself and that may be a bit of a learning curve for you. That is totally okay.

Also keep in mind the strategies that you've learned to beat procrastination and improve motivation. There were several skills and techniques brought up in those areas that may also need to be applied when it comes to developing habits.

Use Your Resources

Your resources include all of the tools at your disposal. I've mentioned several so far. These include planners, lists, white boards, alarms, notepads, apps, music, etc. Even your supports are a huge resource in this process. You have access to all of these and you need to use them as they can fit with your individual needs, lifestyle, and the routine you are building.

Many of these tools will help with forgetfulness and will assist you to establish consistency. They can also be used in the mentally rewarding process of tracking and recording your wins and progress. Additionally, if you struggle with prioritizing and organizing tasks in your mind, using these tools will help with mapping things out in a way that makes sense and give you a visual aid so that you can better conceptualize your plan.

Your support system can be useful in a number of ways. It's helpful when you have a good sense of who is in your corner and how they can each best support you. You may have that friend who is your best cheerleader to encourage you along the way and praise your accomplishments. You may have that person who has their own cleaning or organizing goals and may want to act as a body double so that you both can be on video motivating one another by doing your routines together.

ACCOUNTABILITY

Supports can also be an accountability system. You may feel a greater sense of accountability to accomplish a task once you have told a member of your friends or family that you will be doing that thing. In this case just be careful to not choose supports who may make you feel bad if you don't accomplish the task or who won't understand the importance of being able to adapt your routine to better suit you. Encouragement is great! Shame and guilt are not helpful here.

Make sure to consider all of the tools and resources at your disposal and choose how and when you will use them in your process. They can each go far in helping you develop your system and accomplish your overall goals.

Key Takeaways

- Habit building is harder for people with ADHD, but can be accomplished by choosing ADHD friendly strategies
- Identify the ultimate goal, this means understanding the connection to your primary or secondary rewards
- Write down your new habit being as specific and clear as possible to reduce avoidance, forgetfulness, or procrastination
- Use habit stacking wherever possible, by attaching new habits to your already existing habits
- When it comes to building habits, start really small and build on to it as the habit gets easier and more automatic
- Your habits and routines don't need to work for other people, they need to work for you
- Be flexible, if something is not working you can change it at any time
- Use the reward system throughout the entire process, from start to finish
- Don't beat yourself up, we want progress, not perfection. When something doesn't work, that's information you can use.
- Don't forget everything you've learned about how ADHD works and what that means for you, including tips to address procrastination and low motivation
- Use the resources and tools at your disposal. That's what they're there for!

CHAPTER 4.

DECLUTTERING WITH ADHD. CLEARING THE MESS, ONE DOOM PILE AT A TIME

One of the most significant barriers to getting organized is often the clutter that sits in the way of it all. Making actual organization feel close to impossible. As you've begun to learn in this book, executive function deficits can do a number on people with ADHD. When you combine our poor working memory, weak impulse control, and lower levels of dopamine, it's no wonder we struggle with clutter! These issues are at the core of how ADHD impacts our brains differently from people who don't have ADHD and why we often have such a hard time organizing our tasks and our environments. People commonly struggle with clutter to the extent of feeling like achieving organization is an insurmountable goal.

As we have explored and outlined earlier, our challenges can absolutely be overcome. That is not to suggest our symptoms will be cured by the strategies presented here. Rather we can mitigate their impact on our lives. Once we learn to leverage what works for us and work around the triggers that throw us off in a strategic way, we learn that a clean and organized space is something that we can achieve.

Didn't Organize, Only Moved

If you've seen any discussion of ADHD struggles and behaviors on social media lately, you've probably heard of doom piles. There are also doom boxes, doom bags, and even doom rooms. These are clusters of items that, rather than organizing, we just piled all together. Imagine the classic junk drawer that even organized homes have. Except we've got lots of these, in various forms and sizes throughout our home, taking up space on counters, chairs, tables, bags, bins, drawers, and even entire rooms.

Doom stands for 'didn't organize, only moved.' That's how these piles came together, and it's also an excellent way to describe the feeling you might have when trying to deal with these areas of clutter. Not only do these areas make it less likely that you can find what you are looking for, but they also make your space more congested. Clutter like this often leads you to have to step over things, it takes up space on a chair that you would otherwise sit at, or fills up a counter or tabletop that you would otherwise use but can't because things are in the way.

When your home environment is in a constant state of clutter, it can wreak havoc on many areas of your life. Clutter can be the reason your morning starts out feeling scattered and stressed. You've likely had mornings where you can't find your keys, you spend half an hour trying to find what you intended to wear, and you can't find the AirPods that help you stay focused while you're working. Whether you go to work or work from home, it can lead to moments of embarrassment in front of your colleagues, boss, or clients when you can't find something they ask you for that you were supposed to have. Even worse, perhaps you forget to do something because you lost track of the post-it note you wrote it on.

Then after a stressful day of work, your dopamine is even further depleted, and the last thing you want to do is clean or organize anything. At this point in the day, if you don't have a system, it's very easy to just keep adding to the clutter, making it a vicious cycle. This extent of clutter can make you feel out of control, stressed, anxious, depressed, and further isolated because, frankly, it's an embarrassing problem that many people with ADHD tend to shame themselves about.

How Did it Get this Bad?

As I've mentioned, working memory plays an important role here, and our deficits in working memory are largely responsible for our issues with clutter. Because we don't already have a solid organization system, things in our house can easily go from being held in our hands to being set down on the next available surface, wherever that might be. Surfaces that accumulate clutter can include the floor, couch, bed, desk, counters, tables, tv stands, shelves, and chairs. Essentially any flat surface that can hold a thing is likely to accumulate clutter in a house belonging to a person with ADHD.

Once we have it in our hands and don't need it anymore, we don't know where exactly to put it at that moment, and we might even try to help ourselves out by deciding, "I don't want to forget this," or "I don't want to lose this." So we might put it down in an *extra safe* place, which we promptly forget, or we intentionally leave it in sight because we are confident that this will lead us to address it later. You know how that story ends. A good amount of your clutter likely consists of things you left out to address later.

Another fun thing about clutter and ADHD is that we have a tendency to stop seeing it. Many have reported becoming so accustomed to their clutter that it starts to feel and look normal, so there is even less incentive to get rid of it or get it organized. In these cases, the clutter may as well be part of the furniture because it no longer looks like or feels like a task that needs to be addressed.

Impulsivity is another significant factor. It's no secret that people with ADHD can struggle with impulse buying. We often buy things we don't need, further adding to the clutter in our homes. This is related to both our lack of control over inhibitions as well as our old friend dopamine. We love immediate gratification, and a new purchase is sure to give us that quick feel-good boost we needed. So, part of our system to stay decluttered once we have cleared the chaos is to be deliberate about controlling our impulse buys. We have to stop accumulating things we don't need.

Finally, while you may have decluttered and organized tons of times before, up to now you have likely had a really hard time being consistent. I have zero doubt that you have gotten areas of your home or even your entire home beautifully decluttered and organized at one point or another – only for it to fall back to its old messy ways – and the first slip down that slippery slope was the clutter, one piece at a time. That one piece of paper, that empty water bottle, the post-its, the items that legitimately felt like they had nowhere else to go at that moment or that you told yourself you would take care of soon. Except, they just stayed there, the area got worse, and before you knew it, the clutter and mess were back with a vengeance.

But There is Hope

On the flip side, gaining control over your clutter can make a massive difference. Freeing your space from the chaos and being able to move about freely, using the space in your home as it was intended, and finding the things you need when you need them can make your day better from the get-go. When you can make sense of your environment in this way, you won't be scrambling to get ready to leave the house, forgetting things you needed, and you won't be embarrassed to have friends and family come over. This seemingly small change can significantly improve your life, productivity, efficiency, and overall sense of well-being.

Reiterating the Foundation

In previous chapters, we emphasized the importance of having a home for your most important things. This refers to the 4-5 items you need to use on a regular basis and cannot or prefer not to leave the house without. These are the things that, when you lose them, can literally stop you in your tracks or ruin your day. This can include your wallet, keys, planner, earbuds, phone charger, or anything else that is integral to your daily functioning – I'm assuming that you generally have your phone on or near you and, therefore, not including it in the list of things that need a home. But if you are not someone who always has their phone within reach, and if you tend to frequently lose it long enough to feel like it's a problem, then include your phone on this list as well.

Assigning a home for these items means storing them in the same place every day. You are giving them a place to live whenever you are not actively using them. Perhaps your keys live on the key hook near your door, while your wallet or purse lives on a specific shelf in your bedroom, and your charger is always plugged into a particular outlet in your living room or kitchen. These are just examples, but what works about them is that they remain consistent. You will get a sense of what feels like a natural place to keep these things. Anything that doesn't work can get re-assigned to a home that makes better sense for that item.

For example, you may prefer to have everything you need for the day stored in a basket on a table near your door. This may be especially true if you work outside of your home and you don't want to be walking around to different places to gather the things you'll need to go. CHADD, the leading non-profit national organization for children and adults with ADHD, refers to this type of space by the door with all the things you need to leave as a launchpad. You may find that your own version of a launchpad is exactly what you need for your mornings before leaving the house.

Once you have the important items essentially out of the way and accounted for, it's time to start decluttering. You'll start to see how the chapters and skills in this part of the book build on one another. We've covered the prerequisites for decluttering. Next, we'll learn about how decluttering your space is a necessary step before you can truly get organized.

Where to Start

Pick one cluttered spot to work on. Don't set out to declutter your whole home or even a whole room. It's simply too much. Remember some of the simple strategies targeted at your ADHD needs in previous chapters. Breaking things down into small achievable tasks, using small blocks of time, keeping yourself motivated, and building one small habit at a time are all foundational to making real progress.

So once you have chosen your area – take a good look at it. Chances are, you often don't assess your clutter for what it consists of. ADHD makes organizational skills a challenge, and this would include your ability to look at something that is complex, messy, and comprised of lots of smaller pieces and make sense of it. Your cluttered area is essentially a blob of smaller pieces that may or may not even be related to each other. I want you to assess what categories of items you see.

Our ultimate goal is to take all of those little things and either:

- get rid of them,
- arrange them to be more neat and accessible, or
- put them somewhere else that makes sense for them to go

So first, we need to have a better understanding of what is there. Then we can start pulling them out of the pile and figuring out where they will go.

So look at your cluttered area. Remember the importance of breaking things down into small pieces. A cluttered area, in this case, does not refer to an entire room or one side of a room. Depending on the size of your room, the area you'll start with is maybe a quarter of it, if that. It's a small area that could be one cluttered shelf, one section of the countertop, a section of the couch, or a portion of your desk. This may not sound like a lot, but when it's full of clutter, that's about as much as you might be able to work with at once. You also don't want this to feel like a huge job. It should be small enough that you can sit or stand in front of it and reach everything in front of you without having to get up or take any steps.

Now that you are focused on this little area, what do you see? Take a quick mental note, or jot it down. For example, if you're in the bedroom, you might see a bunch of clothes. That is what your cluttered section might look like, but the next step is to specify further. You might see shirts, jeans, sheets, towels, socks, etc. Do you see any other categories of things in that area? Paper? Toiletries? Office supplies? Ultimately we will want to physically take things out of the cluttered spot and form smaller piles according to the item category.

Make sure you have 2-3 garbage bags available. One is for garbage. One is for donations. One is for recyclables if you recycle. Now depending on the contents of your clutter, you may find that one type of those bags does not apply. That's fine, just keep the ones you need. But generally, those are the bags you want to have in mind or on hand when you start decluttering an area.

As you start going through the pile, you want to start putting things in these bags. Do yourself a favor and mark the bags. This way, you are not continuously having to check the contents or find that you put the wrong things in the wrong bag and end up having to work backward.

Now, in addition to these bags, you're going to make piles. The piles are for things that you will keep. They will be arranged based on what type of item they are. Do not worry about where they will go yet. Just separate them because, ultimately, we want to keep similar items together. These piles will be made up of things that will be either staying here and going back in a more needed and accessible way, or that will be going somewhere else more appropriate in the house. You don't have to have that figured out yet. Just know what they are and what their function is and start grouping them that way.

Be aware that people with ADHD can have a harder time letting go of possessions based on emotional attachments and sentimental value (Lynch et al., 2017). We can also be fans of the concept of "you never know when you'll need it." These are mindsets that contribute to clutter, and we need to be mindful of these patterns in our thinking as we are going through items and considering what to keep or not. When in doubt, let it go. If you can't make an extremely strong case for keeping the thing, chances are you really don't need it. If you haven't used it in a few years, you definitely don't need it.

For example, if you are going through clothes, follow these suggestions when you start decluttering:

GET LARGER ITEMS OUT OF THE WAY FIRST

If there are obviously larger items in the cluttered area, pull them out first. We're talking about prominent items that would otherwise be in the way while you are trying to sort. If you are working with clothes or laundry, this usually means towels, sheets, sweatshirts, and jeans. Larger bulkier items make your whole pile look larger and make it harder to get to the smaller things. Getting rid of these first will make the biggest and quickest dent in your cluttered area, giving you some immediate gratification in the much smaller and more manageable pile you have after only a couple of minutes of work.

DECIDE WHETHER TO DONATE OR TOSS IT

If you are debating about whether to keep an item of clothing, consider whether it is in good condition. If so, but you haven't worn it for a full year, I strongly suggest donating it. This means you have gone through all of the seasons and did not wear it. This also goes for clothes that don't fit. If they are not your current size, get rid of them. If it's in poor condition, toss it. It's just taking up space.

"SOMEDAY" IS A CLUTTER BUZZWORD

If the only reason you are holding onto it is "because I might want to wear it someday," but you cannot think of the last time you wore it, get rid of it. Reasoning like "someday" or "just in case" should set off your decluttering alarm bells.

SORT QUICKLY

If you are keeping the item, quickly make a pile for it. It can be its own new pile if it doesn't fit easily with any of the others. Don't spend too long thinking about your piles or thinking about any one individual item. This will slow you down or make you stop altogether. Give the item a spot off to the side, close enough to you that you can reach it but away from the actual clutter area being addressed. As you go through the cluttered area, you are creating more piles and adding to your existing piles until they have been sorted.

This is the same process that you will use for other kinds of cluttered areas. Let's take your home office desk, for example:

- Gather your bags: donate, garbage, recycle
- Start with the most prominent items that are in the way. If there is obvious garbage lying around, get rid of that first. The same goes for water bottles or books. Essentially, start with the biggest bulkiest type of items.
- Next, go for the smaller items that might be in high quantities. For example, if you have 30 post-it notes spread across your desk, pick those up.
- Now start picking up things that are closest to you – if it's a desk or countertop and things are spread out enough – you may be able to go for things in a certain category first – for example, I'm going to grab all the pens I see, or all the paperclips, all the random non-office things.
- If categories like that do not seem readily obvious, go for what is closest to you and move outward. Or move from one side to the other.
- However you decide to start, it should come quickly to you without much thought. Imagine you are on one of those game shows where you have to pick up things fast. Start grabbing and sorting. No thinking, no addressing anything in that pile at the moment, Just grabbing and sorting.

- You might even add the time-blocking component and give yourself a challenge by saying, "I'm going to have everything in this pile sorted in less than 15 minutes.This gamifies the experience, making it more of an engaging challenge you want to win.
- If we're talking about your home office space, categories you might have could be writing utensils, paperclips, and items with similar functions like staples, unused paper, notepads, and notes you've written (don't read them now) just put them in the "need to read this and figure out where it goes" pile, books, invoices, etc.

Once you've gotten rid of the biggest things, you'll realize that it looks much better. You have no more garbage there, and all of the things that remain are things that you know you will need or use. This is no longer a pile of unknown things that intimidates you to look at or go through. Instead, you have been able to be intentional about what remains in a very short amount of time.

This systematic method of picking things up and getting them out of the way will make the rest easier to tackle, and getting rid of them first will give you a quick sense of accomplishment at how much of a difference you just made in just a few moves.

A word of advice in your sorting process. Try your best not to have a miscellaneous pile. That's how you got here, to begin with. All of this was essentially filed as miscellaneous or to be dealt with later. We need to sort it out more specifically now so that we can figure out what to do with it. If you only have one or two of this type of item and it really doesn't go with other items or have a home anywhere else that you can think of, consider other aspects of it, such as its function or what actions it applies to. This may help you to better sort it into the existing piles that you have.

Once you've sorted your garbage bags, make sure you get them out of the way. If a bag can go outside, take it there. If it needs to go by the door for now, then bring it there. It's time to focus on the piles you have made. When decluttering with ADHD- it's best to go for the low-hanging fruit first. Because quick wins are more likely to keep you moving, we know that more complicated and time-consuming tasks can shut us right down.

So if you find one of your piles looks easiest to put away or deal with, do that first. With ADHD, one of our biggest barriers to getting organized, aside from lack of consistency, is demotivation. Once we get bored or feel like a task is too hard and we're not getting enough of a reward from it, we quickly give it up. So do your best to keep your motivation up by making this entire process a continuous feed of small successes.

Keep Going for the Quick Wins

You've sorted out the cluttered area, you got rid of the garbage, donations, and recyclables. Now you know that what remains in the piles are things that need to be put away. If you are working with clothes or another form of textiles, now is when you'll fold them. If there is a pile of things that needs to be hung, you can do that before or after you fold the other piles. Remember – quick wins. If you know a pile needs to get hung. Go hang it up, but do not get stuck in the closet trying to organize it all. Resist that urge because it will slow you down and threatens to derail the whole process. Remind yourself that organizing is a different task. You are still decluttering. So you're not getting sidetracked, and you are prioritizing decluttering at this moment. Because decluttering is less detail-oriented than organizing, we are aiming for speed and continuous movement.

Choose the pile that looks easiest to you. If you are having trouble identifying what to start with, there are a few ways to choose.

- Go for the big things. There are likely fewer of them.
- Go for piles that have the most similar items. These tend to be easier to deal with. The pile of unused notepads, the pile of post-it notes or office supplies, the pile of jeans or t-shirts, the pile of books.

- Go for the things that do have a somewhat established place to go – it doesn't have to be a perfect spot for them – but if you know your top desk drawer holds the pens and office supplies, get them in there.
- Again, resist the urge to organize that drawer perfectly. Speed is the goal here. Slowly enough to not throw things haphazardly, thereby creating more clutter, but that's about it. We're not getting super organized, we are putting things in the vicinity of where they go in a way that's not a disaster. If you can put it away and leave it looking somewhat organized, great. If the organizing aspect will take you more than 2-3 minutes, then keep it moving, and you'll get organized later. We are getting rid of the absolute nonsensical chaos. So it won't be beautiful just yet, but it certainly won't be a mess anymore.

If you have something that literally does not have any home at all. Make one. Even if that home is temporary. How do you choose a quick home for this category?

- Have you been putting this thing in a certain area naturally?
- What type of area makes sense for this thing?
- Does it need to be visible?
- Can it go in a drawer? In a basket? In a section of the desk?
- If you picture this item in others' homes, where does it tend to go?
- Remember, this does not have to be the item's forever home. We are just decluttering and making a space for that category of item. Keep it moving.
- Do not choose a space that requires you to reorganize a different space you are not currently focusing on.
    - For example, if I decide that my unread mail should go in the basket on my kitchen counter – but that basket is currently holding a bunch of other items that are not included in the area that I'm currently decluttering, then I can either dump the basket quickly and decide

> to go through those things later when I'm done with this section, or the unread mail gets a different temporary home for now. But I don't stop organizing one section midway, just to start another. We need to keep the momentum going.

Now start putting things where they can go. What often holds up the decluttering process or stops it from happening altogether is the fact that we too often try to combine it with organizing. We are not organizing yet, we are just getting rid of the chaos. We will make it beautiful later. The quickest way to overwhelm yourself or take so much time that you cannot complete the task is to confuse organization with decluttering. Focus solely on getting rid of the clutter.

This means our piles are getting dealt with. The items in the piles are going somewhere. Office supplies get put in the drawer if there is room for them. If there is other stuff in there, that's okay. If they still fit, you can put them in there. If they don't fit and you would have to dump the drawer first, consider putting them in a different drawer or spot, and you will address that drawer later. Clothes get hung, linens get put away, jeans, sweatshirts, and unused paper. They all get a home. They each go together with other items from their category.

Once you've done this, that section is decluttered. It should not have taken you very long. An hour at most, but more likely half an hour if you maintain your momentum and keep it to a small space. Decluttering in small spaces like this helps you realize how achievable it is to declutter an area and makes you more likely to commit to decluttering another small area next.

If you were able to declutter a small section in 30 minutes, then pick another spot that day. If you commit 1 hour to decluttering each day, before you know it, you will have decluttered a whole room. Making a series of small achievable commitments helps you to keep making progress. It also addresses one of the major issues surrounding clutter for the person with ADHD, which is feeling overwhelmed to the point of impossibility. In this process, we are showing ourselves that it can be done, it gets done quickly, and it's no big deal.

So the lessons we learned in this section are: commit to small spaces, speed over perfection, remember the distinction between decluttering and organizing, go for quick wins, sort things based on type or function, and be willing to give them temporary homes when their forever home is currently taken or when you haven't figured out where you really want them to go yet. That is totally fine. Decluttering is very much about speed, quick wins, and progress, not perfection. Try to engage a flexible mindset by being willing to try different spaces for different things later on and knowing that the place you choose for it today does not have to be permanent if it ends up ineffective. This takes the pressure off making the right choice and allows you to try different things.

Your Ongoing System to Stay Decluttered

Staying decluttered relies on something that, quite frankly, we are terrible at – consistency. Research has shown that we don't struggle as much with the strategies of getting things done as we do with the ability to persist (Durand et al., 2020). We tend to let things fall off, as you are well aware.

This is where it's crucial to start implementing some of the habit building strategies that you learned in the previous chapter. Keep in mind that by now you know how to get heavily cluttered areas decluttered. It takes a bit of time, strategy, and rolling up your sleeves to address the piles of chaos, but it can absolutely be done. Beyond that, we know that small areas can be decluttered fairly quickly and that the process can be pretty rewarding along the way. This is meant to reassure you that it is very possible to get back on track if you do have a lapse in consistency like many of us do. As we move forward we'll show you how to catch your slips early.

Don't forget some of the strategies that you have learned to maintain your motivation. And build daily habits. Listen to music to keep your pace up, good options can be upbeat music or workout music playlists. Steer clear of movies or shows which will potentially take your focus away.

Now, to maintain the work you have done, let's assume you do plan to have some consistency around staying decluttered. You'll want to create a habit of running through each room in your house daily. By doing it this way, it will take you less than 10-15 minutes total each day to stay decluttered. Low-traffic areas, such as a bedroom, dining room, laundry room, etc., may only need to be addressed once toward the end of the day.

High-traffic areas should get decluttered twice. Once in the afternoon and again in the evening. While I mention that your entire daily decluttering process should only take 10-15 minutes, that's because each time you are decluttering a room, it is only taking 2-3 minutes at most.

Don't forget that next up is our organization system. So that means that once you are decluttered and fully organized, your daily decluttering will consist of taking 2-3 minutes in both the afternoon and before bed to declutter the living room, kitchen, bathroom, and whatever other areas get high traffic. Each of those spaces gets 2-3 minutes of your time. The low-traffic spaces will get a once-over in the evening before you wrap up your day. These areas should only take 1-2 minutes at most.

What you are doing during this daily decluttering process is looking for anything that you may have left out or absentmindedly put down. You're also scanning for garbage or anything you should have tossed out at that moment. An empty water bottle, a napkin, a sticky note that you started to write on but don't actually need anymore. It's that quick.

How will you remember to do it? You've got two options. You can set yourself a reminder – which may be a good idea in the beginning, regardless. Set the alarm in your phone at times that will work for you, generally in the afternoon and evening, to take a few minutes and scan each room for clutter to get rid of.

These brief moments of decluttering should ideally utilize habit stacking and other strategies that you learned in the previous chapter to start generating some consistency. It's simple enough to choose two times during your day where you can devote 15 minutes or less to decluttering your space. Examples of when this could take place is after you finish work and before you go to bed. Or when you wake up in the morning if you don't want to do it at night. Either way, just twice a day when you can commit a few minutes will go far in keeping the clutter from building up again.

So for your daily decluttering – you might stack your afternoon run-through onto the end of lunch if you work from home. Once you put your plate in the sink – you do a quick run-through of the clutter in the kitchen, then prompting you to run through the other high-traffic areas real quick and just pick up anything you see that is lying around.

If you work outside of the home, I would suggest doing your afternoon run-through close to when you get home. Chances are you might have left a bit of clutter around when you were getting ready to leave in the morning, and walking through the house just to pick these things up is a good way to separate the first half of your day from the second. Once you get home and do a quick declutter that should take you less than 5 minutes, you are ready to transition into your downtime. Then you'll repeat this process at the end of the day, just doing a quick walkthrough of each of your rooms with the intention of being able to wake up to a nice clutter-free space in the morning.

Pro tip – try to do your daily decluttering at the same time or associate with the same regular habits each day – this way, it becomes automatic. Sticking to it daily will prevent you from having to do the declutter deep dive that we did earlier in this chapter.

How to Recognize When it's Accumulating Again

Have you been decluttering daily? If not, then it's probably accumulating again. Look around and check out your surfaces. Are there things on them that don't live there, even if they seem benign? Then it's starting again. As a general rule, your surfaces should look clear or very well organized. If they do not, this is a sign that your clutter is picking back up. If they do look clear and well organized at the end of each day, and they just get a bit cluttered during the day before you've picked things up, then you are still fine.

Work with yourself rather than against yourself

Are you realizing that your unread mail is always the outlier? That this is always the type of clutter you find yourself picking up? If you recognize patterns like that, something about that system is not working for you. Don't be afraid to make changes. In fact, this whole book and process is about better learning yourself and what works for you. Don't spend too long fighting it and trying to force systems that don't work for you. You're unlikely to win that battle. You are much better off leaning into it. Think about why that one type of thing is always out. Perhaps the location you chose for it is not the best place for it. Perhaps you need a different habit for addressing that thing altogether. Consider other ways you might address it.

Less is more

Mind your impulse buys. Your wallet and your newly decluttered space will thank you. People with ADHD tend to buy things more impulsively than those who do not have ADHD. This can result in having a lot of extra things that we really don't need. While fully addressing impulsive spending and shopping is well beyond the scope of this book – I would suggest really asking yourself if you need that thing before you buy it. What will be different in your life if you buy it versus if you don't? Can you wait a day or two to decide whether you really have to have it? If you do buy it, are you able to get rid of something in its place? Applying the one-in, one-out rule. Something comes into the house, something goes out – with the mindset of reducing clutter. Being aware of this behavior and using some of these strategies can help you to accumulate things at a slower pace and ideally avoid building up the same clutter that led to more donations and garbage bags than you thought was even possible.

Additionally, when you have fewer things, your entire space is easier to organize, easier to clean, and easier to maintain.

WAYS TO LIVE MORE MINIMALLY

How many dishes do you really need?
When was the last time you used that?
What would the impact on your day-to-day functioning be if you got rid of that?
Is this a "just in case" item?
Is the sentimental value really worth holding onto this item?
Do you frequently look at it or engage with it in some way?

Often we think we need more than we actually need. Clutter doesn't only come from things lying around chaotically, it can also come from having too many of that type of thing. 'Just-in-case' items are most often forgotten about when those 'just in case' moments arise. At one point, I owned 3 tape measures and 2 small toolboxes. You would think I was a handyman. When in fact, I used these things so infrequently that I forgot I had them and mistakenly bought duplicates. I also had bins of things full of just-in-case items under my bed. While I thought I was being organized by having them in bins, the entire storage space under my bed was full of just-in-case bins. That space was later put to much better use by getting rid of the just-in-case stuff and using that area to hold my out-of-season clothes.

So thoroughly consider the things you are holding onto, don't be afraid to let things go, and choose quickly. We are talking about material things here. You will know if you absolutely need something, but if you are in doubt or have to think too long, chances are you really don't need that thing. When it comes to decluttering, we need to keep it moving.

Key Takeaways:

- Clutter is common among people with ADHD and will be a significant barrier to organizing if not dealt with.
- Start with relatively small areas. You want to aim for short periods of intense focus.
- Have 3 bags on hand when you start out – garbage, donation, recycling.
- Create specific piles categories by the type of thing and/or it's function
- Sort items quickly and go for quick wins. You want to avoid getting sidetracked and maintain your motivation to keep pushing forward.
- Prioritize decluttering – NOT organizing. One thing at a time. If you accidentally start trying to organize while in the middle of decluttering, there is a good chance that you won't finish either.
- Progress, not perfection.
- Daily decluttering can become a quick and automatic habit
- Less is more – let things go and think before you buy

PART 2.

Organizing Room by Room

CHAPTER 5.

YOUR SIMPLE ORGANIZATION SYSTEM. HOW TO MAKE ORGANIZING AUTOMATIC AND EASY

Once you've decluttered, you're ready to start getting organized. Despite the fact that ADHD symptoms lend themselves to creating disorganization and chaos, we tend to do much better when surrounded by organized spaces that feel more calm and under control. So this is what we want to create for ourselves and our loved ones if we live with them. We want the home that we live in to be a calm, serene, and functional space where we can get what we need and feel proud of the home that we live in.

There are two aspects to consider when developing your organization system. One is getting organized from a place of being disorganized. The second is maintaining organization with an ongoing system.

What do we mean by organizing?

We mean arranging the items that are contained in your house so that their location makes more sense and is more useful to you and your household. Typically, this involves putting similar items together, making them accessible to you if they are regularly used, or storing them so that they are out of the way, but you can easily find and retrieve them later.

As you choose where items will go, you'll consider not only the type of item that it is, but also its function. For example, if I have a cookbook. Yes, it's a book. But it makes much less sense to put it in your home office or living room, versus finding a place for it to stay in the kitchen.

Ultimately, you'll want items to be in the room they belong in, ideally stored with other similar items, and you'll want to consider whether the area you put them in is efficient, accessible, and aesthetically pleasing.

As you consider this view of organization, you can start to get a sense of why decluttering was such an important prerequisite. People with ADHD often have a lot of extra things that we often don't need. Additionally, those things can sometimes land in the wrong rooms altogether. Upon completing the decluttering phase, you likely got rid of a lot of excess, leaving you with only the essentials, the things that have significant meaning to you, and deserve to have an intentional spot in your home.

Bringing back the basics

As we proceed with organizing – we need to bear in mind the skills that you have previously learned.

SMALL ACHIEVABLE STEPS

Breaking things down helps to address both procrastination and demotivation by reducing the potential to feel overwhelmed and reducing the level of commitment required. It also helps as you work toward building habits by starting with small tasks and gradually adding to them as they become easier and more automatic.

TIME BLOCKS

Small intentional time blocks make a task feel less daunting because you're committing to the time you set rather than the entire task. These time blocks can be put into your daily planner or calendar. For example if you feel overwhelmed at the idea of going through the mail on your counter, you can commit to just 10 minutes. Set a timer and then the expectation is no longer about completing the mail, but about giving it 10 minutes of focused attention. You've now cracked through your avoidance and made a dent in the task. Upon finishing the 10 minutes, you can decide when to come back for the next 10.

REMEMBER YOUR WHY

Your 'Why' is the reason you picked up this book and what you stand to gain if you are successful in your home organizing endeavors. You may also have smaller 'whys' that pertain to each room. Having a clean and organized kitchen as we discussed in Chapter 3 can contribute to your sense of control and confidence at the beginning of your day. While having an organized bedroom space can provide you with a peaceful sanctuary at the end of the day or a place to connect with your partner away from the rest of the world. What matters most is that it feels important to you and provides the foundational incentive you need to take steps forward.

INCLUDE REWARDS THROUGHOUT THE PROCESS

Incorporating rewards prior to, during, and after tasks can boost your dopamine and your ability to complete tasks. If I want to feel more confident in my work life and improve my productivity, I may realize the importance of having an organized home office – my 'why'. So I set goals to get organized and stay organized. I break down the tasks involved and I work on them while doing things I enjoy like listening to playlists or TedTalks. I check the task off my list each time I accomplish it and

I add $20 to a fund for each week that I don't miss a day. This reward goes toward a new design software I've been wanting to splurge on.

MAKE THE TIME

We don't find extra time to organize our homes, we need to be intentional about making the time because we establish that having a clean and organized home is a priority. Putting the time into your calendar makes you more likely to accomplish the tasks you set out to do, rather than vaguely expecting that you'll do it at some point in the day. This leaves much less possibility for procrastination, time blindness, and poor working memory to get in the way.

USE TOOLS AND RESOURCES

We have thoroughly explored the various tools and resources at your disposal that will make cleaning and organizing more feasible as they will help to address some of the additional needs we might experience with ADHD. Once you establish clear plans for how to use each of these resources as part of your organization system, you no longer need to worry about forgetfulness, working memory issues, and time blindness as you actively change and reward your new daily habits.

Getting organized

Get a label maker. This helps in a few ways. First, you'll be able to find the things you are looking for more easily. Second, it can make you more likely to put the item back in that place and to not let other things that don't belong go in there. It's like a little added nudge against getting disorganized again.

If that drawer says "office supplies," you'll have a quick reminder that you are deliberately working against yourself if you put something else in there. This helps to address your impulsivity at that moment. It's impulsivity that says, "who cares? I just want it out of the way." That's how doom piles get formed. Seeing that label makes you second guess that impulsive decision for just a moment so that you can recognize what you are doing and think, "Okay, it doesn't actually go there.

One of the antidotes to impulsive behavior is consequential thinking. This means assessing the potential consequences of your impulsive decision before you go through with it. When we deliberately and impulsively choose to put something in a space that is clearly not labeled for that thing and is, in fact, labeled for something else, we are very quickly reminding ourselves that we may forget where this thing is in the future. We are also forced to recognize that we are choosing to be disorganized at this moment which could be the first step or one of many steps on our way back to chaos. That split second of consequential thinking could be the helpful nudge that pushes us back in the right direction. When it comes to ADHD, we may need lots of those nudges.

STORAGE TIPS

Now that you have decluttered, do you actually have enough storage space? This is when we start to carefully consider whether we need additional storage shelves, bins, baskets, etc. But do not buy them without having a sense of what will go in them and where they will go. You'll consider this more closely as you work on bringing organization to the chaos. See our previous section on impulsive buying. If your purchases, even for organizational purposes, are not well thought out, you could inadvertently be adding to your clutter.

As a kid, I LOVED getting the backpack that had the most storage pockets. I was obsessed with all of those storage pockets and all the potential they had. But I fully lacked organization skills or any sort of system. And every year, no matter how many cool storage areas my backpack had – everything would end up shoved in random places in the most ineffective, inefficient way possible. You don't want that to happen with all the poorly planned storage bings you could impulsively buy. Getting bins or containers, with no plan or system in place for those exact bins or containers, will only add to the problem.

Putting it All into Action

STEP 1:
BUILD YOUR ROADMAP

Here is where we create the plan. We'll use the example of your living room, as it is important to start with the areas you spend the most time in. You want to avoid going in haphazardly and instead start organizing in an order that has some strategy and intention behind it. This doesn't mean it needs to be perfect or that it can't be adjusted. But ultimately, you want to approach all of your rooms in a way that feels as manageable as possible. Creating a plan or roadmap helps you do that.

Grab a piece of paper and a pen. Go to your living room and stand in the center so that you can get a good visual of what every area looks like, including getting a good assessment of its current state. You're going to be writing a list of the areas in your living room in a particular order. As you get to areas that require more work, you'll also be jotting down some notes about those spots.

As you look at your living room, start by identifying the areas that look the best. These are the areas that don't really need rearranging or reorganizing, rather, they just need to be straightened up. Say you have a bookshelf, and you're happy with where your bookshelf is in the living room. It's mostly filled with books and maybe random papers. But overall, it looks pretty good. If this is the spot in the room that looks to be the most organized, put it at the top of the list. You're going to list the areas in your living room, starting with the spots that need the least work, and moving down to the spots that need the most work.

If your living room feels so chaotic that you can't even begin to make sense of individual areas in the way I've mentioned above, then picture your living room as a big clock. Straight ahead of you is 12, a bit to the right of that is 1, directly to your right is 3, behind you is 6, and so on. You can break it up into 12 small sections like this. If you can notice any 'hours' of the clock that seem like they would be the easiest and quickest to address, then list those first, moving along your list down toward the areas that need the most work.

If you feel there is really no way to discern better condition from worse condition in your living room. Then you'll simply start at 12 and work your way around. That will be the order that you complete sections in your living room. However, make sure that if you are at this stage and ready to organize, you have decluttered first. If you skip over decluttering and jump straight to organizing, you'll likely run into problems. Remember, we got rid of a lot of excess in the decluttering phase so that we could effectively organize now.

Now let's run through the list quickly. You have sections of your living room listed – either by name (bookshelf, couch, mantle, coffee table, etc.) or by hour on the clock. This list is quick, and it demonstrates that once you have gotten rid of the clutter, the remaining areas in the room are quite manageable. It also means you can check it off as you make progress, and if you break it up over the course of a few days, you can pick right back up where you left off.

Go through the following steps for each location on your roadmap. Once you're done, each room should be fully organized.

STEP 2:
DETERMINE WHAT TO KEEP IN THE ROOM

Things that make sense to stay in a room are the things that will be used in that room. Start with the first area on your roadmap. Now, as you approach areas that need more work and are a bit messier, there are a few questions to ask yourself:

- Does having this piece of furniture here make sense?
    - If no, move it to the area where it would make more sense before going to the next question
    - If yes, continue to the next question

- Do the objects in or on this piece of furniture belong in this room?
    - If no, move it/them to a bin for now so that you can bring them to the right room later
    - If yes:
        - Move on to step 3

STEP 3:
PICK A SPOT THAT MAKES SENSE

If the items make sense where they are, then move on to step 4.

If not, then consider the following when deciding where they should go:

CONSIDER THE TYPE OF ITEM AND FUNCTION

You'll usually want to keep similar items together, but you'll also need to consider how they are used. A cookbook is a good example. You'd generally want to keep your books together on a shelf that's not likely in the kitchen. More likely a bookshelf in the living room, home office, or even bedroom. But a cookbook would more likely be stored in the kitchen if we consider when and how it is used. For another example, coffee beans and sugar are often pantry items. Yet if they are used daily when you make coffee, you might store them closer to the coffee machine.

CHOOSE LOCATIONS AND STORAGE METHODS WITH CARE AND PURPOSE

Think about how that item will be used. Envision yourself, or if anyone else lives with you, envision how they or you might go to get that item. If you are putting away the salt and pepper in your kitchen, don't put it on the back of the shelf on the highest shelf of the cabinet. Consider what the moment looks like when you might reach for it – keep it within easy reach of the stove and likely toward the front of that shelf or cabinet. If you only use the slow cooker once a month, it can probably go in a cabinet to be pulled out when you need it rather than sitting on the counter next to your toaster.

In your process of getting organized, you will likely find items that don't belong in that section. This is another area that can pose a risk of getting sidetracked. Have on a hand a bin/basket/container where you can keep items that go somewhere else. As you are going through this section, you are only keeping items here that should be here. If you are finding things that need to be tossed, they get tossed. If you find items that need to go in a different room or a completely different section of this room, they just go in this bin. To be dealt with after this section is done and possibly in another time block that you have set aside to address the things in this bin.

Now that you've deliberately chosen where everything should go and you're satisfied that those locations make sense, you're ready to move on to step 4.

STEP 4:
ARRANGE IN A WAY THAT WORKS FOR THAT SPACE

Once you've decided where items belong, you'll need to arrange them. Consider the following:

HOW OFTEN DOES THIS ITEM GET USED?

My planner sits in front of a kitchen organizer on my counter. It typically sits there open to the week we are on because I refer to it and may write in multiple times per day. My checkbook gets used much less often. It sits in a drawer of that same kitchen organizer. It's important and can't be lost, but I generally use it once a month so it can stay in the drawer. The same goes for your travel mugs – if they don't get used often, they don't need to be up front with your daily cups and mugs. Instead, they can go toward the back of that cabinet.

This rule applies to clothing as well. If jeans are not your favorite thing to wear and you prefer sweatpants, the sweatpants need to be more visible and more easily accessible than the jeans. Your organization system needs to be individualized and cater to your lifestyle and your individual preferences while also making sense for the space and storage of the items themselves.

DISPLAYING AND STORING ITEMS

Wherever possible, store items neatly and away unless they are used every day for most of the day or unless they make sense to display, like books, DVDs, or collections that are meant for display. The fewer things you have out, the more spacious and organized your living room will feel. Consider placing appropriately sized baskets on shelves so that the shelves are still easy on the eyes while being able to still hold everything you want.

Items tend to look better, and spaces look cleaner when things are in an order that makes sense. For example, the books in my living room. They are children's books, and they are arranged according to size.

Biggest to smallest. It's pleasing to the eye. The bookshelf in my room with my own books on it is arranged according to the genre. These are both sets of books, but they serve different audiences, and the way they are currently arranged suits the person who is looking through them. This makes them more accessible and efficient. Both sets of books also look clean and neat in how they are set up.

As you follow your roadmap, repeating these steps for each area in the room, you'll fall into a rhythm where the tasks start to flow from one to the next. Before you know it, you'll be standing in an organized room that you can feel proud of.

Stay on Task and Don't Let Perfectionism Derail You

Where ADHD is concerned, our tendency toward perfectionism more often results in not getting the job done because we spent all of our energy and motivation arranging our shirts by color or getting our Tupperware drawer to look like the one we saw on Pinterest. If you want to do these kinds of "extras" after you've gotten organized, have at it. But our task at the moment is getting organized. Arranging things in a way that is efficient, accessible, and looks nice, not looks 'perfect.'

Along with time blocking and breaking the task down into bite-size pieces – make sure you choose a time of day that works for you. You may be more of a night owl. Or you may find that your energy burst only comes mid-day while you are at work, meaning that weekends may be more important for your organizing plans. Ultimately, you may need to experiment with different times of day for this. Don't expect to get organized in one day. You'll likely be doing this process over several days and possibly a few weeks, depending on the time you can set aside for it. How long it takes will also depend on the size of your home and the number of things that need to be organized. Don't let this deter you. This process is achievable for anyone who follows the guidelines and suggestions. You also have practical strategies that directly address *how* you can follow through on the suggestions without your symptoms derailing you. This book allows you to create plans and systems that are individualized so that you can do what works for you, your home, and your lifestyle.

It's all about addressing our biggest issues which include procrastination, motivation, focus, and seeing tasks through to completion. By making the individual goals small, making the process rewarding, and setting your sights on one small task at a time with minimal allowance for distractions or sidetracking, you will steadily chip away at the organization project that is your home.

One of the methods I prefer to use involves tiny bursts of productivity spread across my day. So I'll take half an hour in the morning, I may take another half an hour mid-day, and another in the evening. These small bursts of time and focus are much more powerful for me than if I tried to commit to an hour or two of organizing. That often feels daunting and overwhelming to someone with ADHD, especially since time blindness can make that level of time commitment to a task that you already did not want to do feel like forever.

So again, experiment with the times. Set reasonable expectations where you understand that the entire process of getting your home from a state of chaos into a state or organization can take a few weeks. Know that the exact amount of time it takes will vary depending on their homes, items, behaviors, and choices throughout this process. I can assure you that if you stick to the strategies outlined in this book, you will have success, and you will have the skills you need to sustain your results.

Maintaining Organization

Just as things in your home can often get cluttered easily, they can also get disorganized easily. Whereas your decluttering plan involves tiny daily moments of decluttering, I also recommend 15 minutes of daily organizing and once-weekly organization upkeep of about an hour. The hour-long session could be adjusted depending on the size and needs of your house.

The idea is that once you are organized, it should only take a couple of min per room to stay organized. A book on the shelf may get out of place, the spices in your kitchen may have been taken down while cooking, and you can put them back up on the rack. Each room should take no more than a couple of minutes at most. You also reserve an hour at one point each week to run through each room, doing a deeper organization as needed for your situation.

This means that during your quicker run through you're not worried about making it perfect, but you still maintain an organized feel in your house while knowing you can perfect it during that longer session if needed. Maybe your spices went back in the cabinet or on the rack when you quickly got them off the counter earlier in the week, but now you want to arrange them so they look better. Perhaps you had an event to go through, and you went through a bunch of clothes figuring out what to wear. In your 15 minutes, you got everything back up on the hangers and put it back in the closet, but you still want to fix up where you put everything. This weekly deeper organizing session is really taking the time to re-set exactly where you want things to go.

As you create your organization system, don't forget to accommodate yourself. In addition to the dirty laundry hamper in my bedroom, I also have a clean laundry basket. These baskets are from the same set, slightly different heights and shapes, but they have the same aesthetic, they go with the bedroom, and they are both super important and intentional. Just as I wouldn't leave my dirty laundry to lay around anywhere and I leave it in the hamper until I get a moment to put it in the washing machine, I also acknowledge that I am not always able to fold my laundry as soon as it is done drying. Although I believe it is good practice to do so, I know myself and my lifestyle, and it just does not happen this way. So I have a clean laundry basket. This stops the laundry from piling up on a chair or on my bed, or on top of a dresser. It goes into its designated spot until I fold it. Now if I have time or make time to do it during the week, it gets done, but if I don't and I get all the way up to my organization upkeep day – then that is when it gets folded.

So, your hour devoted to organization each week is when you go through that clean laundry that you still haven't put away and get it put away; you fix the books if they got disorganized and left in different parts of the living room, and you address anything that is left in the 'to be addressed' paper basket in your kitchen or wherever you keep it. Those papers that need to be tended through get looked at least once on the weekends so that you can address them or decide that they need to wait till the following week, but either way, they get looked at, and a decision is made about what to do with them.

So between decluttering and organizing, that's a max of 30 minutes daily and an hour on one chosen day each week. Just to put that in perspective, that's less than the time it would take for you to watch one show or movie on Netflix each day. It's closer to listening to 10 or fewer songs. And your 'long' period of organization that occurs weekly is about as long as one show, and that's only happening once per week.

If you're someone who spends time on social media and this time commitment to organizing feels daunting, try to change your perspective on it. Imagine you could only use social media for 30 minutes per day and an hour on the weekends. Does it still feel like a lot of time? This is not to shame you at all. This example is to demonstrate how our perception and our dopamine reward response can play such a huge role.

You've already learned some specific tips on increasing motivation, rewarding yourself, and beating procrastination – so if those things come back around and threaten to make your goal of getting organized seem impossible, I urge you to revisit those chapters. Once you understand what your needs are and how your brain works, you absolutely can achieve your goals.

The time when you are getting organized is super important to stay on top of your symptoms. Try to make sure you are enjoying this time – by playing music, audiobooks, etc., sipping a latte, and stepping back every 15 min or so to admire your progress. Keep moving fairly quickly. Setting milestones for yourself can help with this. I'll be done going through this drawer in 10 minutes. This particular piece of the task will be completed at this time. Little milestones like this can also gamify the experience a bit which can be naturally rewarding, especially for people with ADHD.

Assess and reassess your storage strategies

Once you have gotten things organized is when you will have the opportunity to determine if particular strategies are working for you. Remember, we want to create habits that are easy for you to maintain.

Does it work that you keep jackets in the coat closet? It may look 10x neater that way, and it's easy to tell why you put it there, but if in the day-to-day that results in you not wanting to take the time to open the closet door and put the jacket on a hanger, so instead you just throw it on the couch or on your bed, then you may need to re-assess that strategy. An over-the-door coat hook may be more beneficial for your daily jacket because you're simply more likely to use it.

The systems that work are not necessarily the ones that look the best or make the most sense. The systems that work are the ones that you'll use. Yes, we want them to be more efficient than the chaos, and we want your new system to look better than the chaos. But remember that they are literally no good if you don't use them. So if something is not working after a few weeks of trying to do it according to your original setup, then it is time to try a different system.

Key Takeaways

Have a step-by-step plan:

- **Step 1.** Build You Roadmap
    - For each room, list the areas you'll be going through from most to least organized
    - If this type of breakdown doesn't work for that room, than picture it like a clock and break it down into 12 small sections
    - You'll use this list to keep track and check things off as you go
- **Step 2.** Determine What to Keep in the Room
    - Start with the first area on your list
    - Follow the steps from here down through step 4, then come back up to this step for the next area and so on.
    - Does the furniture make sense where it is? If not, you'll need to move it.
    - Do the items belong in this room?
        - If not, place them in a bin to be moved to the room they go in later, then move forward to the next step
        - If so, continue to step 3.
- **Step 3.** Pick a Spot that Makes Sense
    - If the items there make sense in that spot, and just need better arranging, proceed to step 4
    - If you're not yet sure where they should go:
        - Consider the types of items, as you'll group similar items together
        - Consider how you use them
- **Step 4.** Arrange Items in a Way that Works for that Space

    - Consider how often you use the item
    - Similar items look better together
    - Arrange neatly and out of sight where possible

- Make sure you declutter before attempting to organize
- These chapters build upon one another. Keep in mind what you have learned in previous chapters
- Organize one room and one small section at a time
- Start with the high-traffic rooms first
- Labeling, storage containers and organizers, and careful choice of where you store things will come in handy
- Individualize room plans to meet your needs, preferences, and lifestyle
- Use the skills you've learned to curb perfectionism, procrastination, and low motivation
- Maintaining means
    - Decluttering for a max of 30 min per day broken into two 15-minute blocks. It will likely go faster.
    - Reorganizing for one hour per week, this time will also likely go faster.
- Assess your storage areas and be willing to change them to find what works best for you in the long run

CHAPTER 6.

THE LIVING ROOM

Your living room is likely the most high traffic room in your house. Because you spend most of your time here and any guests you have would undoubtedly spend most of their time here as well, this is where we'll start. Once you see that you can tackle the most frequently used room in the house, you'll start to get a sense of just how achievable getting and staying organized really is.

Although everyone's living room space can differ, you likely have some of the following areas:

- Seating areas, including couches, chairs, and ottomans
- Coffee table and End tables
- TV stand
- Book shelf
- Display shelves or mantel
- Additional storage cabinets or shelving

SEATING AREAS

There are endless ways to arrange the furniture in a living room, but ultimately you want it to be intentional. If the focal point of your living room is the TV, then couches and chairs are oriented toward that. Seating areas should be conducive to a conversation between people seated in different spots. Furniture shouldn't be cluttered and awkward to move around. The seating that you have in the room is useful, and if it is more of a display piece, make sure it's not just creating another surface to collect clutter.

Too many decorative pillows on couches and chairs can get disorganized quickly. If you have throw blankets, these can be arranged neatly on a couch or chair. If they have a tendency to look messy, keep them in a storage ottoman, nearby drawer, or basket.

COFFEE TABLE / END TABLES

Ideally, there should be at least one table surface within reach of every seating option so that people have a place to put things down while in that space. But bear in mind these surfaces can be clutter magnets. Make a point to leave these spaces open. You might have one decorative item in the middle of your coffee table. You might have a lamp on an end table.

These areas are meant to be useful while you are in the living room if you need to put down a book, laptop, or drink. Outside of being used at that moment, they should be clear. This makes the room look more open and organized.

TV STAND

This is where your consoles will go. Refrain from putting decorative items around the TV or on the TV stand. This makes the area look cluttered and messy. Try to keep wires out of sight or neatly tied together. Whether you keep the remote controls here is a personal preference. You might opt to keep them on the TV stand when the living room is not in use, or you might keep them in a drawer of the coffee table or end table since you typically watch TV when seated on a couch or chair.

Any drawers or cabinets in your TV stand should contain things like videos, DVDs, and games for the consoles you have. If you have a TV stand with lots of extra storage space, this is where you might keep other items that are relevant to the living room, such as books or board games. If you have large shelves on your TV stand – choose simple-looking baskets to hold your items. This will look more organized than placing things directly on the shelf.

SHELVING

If you are using a shelf for books, only have books on that shelf. Don't mix books with other items. This can look messy and disorganized. Arrange the books in a way that makes sense for you. This might be by genre, by author, or alphabetically. Choose one way that makes sense and stick to that so that you always know where to find the book you need and where to put it back.

Display shelves are often used in living rooms to hold pictures or other sentimental or decorative items. Be intentional about the items you place on these shelves. Too many things, too close together, will look chaotic. Choose a few times, and space them out. Try to have similar items on the shelf. Whether it's pictures, trophies, or figurines, the shelf should look cohesive rather than a mashup of random items.

For additional storage shelves, keep their size of them in mind. Whenever possible, use a bin, basket, or some type of organizer. Otherwise, the shelf is likely to quickly gather random items. Use labels ff you have a lot of storage shelving in your living room. This will make it more likely that you know where things are and that you put them back in their place. It will also make your organization maintenance quicker.

Pro Tip for the Living Room

Because this is a high-traffic area used in many different ways, it can easily get messy and cluttered. Consider having one basket, bin, or drawer that is a small catchall area. This acts as your backup. If you are in a moment where you don't have time to put something where it goes, you can put it in this basket. It's better than leaving it on the couch or coffee table. It will then become part of your normal routine to check and address the things in that basket daily or weekly, depending on how quickly things might accumulate in it.

If a room looks messy already, we are more likely to leave things lying around. But if a room appears to be neat and tidy, it's more obvious to us when we go to leave something out. This basket helps keep the room looking neat and organized while still acknowledging that you might not always have the time to put it where it goes.

CHAPTER 7.

THE BATHROOM

Your bathroom is likely much smaller than your living room and is typically made up of sections that are easier to define and generalize.

- the closet, if you have one
- additional cabinets or shelving
- linen tower
- medicine cabinet
- storage areas beneath your sink which can include drawers
- inside the shower/bath area
- countertops

Primary strategies that you'll want to remember in the bathroom are that you want to limit the appearance of clutter in this small space and you also want to group like items together.

COUNTERTOP

Consider what items really need to be on your countertop. At a minimum, you should have soap and a hand towel. Anything else is a personal choice. Bathroom organizer sets are typically a nice way to store the items that go on your countertop. This could also include toothbrushes, toothpaste, hand lotion, and tissues.

If you have a large bathroom countertop, you can probably have these things out in their organizers and still have space to spare so that it doesn't look too cluttered. If you have a smaller countertop in your bathroom, you'll want to stick to the soap and hand towel and keep your other items stored out of view.

CLOSETS, LINEN TOWER, AND CABINETS

The linen tower or closet should be used to hold your towels, bathmats, hand towels, and bathrobe if you use one. If you have more space in there, this is also a good spot for extra toilet paper and tissues. If you have even more room, you can store backup shampoos, conditioners, soaps, shower gels, etc. Again, this is where your individual preference comes into play.

Underneath the bathroom sink and among the drawers will also depend on your personal preference. You'll likely be storing additional cleaning supplies, possibly larger items like hair dryers, straighteners, electric razors, brushes, etc.

Ultimately the way you use this space is completely based on your personal preference – but keep similar items together and consider how often and when you use the items. This will better inform where you choose to place which items. The same goes for additional cabinet space. It comes down to what items you have, whether you feel you need to keep those items or if they are never used, and how often and in what context you use those items.

SHOWER/ BATH AREA

The shower or bath area definitely benefits from an organizer. Get one that you like the look of, and that will stay up on the wall. Many of them can slide down if they don't hang on the shower head, and that will quickly lead to more disorganization.

If your shower has built-in shelves, those are usually not large enough to accommodate everything neatly. So find an organizer that you like, and if possible, check reviews to make sure it stays up. Here is where you'll store conditioner, shampoo, soap, razors, moisturizers, hair masks, body scrubs, loofahs, and anything else related to your shower or bath routine.

Pro Tips for Organizing the Bathroom

YOU'LL NEED SMALLER ORGANIZER BINS AND/ OR DRAWER ORGANIZERS

There tend to be a lot of smaller items that can gather in the bathroom. If you have large cabinet spaces or large shelves, the bathroom is typically a place where you will benefit from smaller organizers to put on those shelves, in the cabinets, or in the drawers. Even if you don't have incredibly large spaces under your sink or in the cabinet/closet area, it's still very likely that you'll need some smaller organizers to group like items together and to keep them from becoming a doom pile.

GET OUT THE LABEL MAKER

With the organizers that you purchased, it makes sense to label them. If you store makeup, you'll want to group it by area of the face and potentially even more categories depending on your collection. These things get labeled clearly. Over-the-counter pain relievers, allergy medicines, first aid – these things get labeled as well. You'll also want to clearly separate cleaning supplies from any products that you'll use on your body. Depending on what goes in your bathroom and the space you have, it is very likely that labels will be helpful here.

HAVE SMALLER JARS AND BOTTLES AVAILABLE

Have you ever had a large bottle of conditioner sitting in your bathroom for over a week with less than a quarter of the original contents still in it? It's still more than enough to use a few times, but it can become annoying when you have a large, mostly empty bottle taking up space. They always fall over much easier too. This is where small reusable jars or bottles come in. Use these as soon as your products start getting low to keep things neater. And again, label them.

TAKE THE TIME YOU NEED TO DO IT RIGHT

The bathroom is another area of your home that you are likely to frequent several times per day. It's also an area that can easily start to look cluttered due to its small size, and it can easily be embarrassing if it looks messy to guests. Depending on the amount of items in your bathroom and the level or organization you still need to do with all of the small things, this room may take you anywhere from 1–3 sessions, which you might decide to spread across a few days. That is totally okay. It's not about speed, it's about getting it done in a way that can be maintained. Quick fixes might look nice at first glance, but they often don't get maintained due to the lack of intention and consideration of where things are placed. Putting in that extra consideration really goes a long way to creating an organization system that you can maintain in the long term.

CHAPTER 8.

THE KITCHEN

The kitchen is another main hub of every home. It gets traffic from the beginning to the end of the day and is often frequented by guests as well. Your kitchen is one of the rooms that require the most structure, considering the frequency of use and the way that it needs to function.

Kitchens can also have a lot of variation in how they are laid out, but ultimately we all tend to have similar areas despite the difference in layout, size, shape, etc. You likely have an area where you cook and prepare food, areas to store foods that need to be kept cold and areas where you can store food at room temp. You likely have a sink, dishwasher, or both, and countertops connecting or nearby to all of these things. Some kitchens have enough space for a table, breakfast bar, or both.

- Pantry
- Cabinets
- Countertops/Island
- Table/Breakfast bar
- Refrigerator
- Sink/Dishwasher
- Trash/Recycles

PANTRY

If you have a separate pantry in addition to your existing cabinet space, this is where you'll keep:

- Canned goods
- Cereals
- Snacks
- Various baking/cooking ingredients

Pantry organizers are a good idea to reduce the clutter of packaging that your goods come in – especially when this package stops you from seeing how much is actually left in the box or bag. This type of packaging can become a major waste of space and make the entire pantry look and feel messier.

Get out your label maker because you'll be taking things out of their bulky packaging to place things in more uniform containers that make finding things a breeze

Try to choose containers that are both transparent and stackable. Often pantry shelves can be tall, but you'll realize that most items don't use that height, so stackable organizers can make the most of this small space. Lazy Susans can also be great for similar items like oils, baking ingredients, or spices.

Before you start organizing this space, make sure that you've already gotten rid of anything that is past the expiration date. Sometimes it can be easy to miss these – just do a quick check as you go through the items you intend to keep in the pantry.

If you are short on space in your pantry, look for door organizers, hooks, and wall dispensers to add additional storage. Organize areas in your pantry by how the things will be used. You can have an area for baking, dinners, snacks, quick lunches, breakfast foods, canned goods, spices, condiments, etc.

CABINETS

When it comes to organizing your cabinets, it's important to consider whether you have a separate pantry like what is described above or if you are using cabinet space to hold everything. Typically things like canned goods, cereals, snacks, extra paper towels, garbage bags, etc. would go in the pantry, but if you have no pantry, these things are being organized within your cabinet space.

First off, when considering what will go into which cabinets, you'll first consider the location of the cabinets. For example, cabinets near the stove or your food-prepping area will likely contain the items you need for cooking and food prep. Items such as oil, spices, colanders, pots, pans, cutting boards, Tupperware, etc.

While cabinets near the sink area will hold your dishes and glassware. The cabinets underneath the sink typically store cleaning supplies, extra soap, and garbage bags if you don't have a pantry. Consider how you use the items in your kitchen and keep them in the areas that are closest to where they'll be needed or used.

In the absence of a pantry, store food together and organize it by size and type. Similar to the breakdown of areas described in the pantry section, you can do the same with your kitchen cabinets. Areas for breakfast pantry items, dinner pantry items, snacks, condiments, spices, etc. Keep similar items together and taller items toward the back. Keep very large cans or jugs in your bottom cabinets, while smaller items will go toward the front.

As described in the pantry section, clear containers work best to avoid bulky packaging, and labels can be your best friend.

COUNTERTOPS

Countertops are often magnets for paperwork doom piles. Try to be intentional with the items on your counter. This will keep the room looking more open and organized as well as more functional.

Some things that will likely stay on your countertops are your small appliances, such as your coffee maker, toaster oven, and your blender – if you use them daily. If you only use it sparingly, this is something that should be stored in a cabinet. The same goes for your slow cooker, food processor, etc. If they are not used frequently, put them away.

While your paperwork should be kept in a spot that makes sense for you, many people often use the countertop as a quick drop spot for mail or other household paperwork that needs to be dealt with. This can result in a paperwork doom pile. If your paperwork doom pile is on the kitchen countertop or anywhere else in the house, you'll want to break it into at least 3 clear categories.

- To pay
- To review/fill out
- To file

If there are other categories that you frequently use, such as coupons or scheduled activities to attend, that need to be put in your calendar, then add those categories. Don't overcomplicate it, but make sure that you've addressed the main areas that typically make up your paperwork clutter. When mail comes in, you'll quickly toss it into one of these baskets or files, and then it will be addressed at least weekly in your organizing routine.

TABLE

The table is only useful if it's clear of clutter. Get into the habit of leaving the table clear. Nothing gets stored here aside from a centerpiece if you like and possibly placemats if you want to leave them on the table and ready. Things like napkins or salt/pepper can come out when needed.

REFRIGERATOR

Chances are, you already know what goes in the fridge and freezer. But the trick can be organizing them so that things are easy to find and don't look like chaos when you open the fridge. This is another place where clear uniform containers come in handy. First off, if you have those drawers at the bottom of your fridge, they're typically meant for your produce. If they have vents, you can slide the vents more open or more closed depending on what you put inside. If you don't have vents, they are just meant to be high-humidity drawers.

Things that go in high-humidity drawers are typically your leafy green vegetables and herbs – things that have the potential to wilt when they dry out. These drawers keep them fresher longer – but don't forget, with ADHD, you might struggle with things being out of sight, out of mind. So pop a label over these drawers to remember what's in there. Low humidity works best for your fruits and just means you leave the vents open to allow the airflow.

Chances are, not all of your produce fits in these drawers, so having clear containers to better sort items and keep them from rolling into each other will help keep the fridge organized. When possible, get rid of extra packaging, just like with your cabinet items.

SINK/ DISHWASHER

This section is more about what goes around these areas. If you have a dish rack for dishes that are drying, use it, but try not to let this just become a space where your dishes live all the time. From the dish rack to your meal, back to the sink and dish rack. Make a plan in your organizing routine for when you will empty the dishrack and dishwasher to put those items away.

I have decided not to have a dish rack for this reason. I have a dishwasher, and for anything else that gets hand-washed, I use a hand towel to dry it right away. Otherwise, my dishrack becomes a permanent home for my dishes. Again, it's about knowing yourself.

Having a sponge holder in your sink gives you a place to leave the sponge that's not out on the counter or lost somewhere in the sink. Keeping the dishwasher pods or the dish soap right under the sink keeps your counters neat while keeping what you need close by.

TRASH/ RECYCLES

Trash is pretty straightforward, Keep it in the bin and have a routine for when it gets taken out. If you find it doesn't get taken out frequently enough, get a smaller bin. If you find your bin is too small, consider a slightly larger one while still staying within the realm of normal kitchen bin size.

Have a recycle bin or basket nearby. If you separate your recycles, your bins should also account for this. Recycle bins can usually be smaller and still do the job. If you don't want a bin, you might be fine with a recycle bag. I've seen clients be successful with a dedicated bag that hangs on the bag of the island to keep used water bottles. I personally have a small bag that hangs on the backdoor because that door is situated right between my kitchen and where the bins are outside. So it's easy to grab and move it right out the door.

Key Takeaways

- Clear uniform containers and labels are best for avoiding clutter in the pantry, cabinets, and refrigerator.
- Get rid of unnecessary bulky packaging.
- Keep everything closest to where you'll use it.
- If you notice any doom piles like paper/mail, get a dedicated mail organizer, thin baskets, or paper organizers and label them.
- Keep trash and recycle bins near eachother and in a spot that's easy to take out.

CHAPTER 9.

THE BEDROOM

Bedrooms are another space that can be entirely unique to each individual but for the most part we can assume to include certain things. Like clothes, shoes, a bed, etc. The main areas to consider when organizing your bedroom are:

- The Bed & Under The Bed
- Closet
- Dresser(s)
- Night Tables

THE BED AREA

The only things on top of the bed should be your sheets, blankets, and pillows. If you have space under your bed, this can be a great storage area. You can get storage bins and bags of almost any height to fit under your bed. If you have a smaller living space that doesn't have ample storage, don't let this space go to waste. Use this space for the things that you don't need on a regular basis, like your summer or winter clothes and shoes.

CLOSET

The closet is usually the biggest challenge in the bedroom. For someone with ADHD, this often ends up becoming a problematic catchall space. But since you've already decluttered, you've got the hardest part out of the way.

To organize your closet in the best way possible, you'll want to consider the various items that need to be organized. You'll also need to consider whether your current closet setup has the kind of organization space you need. For example, big open spaces can often benefit from adding some additional shelving. But don't go overboard in buying additional organizing units until you see how everything fits.

In general, you'll need to organize:

- Clothes
- Shoes
- Accessories

CLOTHES

Break down your clothes into categories. Coats or dresses will get hung on higher racks, while shirts and pants can get hung on mid-level or lower racks. If you have a closet with only one rack, keep the coats furthest toward the back, then dresses, then shirts, then pants closest toward the front. This order works so that you can still see everything. If you have a smaller closet, don't worry about hanging everything. At bare minimum, you'll just want to hang materials that can easily become wrinkled. If you have a bit more space, you'll generally hang any pants, dresses, jackets, and shirts – depending on whether they're likely to wrinkle. Materials that are likely to get stretched out or deformed when hanging should be folded.

T-shirts and Jeans can go either way, and this will depend on what kind of space you have. If you have a small dresser but ample hanging space, you might hang your jeans, but if you only have a small area for hanging and you have a lot more space for folded items, then these items should be folded.

SHOES

Unless you only own 4 pairs of shoes, you'll need an organization system for them. Without a clear place to put them, shoes can easily pile up on your closet floor or near your front door.

Options to organize your shoes include free-standing shoe racks, under bed shoe organizers, shoe racks that hang on the closet door, or individualized shoe cubes that can stack and sit on your closet shelf. You can also combine different options if needed. Consider how many shoes you need to store and what kind of space you have.

ACCESSORIES

Accessories in your bedroom may include jewelry, purses, belts, ties, hats, or scarves.If you have a closet with space for these items, they'll be stored here. If not, you can also use areas in or near the dresser. For many of these items, some strategically placed hooks can do the trick.

Hats, purses, belts, and scarves can all be stored on simple command hooks hung on the wall inside your closet or a wall in your bedroom. Hats and purses can also be stored on shelves or in bins/baskets as long as nothing heavy is placed on top of them. Scarves and ties can also be placed in bins. Ties can be rolled to fit in smaller spaces or hung on a tie rack. How you store jewelry depends on the kind of jewelry and how much of it you have. Long necklaces can also be hung on small hooks, while other jewelry does best in jewelry boxes or organizers, which come in all shapes and sizes to fit your needs.

DRESSERS

If you have a dresser you'll want to be strategic and consistent with where you store items. Ideally, the top drawer holds smaller items such as underwear, socks, or jewelry if it didn't get placed in a jewelry organizer in the closet. To help keep smaller items spaced from one another, use drawer inserts to keep items separated.

Heavier items go toward the bottom of the dresser. These include sweatshirts, sweatpants, jeans, etc. In the middle, you can place pajamas, t-shirts, or other lightweight clothing items that don't need to be folded. Consistency is key when you decide what will go in each drawer so that they don't become a mess.

NIGHT TABLES

Try to keep your night table clear. This is where you might just have a lamp to read at night, you might store a book you are reading or your Kindle in the bedside drawer. Others keep nighttime medications in this area so they don't forget to take them. Always keep medications out of reach if there are children in the home. Essentially your night table is not a major place for storage. Just a few personal items inside and a mostly clear surface aside from maybe a lamp, a photo, or another decorative item.

Pro Tip for Organizing the Bedroom

Keep in mind that your bedroom should exude peace. This is where you wind down at the end of the day. You really want to keep surfaces clear aside from intentional decor. There's also a good chance that you are underutilizing available storage space that's in your closet, your dresser, or under your bed. Once you organize everything, look around for areas that you can see becoming highly disorganized quickly again. This means that while everything fits, you may need to add an organizer or move smaller things to an even smaller space to avoid items piling up.

CHAPTER 10.

THE HOME OFFICE

Your home office needs to be well organized. This is where you work. You want this space to foster productivity. Many of us have rapidly learned to work at home over the past few years, while others may have been doing it for a while before that. Whether you love it or hate it, if you have a home office, you'll need to make sure it is well organized so that you can work efficiently and feel well-prepared when you jump on calls or need to produce something quickly for a client or colleague.

Most home offices have similar components:

- Computer
- Printer
- Books and Files
- Office supplies

COMPUTER

Considering most things have gone digital, it's possible that your home office space is nothing more than a desk, chair, and computer. Many find that they no longer have a need for anything paper related, while others still need to print and store things.

While a thorough explanation of digital organization is outside the scope of this book, you'll generally approach it with some of the same concepts you have already learned. Keep your desktop from becoming too cluttered with random shortcuts. Your desktop should have just the shortcuts that you'll need. Keep shortcuts with related functions near each other. Create files to categorize items so that they can easily be found later. Use files or labels in your email folder to categorize your emails. Consider adding filters in the settings so that specific emails automatically go under the correct label, rather than piling into the general inbox.

Regarding your actual desk space, it's important to keep the space around your computer clear and ready to work. Having a lot of things around you, like papers and post-its can be distracting. It can also be unpleasant to work in a space that feels overly cluttered. Additionally, keep your cords neat and out of the way.

PRINTER

This should be on or near your desk area so that you're not having to walk to another area of the office or to another room to get what you printed. Additionally, keep things like extra paper and ink stored nearby.

BOOKS AND FILES

These can be pretty straightforward. Books should be stored on the bookshelf. If you don't have one and you only have a few books in your office, you can use bookends and put them on any nearby shelf or on one end of your desk, depending on the size of your desk space.

Files would be considered any paper that you need or want to keep. To avoid these piling up on your desk, either use a paper organizer that goes on top of the desk with labels to categorize the papers or use a filing drawer with hanging file folders that you can label and store papers that way.

OFFICE SUPPLIES

These include pens, highlighters, post-its, extra notepads, paperclips, etc. Have one drawer where you can store extra office supplies. Use smaller containers that can sit in that drawer to keep things separated and organized. This way, when you need something, you know exactly where to look.

Pro Tip for the Home Office

Each time you leave your desk for the day, make sure these items are back where you initially arranged them. It's easy to get disorganized when you are busy working. But your workspace should never feel cluttered or difficult to navigate. You want to look forward to being productive and efficient in your space.

Make your home office space enjoyable to be in. This will also help your productivity. Intentionally choose lighting that you enjoy working in, have a smart speaker so that you can play music while you work, and decorate in a way that inspires you. These things will help you want to maintain the organization and keep this space being one you want to come back to again and again.

CHAPTER 11.

LAUNDRY AND THE LAUNDRY ROOM

Now you might have a separate laundry room, or you might have a smaller living space that doesn't include this room. But either way, we know you have laundry. So let's consider the various aspects that go along with your laundry and how you can keep it all organized.

- Dirty laundry
- Laundry soaps, dryer sheets, fabric softeners, etc.
- Clean laundry

DIRTY LAUNDRY

If you sort your clothes before washing them, have a 3-section laundry sorter so that dirty clothes get immediately sorted after taking them off. Label the sections for your darks, whites, and colors. Keep this sorter in your bedroom because that's where you're most likely to use it. If you put it in the laundry room, chances are your laundry goes on the floor rather than you getting undressed and walking it over the laundry room. You want your system to cater to the path of least resistance.

LAUNDRY SOAP, DRYER SHEETS, FABRIC SOFTENERS, ETC.

Having a wall rack, a small laundry cart, bins, or baskets to hold the supplies that you'll need to do your laundry is essential. These things should be quick and easy to find and always located closest to where they will be used. If you are using bins or baskets, don't forget to label them.

CLEAN LAUNDRY

Keeping a drying rack in your laundry room is ideal for the clothes that you don't want to put in the dryer. You can find free-standing or wall-mounted foldable drying racks to keep in your laundry room without taking up too much space.

It's also a good idea to have a small basket near the dryer for unmatched socks. They usually have a way of turning up, and you want one designated spot for them until you find their match. You'll also want a small trash bin for lint after clothes come out of the dryer.

Ideally, you'll be folding your laundry as soon as you pull it out of the dryer, but if we're being realistic, that may not happen every time. This is where a clean laundry basket comes in. If it's one of those times when you are in a rush, or you are in the middle of doing something else, and you had to pull the clothes out of the dryer to start another load, but you don't have the time or patience to fold it all right now, you can put it in a basket in your bedroom designated just for clean clothes. Establish a routine for how frequently you clear this basket. This stops the clean laundry pileup from happening in other places like your bed, a chair, or your couch.

Pro Tip for the Laundry Room

Depending on the setup of your home, the laundry room can also be a great area to store additional cleaning supplies such as the mop, swiffer, vacuum, etc.

CHAPTER 12.

STORAGE AND HALLWAYS

Hallways should remain clear aside from any hallway closets or built-in shelving. Shelves that are in the halls should hold minimal decor or deep baskets that give a clean and uniform look to the space.

If the shelves are near an entryway, you can keep things that would be useful when leaving the house, such as a small umbrella, gloves, hat, or sunscreen. If you have built-in shelves instead of a linen closet, these baskets are where you might store extra blankets. These shelves could also be used for books.

Generally, the closet nearest to the entryway is used as the coat closet to hold any coats, rain jackets, umbrellas, hats, gloves, boots, etc. While the closet in the middle of the hallway is often used as a linen closet where you might store extra sheets, towels, blankets, tablecloths, etc. Additional storage closets can keep extra things like cleaning supplies, holiday decorations, and other seasonal items that don't really make sense in any particular room of the house.

You can often create additional storage space in almost any room. Whether you do this by finding bins that fit under the bed, hanging hooks on the wall of the closet, installing floating shelves in your laundry room, etc. There are always ways to create more storage space.

When storing items, make sure they are clearly labeled so that you know where to find things and you have a clearly designated spot to put them back. Storage spaces can easily get cluttered and disorganized, so make sure you are intentional about where things go so that anyone looking at that space could find what they are looking for.

PART 3.

Cleaning Room by Room

CHAPTER 13.

YOUR CLEANING SYSTEM

If you are someone who has ADHD and struggles with clutter and organization, chances are your cleaning routine doesn't come naturally either. But once you have a plan and a system for how to address keeping your home clean, you'll find it easier than you think.

By now, you've really begun to master the application of the skills you need to initiate tasks and to see them through to completion. You've done it in the decluttering phase, and you've done it as you reorganized your home and set up systems to keep it decluttered and organized.

Cleaning is really just an additional step. It's essentially an add-on using the same types of skills that you've already been working on. Once you can start to think of cleaning as just an extension of the skills you've already been successfully using, you can break up the tasks into small, manageable, rewarding pieces, and you can start to create a routine that is both structured and flexible enough to keep working for you.

How Often Should You Clean

How often and in what ways you use a room helps to determine how often you should clean it. Places that get used more often will need to be cleaned more frequently. Places where hygiene is essential, like the bathroom, or where food is involved, like the kitchen, will need a deep cleaning that includes more attention to detail and disinfecting more frequently than, say, the bedroom or laundry room.

Generally, your entire house only needs a solid deep clean 2-3 times yearly. This is the kind of cleaning you see people doing during Spring cleaning where they go through everything, removing extra clutter, dusting and wiping from the ceiling to the floor, and getting behind and under all the furniture.

Daily cleaning is usually pretty simple spot cleaning, general wiping down of areas, and keeping high traffic spots swept. While a weekly or biweekly clean will be more detailed than your daily cleaning including mopping and getting into smaller areas that you might not pay attention to every day. The kitchen, for example, gets a general simple cleaning daily and a more thorough cleaning at least every 1-2 wks.

What Supplies You'll Need

- Paper towels or reusable clean rags
- Broom
- Mop
- Vacuum
- Multi Surface cleaner
- Disinfectant spray
- White vinegar
- Spray bottles
- Microfiber cloth
- Microfiber mop or duster to reach high places
- Daily shower spray
- Squeegee
- Cleaning caddy

MAKE A WHITE VINEGAR CLEANING SOLUTION

If you pour white vinegar and water into a spray bottle in a 1:1 ratio, you have a cleaning solution that breaks down dirt and buildup, kills most mold and mildew, and is safe and non-toxic. This can be used when cleaning many areas of your home. The smell of the vinegar should dissipate shortly after you're done cleaning.

The Secret to Never Getting Overwhelmed by Cleaning Again

We know that part of the reason it is difficult to get organized and clean and maintain it is that the idea of cleaning your whole house can feel daunting. Executive function deficits make it hard to conceptualize what seems to be a very big task with way too many smaller parts. It becomes difficult to identify what to prioritize, where to start, and how to proceed through all of the necessary steps effectively. So, cleaning can become something we might avoid altogether or only do when we absolutely have to.

There are approaches to cleaning that are meant to make it more focused and approachable. There are also an unlimited number of cleaning schedules that have been published that are really meant to make it as simple as print and checking it off the list. You can even use the Daily Weekly Organizer found at this end book.

Take advantage of the visual aids where possible, either by creating your own or using one that is pre-made for you. Using a visual list for your cleaning needs addresses working memory deficits and means that you won't have to rely on remembering what you need to do next or having to break down the components of thoroughly cleaning your kitchen every time. You'll simply follow the list. Some of these lists can be more ADHD-friendly because you don't always have to do the same task every Monday. Instead, if you have tasks that get completed on a weekly basis, then you make sure that each day, you are checking something off that weekly list. It can be whichever task you would prefer to do that day, but something gets checked off.

Next, we'll explore three different approaches to regularly cleaning your home. These are Zone Cleaning, Task Cleaning, and using a Daily/Weekly/Monthly Checklist. As you consider these approaches, take into account your individual needs and the barriers to cleaning that you have experienced up to now. You'll want to focus on choosing the method that is most likely to overcome your individual challenges with cleaning to make the process as easy as possible.

WHAT IS ZONE CLEANING?

If you've explored different ways of cleaning your house before, you may have encountered the concept of zone cleaning. It's meant to be an effective method of cleaning that's meant to minimize feelings of anxiety and overwhelm. The idea is that you divide your home into about 5 zones. Those zones may include more than one room grouped together. For example:

Zone 1: Living Room

Zone 2: Kitchen

Zone 3: Bedroom and Home Office

Zone 4: Bathroom

Zone 5: Laundry and Storage

Once you've divided your home into zones, you list deep cleaning tasks for that zone. One of the benefits of zone cleaning is also considered to be that deep cleaning is occurring all year round, so you do not have to plan to do it at any particular point, such as Spring cleaning.

Examples of tasks for Zone 1 Living Room might be:

- Clean the windows
- Dust the ceiling fan

- Vacuum the rugs
- Wash the throw blankets

While tasks for Zone 4 Bathroom might include:

- Scrub the floor
- Clean the toilet
- Wash the bathmats and towels
- Deep clean the shower

Once you've made this list, you commit to doing tasks in that zone for 15 minutes. This may mean only working on one task, or you may get to more than one. Each week, you are only focusing on 1 zone, and each day you are only doing 15 minutes worth of tasks in that zone. There are many free templates of zone cleaning examples available online, or it may make the most sense to make your own so that it's tailored to your home and the tasks you need to accomplish.

WHAT IS TASK CLEANING?

Task cleaning differs from zone cleaning by focusing on one particular type of task and applying that throughout the entire house rather than staying in one particular room or zone. The idea is that you may be less likely to become distracted or sidetracked in tidying up other things if you are focused on one particular type of task.

Examples of task cleaning might be:

- Wipe down and disinfect all hard surfaces (tables/countertops)
- Vacuum all carpets/rugs
- Sweep all hard floors
- Dust (remember to go from top to bottom)

You would list all the tasks involved with cleaning your home, choose one task each day, and move through the house completing that task.

MAKING A DAILY/ WEEKLY/ MONTHLY CHECKLIST

If the above strategies don't feel like they do enough to accomplish the cleaning needs of your home, you might want to consider the Definitive Cleaning Schedule created by Good Housekeeping (Smith & Picard, 2019). They established an ultimate guide for how often cleaning tasks must be completed in your home. With a checklist like this, you could establish your daily routines and then also make sure you are checking something off the list on a weekly and monthly basis.

For example, their daily list includes:

- Clean dirty dishes
- Wipe down kitchen counters and table
- Sweep kitchen floors
- Squeegee shower walls
- Wipe down bathroom surfaces

While their weekly list includes:

- Change bedding
- Clean microwave
- Mop kitchen and bathroom floors
- Scrub bathroom surfaces
- Toss expired food

And things on their monthly list include:

- Dust and clean the light fixtures
- Clean the dishwasher and laundry machines

They suggest tasks that need to be done every 3-6 months, such as:

- Wiping down the inside of your fridge
- Cleaning the shower curtain liner
- Cleaning under and behind furniture

- Cleaning inside the oven

While yearly tasks include:

- Cleaning the drapes and curtains
- Clearing out the gutters
- Deep clean the carpet and upholstery

An extensive checklist like this, with specifically identified timing of when things need to be done, lets you see all of the tasks that need to be done and lets you choose what you'd like to pick from that list. The idea here is that tasks won't be overlooked, but also, you wouldn't need a rigid schedule. As long as you set aside time in your daily/ weekly schedule for cleaning, you can choose what goes in those time blocks based on what you prefer to do. You could also change it up on a weekly basis.

ESTABLISHING THE RIGHT SYSTEM FOR YOU

Finding the system that works for you means taking into account which ones you are most likely to do. After reading through these options, you might not be sure, and that is okay. You can start with one and see how that works. However, if you know that you are likely to get sidetracked with different tasks in a room, then task cleaning may be a better fit for you. On the other hand, if the idea of doing one task throughout the entire house seems daunting, then zone cleaning may be a better fit because of the more narrow focus on one area for a set amount of time.

Some prefer the checklist option because they can be certain that things in the house are getting done at the pace they should be cleaned. However, they are not stuck to a rigid schedule. As long as they set aside time for cleaning, they can pick and choose based on what's still left on the list. This adds some novelty to the process and allows more flexibility based on what you feel like or don't feel like doing.

When applying any of these systems, you need to make them work for you. Tailor them to your home and your needs. Having a visual plan that you can check off makes you more likely to complete the tasks that need to be done.

Keep in mind that you'll be establishing some habits around your daily cleaning needs, such as making the bed, wiping down counters, and doing dishes. With these habits becoming part of your normal living routine, they wouldn't necessarily have to be scheduled into your cleaning time. For example, making the bed just becomes what you do when you get out of bed. Wiping the counters and table is just what you do after you've prepared or eaten food in the kitchen, etc. Habit stacking, in this way, frees up space in your calendar and in your day to really consider where the other cleaning tasks will go.

Don't Skip Out on the Details

When going through your cleaning process, it is helpful to have an understanding of some basic details. You'll want to clean in the most efficient way possible so that you're not having to backtrack over work you've already done.

THE BEST ORDER TO CLEAN

SOAK FIRST

Where chemicals and cleaning solutions are involved, anything that needs to soak should be done first. This way, you can spray and allow it to soak while you move on to other things in that room. So that after you've accomplished other things, you can come back to easily wipe it down, and you don't waste time simply waiting for it to be ready.

CLEAN BEFORE DISINFECTING

Disinfecting an area first just defeats the purpose. It should be the last stage of cleaning that area. First, wipe it down, clean it, then disinfect it before you are done.

TOP DOWN

Clean from the top down. In other words, you are not going to clean the floor and then wipe down the counters. This means you are potentially wiping crumbs and debris onto your clean floor. In any room you are cleaning, clean high first and make your way down to the floor so that you are not inadvertently doubling your work.

In addition to making sure that the floors are the last thing to be cleaned in a room, make sure that you sweep or vacuum before you mop. Even if it doesn't look like it needs to be swept or vacuumed, the last thing you want to do is to be swirling around dirt and debris while you mop.

HOW TO CLEAN WITHOUT WASTING TIME AND ENERGY

Not having a plan, doing things in the wrong order, and doing them incorrectly can waste time. You don't want to put the effort into cleaning and organizing only to have to go back over things you have already done. You also don't want a task that should take 10 minutes to take 30 minutes. Take a look at these common time wasters and how to accomplish your cleaning tasks as efficiently as possible.

CHECK YOUR CLEANING TOOLS

Make sure your cleaning tools themselves are clean. When gathering the items in your caddy or verifying that you have everything you need in there, take a look and make sure that the things you are using aren't just going to spread more dirt and grime around. The brushes, cloths, or sponges you are using should be clean.

IT NEEDS TO BE CLEAN BEFORE IT CAN SHINE

Another common mistake is not cleaning surfaces before you expect them to shine. Your mirror is a good example. Often people will apply the glass cleaner, wipe it, and become confused about why it didn't work. Make sure you wipe down the mirror or television set with a clean damp cloth first, then dry, then apply the glass cleaner and wipe.

YOU PROBABLY DON'T NEED TO SCRUB

Don't scrub, soak. Anything that requires sufficient scrubbing should be soaked first. Whether this means you spray it thoroughly and let it set for 20 minutes before you try to wipe it down or you soap up a pan and leave it soaking in the sink before you try to wash it. Don't waste time and energy scrubbing when soaking can break down the mess for you. This is where your white vinegar solution can often come in handy. The acidity in the vinegar can break down dirt and grime when left to soak. So spray it, go clean something else, and come back to it.

DON'T CLEAN YOUR WINDOWS IN THE SUN

Don't clean your windows when the sun is beating on them. Your glass cleaner will dry faster than you can wipe it, leaving you with a streaky finish. Wait for cloudy days, or aim to clean your windows in the morning or evening so that your windows get a nice streak-free shine the first time around.

WHAT ARE YOUR CLEANING CLOTHS MADE OF?

Choosing cleaning cloths that are the wrong material. Nothing is worse than trying to clean and leaving lint or fibers behind as you're cleaning. Go for microfiber cloths in your cleaning caddy. These cloths are more effective at wiping away bacteria, and they can easily be tossed in the laundry.

CLEAN YOUR VACUUM

Empty your vacuum bag or container frequently. Having a full vacuum at best makes it weaker and more time-consuming to pick anything up, but beyond that, some vacuums will start to kick out dust and dirt through the exhaust, making your space even messier than when you started. It's a good idea to empty the bag or container and remove the hair from the brushes after each use so that you're not wasting time the next time you use it.

CLEAN AS YOU GO

Try to clean as you go. Some people make the mistake of saving things for when their cleaning session is scheduled. This is a good way to let a spill set so it takes more time to clean later. Also, you aren't doing future you any favors by adding on to the task and potentially making it more overwhelming than it needed to be. If something spills try to normalize wiping it up right then and there. If you prepare food, get used to wiping down the counters immediately. Spraying and squeegeeing the shower after each use will make your shower deep cleaning a lot easier and less time consuming.

Schedule Your Cleaning in Advance

Just like many other aspects of your decluttering and organizing systems, you have to make time for cleaning rather than waiting for time to be available. While you'll want to make certain aspects of your cleaning system become part of your daily habits, such as wiping down the table after you've eaten a meal, you still want to use your calendar or planner to set aside 15-30 minutes daily to accomplish cleaning tasks.

Depending on the cleaning system you create, you might do 30 minutes every weekday and take off on the weekends. Or you might do 15 minutes each day and have an hour set aside over the weekend to do a deeper clean. Whatever schedule you decide to implement, make sure that it's in your planner so that you see it, you have a reminder, and you'll be more likely to follow through.

Additionally, have a clear cleaning plan. Executive dysfunction makes it really inefficient to approach a room and start figuring out how to clean it right then and there. It's more likely that you'll spend a lot more time figuring things out and accomplishing less than you would have if you had a clear plan to follow. Have it written out so that all you need to do is look at the list, do what it says, and check it off. This takes the cognitive effort out of the equation and makes the task itself more tangible.

Don't be afraid to ask for help

If you live with a roommate, partner, or other family members, ask them to help out in the process. Enlisting help can be more motivating, it can help keep you accountable and it can get the job done!

If you live alone, you can still get help from your friends or family. If it's a big cleaning job, you might ask them to come over to help you get it done. This applies to things like Spring cleaning, or cleaning for the first time in a while. Another way of getting help from friends and family includes body doubling. If you have a friend who has also wanted to get their own cleaning system on track, you can motivate each other by cleaning together on a video call. This helps keep you accountable, it is more motivating to do the activity while you see someone else also doing it, and the reward here is social. You and your friend have a shared goal of getting your cleaning on track and you are both working on it together.

Even if you are not sure whether your friends or family will want to come over to help or body double with you on the phone, it doesn't hurt to ask. The worst thing they can do is say no, and then you haven't really lost anything.

Managing Boring Tasks & How to make cleaning more fun

As we've discussed in depth, if the task is boring, people with ADHD are much less likely to start or follow through with it. You'll need to find ways to make it less boring and a bit more fun. Take into account your preference for immediate gratification, your reward system, and your impulsivity which drives you toward more spontaneity rather than rigid schedules. These can all be leveraged if you are intentional about how you proceed with your cleaning system.

MAKE IT REWARDING

Find something you genuinely enjoy or are interested in and pair it with your cleaning tasks. Listening to podcasts or TED talks, audiobooks, upbeat music playlists, or talking with a friend on the phone. These are all ways to make your cleaning tasks more enjoyable and rewarding because you are incorporating something that you are interested in, that you like to do, or that makes you feel good. These things will also have your mind occupied more with the fun thing while your hands do the cleaning. Time will pass more quickly this way and you won't be focused on thinking about how boring or unenjoyable the task itself is.

BE SPONTANEOUS

Yes, you'll need to schedule time for cleaning. However, you have some wiggle room when it comes to exactly what you do during that cleaning time. Whether you opt for zone cleaning, task-based cleaning, or cleaning according to your daily/weekly/monthly checklist, none of these approaches requires that you do the same thing every Monday at 10am.

The benefit of each of these approaches is in the combination of structure and flexibility that they allow. There is enough structure to ensure that things that need to be cleaned are not being neglected and falling through the cracks. But there is also enough wiggle room to say that if you don't feel like vacuuming right now, you can probably just as easily choose something else on the list. Unless you've done everything else and in that case, yes, it is time to vacuum.

The ability to choose which things you want to do and when also gives you more of a sense of control over the whole cleaning system. So, rather than feeling like this is something that you are stuck doing, this is something that you own and can shape in the way that best suits you and your household.

Now that you've got a good sense of what you'll need and how your cleaning system can work, you can start to establish clear plans for each room in your house. As a foundation, you can start with the information here, and adapt it to what works for you.

CHAPTER 14.

HOW TO CLEAN EACH ROOM

The following sections will take you through the rationale for how to approach each room, the supplies you'll need, and how frequently each task should be done. As with other sections of this book, these things can be adapted to fit your needs. Your frequency of cleaning may be different if for example, you have pets, or if you travel for work and spend several days each week away from home. These are meant to give you a general starting point as you establish your own cleaning routine.

The Living Room

The living room is the main hub of your house. This is where you'll spend time relaxing and also the first place your guests will see and where they will spend the most time. This makes your living room a priority in the cleaning system that you create, but luckily if you don't spend much time eating in your living room and if you address any spills as they occur, this room is not one that requires frequent heavy-duty cleaning.

SUPPLIES

Things you may need when cleaning the living room include:

- A duster
- White vinegar solution
- Window cleaner
- A few microfiber cloths
- A vacuum
- A mop and bucket
- Furniture polish

Depending on the approach you have decided on for cleaning, you may not need all of these items at once, however, it is useful to know which supplies will generally be used in this room.

Assuming you've been staying on top of the clutter and you've been maintaining your organization system, you are ready to clean up! If things have slid back a bit, make sure that you tidy up before you start cleaning.

DAILY

- General upkeep, wiping up spills

WEEKLY

- Dust
- Wipe down surfaces
- Vacuum or Sweep and Mop
- This may be more frequent with children or pets

MONTHLY

- Clean the windows, wipe down window frames
- Clean mirrors
- Polishing furniture and cleaning upholstery if needed

The Bathroom

The bathroom is a high-traffic area that has the potential to get dirty quickly. Luckily it tends to be a smaller room, but this room has more daily and weekly cleaning needs than you saw in the living room.

SUPPLIES

It's generally a good idea to keep these cleaning items stored in your bathroom if you have the space.

- Multi-surface bathroom cleaner
- Daily shower spray
- Glass cleaner
- Toilet bowl cleaner
- Disinfecting wipes
- Toilet brush
- Spray bottle
- Handheld squeegee
- Sponges or microfiber clothes

DAILY

- Spray and squeegee the shower
- Wipe down the sink, counter, and other surfaces
- Change hand towels, especially if being used by multiple people

WEEKLY

- Wash all the towels and bathmats
- Clean and disinfect the toilet
- Mop the bathroom floors

- Cleaning the shower and tub
- Wipe down the mirrors and cabinets
- Empty the trash

MONTHLY

- Clean the shower curtain
- Clean windows

The Kitchen

The kitchen is another high-traffic area that is likely one of the central hubs in your home for both you and your guests. Because you are preparing and cooking food, likely making some daily messes, doing dishes, and cleaning the sink area regularly, this would be considered more of a high-priority area in your cleaning system.

SUPPLIES

- Disinfectant wipes, spray, and floor cleaner
- White vinegar solution, spray bottle
- Rubber gloves
- Microfiber cloths
- Mop, bucket
- Multi-purpose cleaner
- Oven cleaner
- Stainless steel cleaner (if your appliances are stainless)
- Scrubbing sponges
- Dish soap

DAILY

- Do the dishes
- Sweep the floor
- Clean up spills as they occur
- Wipe down the sink, countertops, range top, and kitchen table top

WEEKLY

- Mop the floors
- Wipe down cabinets
- Wipe down the appliances
- Change the dishtowels
- Go through the fridge to toss any old leftovers

MONTHLY

- Clean the oven
- Wipe down and spray the refrigerator shelves to clean and disinfect
- Clean the inside of the microwave with the white vinegar solution
- Clean your coffee maker – running white vinegar mixed with water through to descale it
- Wipe down the outside and inside of the cabinets
- Pull out the food, pull out the shelf liners and clean them, wiping down anything that may have spilled

The Bedroom

Out of all the spaces in the house, this one should be your sanctuary. As such it should be clean so that you can feel comfortable and relaxed. Although you spend time in your bedroom daily, this wouldn't be considered a high-traffic area, the cleaning needs are not too intense here.

SUPPLIES

- Microfiber cloths
- Vacuum / Mop and bucket
- White vinegar solution
- Multipurpose cleaner
- Glass cleaner

DAILY

- Daily cleaning here is more associated with decluttering and organizing
- Making your bed
- Tidying up any clutter
- Clean and Dirty laundry are in the right place

WEEKLY

- Change your sheets and pillowcases
- Dust your furniture
- Mop or vacuum the floor

MONTHLY

- Wash comforters
- Wipe down walls and baseboards
- Clean light fixtures
- Shake out any area rugs

- Clean the mirrors and windows
- Dust the ceiling fans, vents, and air conditioning units

The Home Office

The home office is an area that you'll use almost every day, but luckily cleaning it is typically pretty simple. Here are the things you'll need to keep it clean:

SUPPLIES

- Microfiber cloth
- Duster
- Multi-purpose spray cleaner
- Disinfectant spray or wipes
- Glass cleaner
- Vacuum
- Mop/Bucket

DAILY

- Wipe down your workspace

WEEKLY

- Dust
- Vacuum/Mop
- Disinfect keyboard and mouse

MONTHLY

- Clean windows

Laundry and the Laundry Room

While it is normal to do about one load of laundry per week, exactly how often you do loads of wash can differ based on several factors:

- How many times you change clothes, including:
- Gym clothes
- Work uniforms
- Getting dressed for evening social events
- How many people are in your household
- Whether you do your laundry at home or at the laundromat

All of the above factors will influence your approach to doing the laundry. Generally, you don't want to have to do more than one or two loads to get all of your laundry done. This may mean you do laundry 2-3 times per week, depending on how many clothes you are going through. Otherwise, the task can feel too daunting to complete. However, if you go to the laundromat, then a weekly routine might make more sense – even if that means 4 loads since you can use multiple machines at once.

If you do your laundry in your own home, you may choose to split up when you wash and dry. For example, you might start a load right before you leave for work in the morning, and you might put it in the dryer as soon as you get home from work. Generally, clothing can be left in the washer for up to 8-12 hours without building up any mildew or getting that musty smell. Often laundry can feel daunting because we know a full wash and dry cycle takes about 2 hours. That can feel like a large block of time to set aside. Breaking it up might help you do it more frequently instead of procrastinating until you have no pants left.

If you've left a load of clothes in the dryer for too long, you don't need to run an entire dry cycle or pull out the iron to get the wrinkles out. Simply take a damp hand towel and toss it in with your dry clothes. Then run the dryer for 10 minutes. This should de-wrinkle them so that you can fold them without having to waste more time.

Your clothes will be cleaned more effectively if you do smaller loads. You want your clothes to move around freely in the soap and water versus being tightly packed in and immobile, so that they can actually get clean. Additionally, try to wash similar clothes together. If you have a laundry organizer that allows you to separate your laundry as soon as you put it in the hamper, that makes it easier. Similar colors and materials will have similar washing instructions. Following the instructions on the tag will keep your clothes in the best shape for longer. For example, dark clothes will keep their color longer when washed in cold water.

As for the laundry room itself, this area has a tendency to get dusty. With all of the fabric, dirt, debris, and lint involved, you'll be sweeping and wiping down this area regularly to keep it looking clean. Otherwise, your laundry room upkeep tends to be pretty easy.

SUPPLIES

- Multipurpose cleaner
- Microfiber cloths
- Broom/Mmop/Bucket
- Glass cleaner
- White vinegar

DAILY

- Sweep
- Clean up any soap spills
- Empty lint trap in the dryer

WEEKLY

- Mop the floors
- Wipe down the machines

- Dust/wipe down any other surfaces

MONTHLY

- Clean the windows
- Wipe down the baseboards and walls to prevent any dust buildup
- Run an empty wash cycle with white vinegar to clean your washing machine

Storage and Hallways

Hallways throughout the house will differ in the amount of traffic they get. Storage areas typically won't get much traffic and will really only require monthly maintenance if they're not used frequently.

SUPPLIES

- Broom/Mop/Bucket or Vacuum
- White vinegar solution or another floor cleaner
- Microfiber cloths
- Duster

DAILY

- Sweep high traffic areas

WEEKLY

- Dust any light fixtures, shelves, or decor in the halls
- Sweep and mop or vacuum

MONTHLY

- Wipe down the walls and baseboards
- Dust and wipe down surfaces in your storage areas
- Depending on the storage area, vacuum or sweep and mop the floor

As you consider the things that need to be done daily, weekly, and monthly, you can figure out where you would like them to go in your regular cleaning schedule. Whether you opt for zone cleaning, task-based cleaning, or simply choosing from the checklist based on how frequently things need to get done and fitting the tasks into your time blocks, cleaning should now feel more tangible.

Cleaning can feel overwhelming when we consider all of the tasks that go into maintaining a clean home, but not everything gets done every day, and when you break it down in ways that work for you, your schedule, and your household, you'll find that it's a lot easier to maintain a clean and organized home than you initially thought.

CONCLUSION

By now, you have a better understanding of how ADHD impacts you and how you can leverage the characteristics that are common to ADHD to overcome your challenges and accomplish your goals. Cleaning and organizing become tangible when we break them down and structure them in a way that works for us.

Establishing habits and systems are the key to maintaining a clean and organized home in the long term. The reason it has not worked for you before, is that much of the advice out there is not specific to people with ADHD.

Bear in mind that it is normal for people with ADHD to fall out of a routine. That's okay, and self compassion goes much further than beating yourself up. You have the skills, and once you've created a habit and a system, it's much easier to start again. Keeping this manual as your guide and adapting the skills to suit your preferences and needs, I'm confident you'll be able to master the ability to maintain a neat and organized home that helps you function better and that you can be proud of.

Sample Calendar

Check out the schedule below for an idea of what your decluttering, organizing, and cleaning systems might look like in your monthly calendar. You'll notice that this maintenance system really doesn't require much time each day. It's more about consistency and staying on track with the tasks that need to get done. Remember that this is just one example and the maintenance system you set up for yourself may be different depending on your needs and your lifestyle.

May 2023

Daily: Bathroom - spray/squeegee/wipe shower & sink after shower
Kitchen: Wipe surfaces, sweep after dinner
Declutter x10 min 730am & 530pm; Organize x15min 545pm

Monday	Tuesday	Wednesday	Thursday	Friday	Saturday	Sunday
1 6pm Paperwork x15min	2 6pm Clean Toilet & Shower (30min)	3 6pm Empty Trash	4 Do Laundry 8am Wash 5pm Dry	5 530pm Re-Organize x30min Fold Clothes	6 Vacuum / Mop Floors	7 Clean Windows & Mirrors
8 6pm Paperwork x15min	9 6pm Clean Toilet & Shower (30min)	10 6pm Empty Trash	11 Do Laundry 8am Wash 5pm Dry	12 530pm Re-Organize x30min Fold Clothes	13 Vacuum / Mop Floors	14 Clean Shower Curtain
15 6pm Paperwork x15min	16 6pm Clean Toilet & Shower (30min)	17 6pm Empty Trash	18 Do Laundry 8am Wash 5pm Dry	19 530pm Re-Organize x30min Fold Clothes	20 Vacuum / Mop Floors	21 Clean Fridge & Coffee Maker
22 6pm Paperwork x15min	23 6pm Clean Toilet & Shower (30min)	24 6pm Empty Trash	25 Do Laundry 8am Wash 5pm Dry	26 530pm Re-Organize x30min Fold Clothes	27 Vacuum / Mop Floors	28 Clean Fridge & Coffee Maker
29 6pm Paperwork x15min	30 6pm Clean Toilet & Shower (30min)	31 6pm Empty Trash				

Daily Weekly Organizer

Check out the Daily Weekly Organizer below for an idea of how you can schedule your cleaning systems. Like the monthly calendar above your system might have some differences so it's more tailored to you. Use the Organizer as a template to understand how tasks and rooms can fit into a week and be easy to manage.

Get Your Daily Organizer by using the link if you're reading on an ebook device, or by scanning the QR code below:

REFERENCES

American Psychiatric Association. (2013). *Diagnostic and statistical manual of mental disorders* (5th ed.). https://doi.org/10.1176/appi.books.9780890425596

Arnsten A. F. (2015). Stress weakens prefrontal networks: molecular insults to higher cognition. *Nature neuroscience, 18*(10), 1376–1385. https://doi.org/10.1038/nn.4087

Carr-Fanning, K. (2020). Understanding ADHD and its impact. *Irish Medical Times, 54*(10), 28-28,30. http://library.capella.edu/login?qurl=https%3A%2F%2Fwww.proquest.com%2Ftrade-journals%2Funderstanding-adhd-impact%2Fdocview%2F2448683599%2Fse-2%3Faccountid%3D27965

https://chadd.org/for-adults/organizing-the-home-and-office-space/

Clear, James. (2018). Atomic habits: an easy & proven way to build good habits & break bad ones . Penguin: Avery.

Grimm, O., van Rooij, D., Tshagharyan, A., Yildiz, D., Leonards, J., Elgohary, A., Buitelaar, J., & Reif, A. (2021). Effects of comorbid disorders on reward processing and connectivity in adults with ADHD. *Translational psychiatry, 11*(1), 636. https://doi.org/10.1038/s41398-021-01758-0

Durand, G., Arbone, I. S., & Wharton, M. (2020). Reduced organizational skills in adults with ADHD are due to deficits in persistence, not in strategies. *PeerJ, 8*, e9844. https://doi.org/10.7717/peerj.9844

Khadka, S., Pearlson, G. D., Calhoun, V. D., Liu, J., Gelernter, J., Bessette, K. L., & Stevens, M. C. (2016). Multivariate Imaging Genetics Study of MRI Gray Matter Volume and SNPs Reveals Biological Pathways Correlated with Brain Structural Differences in Attention Deficit Hyperactivity Disorder. *Frontiers in psychiatry* , *7* , 128. https://doi.org/10.3389/fpsyt.2016.00128

Hvolby A. (2015). Associations of sleep disturbance with ADHD: implications for treatment. *Attention deficit and hyperactivity disorders*, *7*(1), 1–18. https://doi.org/10.1007/s12402-014-0151-0

Lazar, S. W., Kerr, C. E., Wasserman, R. H., Gray, J. R., Greve, D. N., Treadway, M. T., McGarvey, M., Quinn, B. T., Dusek, J. A., Benson, H., Rauch, S. L., Moore, C. I., & Fischl, B. (2005). Meditation experience is associated with increased cortical thickness. *Neuroreport, 16*(17), 1893–1897. https://doi.org/10.1097/01.wnr.0000186598.66243.19

Lynch, F. A., Moulding, R., & McGillivray, J. A. (2017). Phenomenology of hoarding in children with comorbid attention-deficit/hyperactivity disorder (ADHD): The perceptions of parents. *Comprehensive Psychiatry, 76*, 1-10. https://doi.org/10.1016/j.comppsych.2017.03.009

Mehren, A., Reichert, M., Coghill, D., Müller, H. H. O., Braun, N., & Philipsen, A. (2020). Physical exercise in attention deficit hyperactivity disorder – evidence and implications for the treatment of borderline personality disorder. *Borderline personality disorder and emotion dysregulation*, *7*, 1. https://doi.org/10.1186/s40479-019-0115-2

Nall, R., & Klein, A. (2021). *ADHD Benefits: What the Research Says, Creativity & More*. Healthline. Retrieved March 20, 2023, from https://www.healthline.com/health/adhd/benefits-of-adhd#personality-strengths

Sjöwall, D., Roth, L., Lindqvist, S., & Thorell, L. B. (2013). Multiple deficits in ADHD: Executive dysfunction, delay aversion, reaction time variability, and emotional deficits. *Journal of Child Psychology and Psychiatry, 54*(6), 619-627. https://doi.org/10.1111/jcpp.12006

Smith, L., & Picard, C. (2019, March 22). *House Cleaning Schedule – The Cleaning Checklist You Need. Good Housekeeping. Retrieved April 21, 2023, from* https://www.goodhousekeeping.com/home/cleaning/a37462/how-often-you-should-clean-everything/

Society for Neuroscience. (2008, August 21). One Sleepless Night Increases Dopamine In The Human Brain. *ScienceDaily*. Retrieved March 24, 2023 from www.sciencedaily.com/releases/2008/08/080819213033.htm

Steel, P. (2011). The procrastination equation: How to Stop Putting Things Off and Start Getting Stuff Done. New York: Harper.

stress.org/mental-health-apps

Tripp, G., & Wickens, J. R. (2009). Neurobiology of ADHD. *Neuropharmacology, 57*(7-8), 579–589. https://doi.org/10.1016/j.neuropharm.2009.07.026

Volkow, N. D., Wang, G. J., Kollins, S. H., Wigal, T. L., Newcorn, J. H., Telang, F., Fowler, J. S., Zhu, W., Logan, J., Ma, Y., Pradhan, K., Wong, C., & Swanson, J. M. (2009). Evaluating dopamine reward pathway in ADHD: clinical implications. *JAMA , 302* (10), 1084–1091. https://doi.org/10.1001/jama.2009.1308

Weissenberger, S., Schonova, K., Büttiker, P., Fazio, R., Vnukova, M., Stefano, G. B., & Ptacek, R. (2021). Time Perception is a Focal Symptom of Attention-Deficit/Hyperactivity Disorder in Adults. *Medical science monitor : international medical journal of experimental and clinical research, 27*, e933766. https://doi.org/10.12659/MSM.933766

Zhao, S., & Toichi, M. (2020). The Effect of Music Intervention on Attention in Children: Experimental Evidence. *Frontiers in Neuroscience, 14*. https://doi.org/10.3389/fnins.2020.00757

Zheng, Q., Wang, X., Chiu, K. Y., & Shum, K. K. (2022). Time Perception Deficits in Children and Adolescents with ADHD: A Meta-analysis. *Journal of Attention Disorders, 26*(2), 267–281. https://doi.org/10.1177/1087054720978557

BOOK 3.

Executive Functioning Workbook For Adults With ADHD

8 Days to Strengthen Focus, Organization, Working Memory and Emotional Control

INTRODUCTION

Throughout my life, I've had to find ways to work around several executive function deficits and it wasn't easy. It can be especially hard when you don't know you have ADHD and you've never heard the words executive function in your life.

Growing up, my dad would always say I was in "la la land". That was his term to describe the fact that I never seemed to notice or pay attention to things that he thought I should pay attention to. This could have been things he was trying to tell me, objects or occurrences in my surroundings, or little ways in which I overlooked important details. But from an early age, it became part of who I was. I was "always in la-la land". Of course, I didn't think so. Most of the time, I was captivated by my own thoughts, and they were way more interesting or entertaining than what was going on around me.

I considered my ability to zone out a gift when I was growing up. Sitting through class was incredibly boring, and I couldn't imagine how that would be if I wasn't so good at mentally escaping. One time a teacher even called home to tell my parents that I was staring at her almost as if I was "looking through her". I'm not sure exactly what the offense was there – but I definitely wasn't staring at her. Maybe that's where my gaze landed, but I was somewhere else. She taught 8th-grade algebra, I was sure everyone wanted to be somewhere else.

College was not much different, except nobody seemed to mind. My biggest challenge was getting things in on time. I hated that almost every time I had a big paper due, it would result in an all-nighter. I consumed a lot of Lipton tea throughout college. After every all-nighter, I swore not to do it again and to start my work earlier the next time. And through all of my college career – starting earlier never happened.

I did attempt to start early on many occasions. But something I couldn't make sense of would happen. It felt like I couldn't understand the assignment or the information when I tried to do it in advance. I would look at the instructions and try to read the content, and it just wasn't sinking in. I couldn't wrap my head around it enough to start the assignment. Then magically, in the eleventh hour, I was able to zone in on the task, I somehow could connect the dots, work with an intensity that I wished I could apply at will, and I'd get an A. That's how I survived college.

In my career, I know better than to assume I'll remember things I need to do. I've learned to make a lot of accommodations. Writing everything down, restating my instructions, repeating things so that I remember them, using music to focus better, and much more. These have just become the things that I know can help me get things done and help me function better.

Had I known what was going on with me earlier, I would have saved myself a lot of sleepless nights and pissed-off teachers. Not to mention the friendships I lost based on my impulsivity and emotional dysregulation. But hindsight is 20/20, and what I have learned since then is that these things can get better.

I wish someone had told me

In this book, you'll learn the things that I wish I had known earlier. Facts and strategies that any person struggling with ADHD needs to know. If I'd had a book like this, it would have made a world of difference in the expectations I set for myself and how I navigated daily life. I could have improved the issues I was having at work, school, at home, and in my relationships. It would have made sense of many of my struggles and saved me a lot of wasted energy as I tried to address them in all the wrong ways, beating myself up every time I failed.

Unfortunately, I didn't start figuring things out until I was diagnosed in my early 30s. At that point I knew, I owed it to myself to understand this disorder as much as I could. Up to that point, the most common treatment I knew about for ADHD was medication.

ADHD is a neurodevelopmental disorder. This means that our brains and nervous systems develop atypically from birth, though these differences may not be noticeable until childhood. So, my assumption at the time was, how could behavioral interventions like positive reinforcement or skills training change anything? Whereas depression, anxiety, and trauma could be affected by examining your thoughts and behavior patterns, we wouldn't change the effects of biology in a therapy session, right? Wrong. Very wrong. It was common back then not to spend much time learning about ADHD and many clinics don't touch neurodevelopmental issues aside from referring clients with these issues to a staff psychiatrist. So, unfortunately, I was lacking crucial information.

I began reading numerous books and poring through tons of academic research on executive functioning. Even the clinicians who had diagnosed me hadn't offered anything in this area. I had met with two separate clinicians, just to be sure, and neither of them brought up executive dysfunction or how learning about it and learning to manage it could help me.

You won't find executive function deficits explicitly stated in the DSM-5 (Diagnostic and Statistical Manual of Mental Disorders, 5th Edition). Instead, you'll find a list of symptoms. Many of which actually describe the impacts of executive dysfunction. Executive function deficits exist in several disorders, so while EF issues don't mean you have ADHD, having ADHD is a pretty clear indicator that you struggle with EF.

This book will help you to see that there is a biological reason you struggle with planning, completing tasks and goals, following directions, retaining information, managing your emotions, and more.

Understanding that there is an underlying cause for these difficulties can make a world of difference. People with ADHD often stop blaming themselves and feel less shame when they realize what ADHD is. What's even better is learning that these issues can be improved.

The Role of Medication in Improving Executive Functioning

When it comes to medication, you should always consult a professional directly for more information about what may or may not work for you. When most people hear ADHD, they think of Adderall or Ritalin. While these medications can be helpful, there are other medication options available. It's also important to note that executive function skills can be improved without using any medication at all (Diamond & Ling, 2016). Both clinicians I met with when I was diagnosed with ADHD suggested medication options they thought could help me while failing to mention anything about executive function skills. Unfortunately, this type of approach doesn't give us the full picture.

Imagine you wanted to tend a garden. An automatic sprinkler that turns on every day could certainly make your task easier and more efficient. Depending on the garden size, the level of moisture in your environment, and whether you have the time to consistently water it yourself, you might find that the sprinkler makes your life much easier. But could you maintain a garden without it? Yes, you could. Several other factors would be crucial to maintaining a healthy and thriving garden, such as good soil, proper sunlight, and regular pruning. Likewise, whether you choose medication depends on various factors that are individual to you. And some circumstances may call for it more than others.

However, there are limitations to treatment with medication. Some people are not responsive to these medications, and others experience only minimal reduction in their symptoms. Additionally, for some, experiencing side effects from these medications can make taking them more of a hindrance than dealing with the ADHD symptoms alone. And while ADHD medications can be effective in improving core symptoms of ADHD, there is limited research on the impact they have on EF skills and emotional dysregulation (Mitchell et al., 2017). According to Dr. Scott Shapiro (2016), an Assistant Professor at New York Medical College who specializes in treating adult ADHD, executive functioning is less responsive to medications when compared to their 70-80% success rate in resolving other core symptoms of ADHD.

So, whether you are taking medication for your ADHD, exploring the possibility of medications, or deciding not to take them at all, it's an extremely personal decision that depends on your unique preferences, needs, and body chemistry. But recognizing that you can't maintain a garden with just an automatic sprinkler system – this book will teach you everything you need to know about executive functioning, how deficits in our executive functioning impact people with ADHD, and how we can train our executive function skills to improve.

The Beauty of Neuroplasticity

It was once thought that our brains stopped developing in our early 20s. The idea that our learning and development solidifies at any age has since been debunked. While your capacity to learn and change will slow down with age, it does not stop. Our brains continue to learn and change based on our experiences. Neuroplasticity refers to the fact that the structures in our brain can further change and adapt throughout our lifetime (Voss et al., 2017). So, what does that mean for us? It means that we can implement and practice strategies that will improve our executive function skills over time.

In people with ADHD, the part of the brain responsible for executive functioning is underdeveloped. This means we need to further develop it intentionally. In the same way, you wouldn't expect to build muscle by sitting on the couch, we can't expect that our executive functioning will improve without some concentrated effort. But just like there are a variety of workouts you could do to build muscle, there are also various exercises that will help you build your executive functioning skills.

How EF Skills Make a Difference in Your Daily Life

For people with ADHD, the impacts of EF deficits can be felt on a pretty consistent basis. These aren't problems that pop up once or twice a week. They're daily. On rough days, a person with ADHD might not go an hour without being impacted by EF deficits in some way. Executive function skills touch everything that we do. Deficits in this crucial area of our brains include, but certainly aren't limited to, the following challenges:

- Not keeping up with chores around the house
- Missing deadlines at work
- Forgetting to follow through on commitments
- Disorganization everywhere
- Overlooking important details
- Terrible time management
- Losing important things
- Interrupting others
- Losing the focus required to complete even a simple task
- Procrastinating on important tasks
- Getting up a bunch of times when you're generally expected to stay seated
- Feeling restless and fidgety
- Having strong emotional reactions and feeling unable to get back to baseline

Chances are you are very familiar with these struggles. These problems impact our personal and professional lives every day. And unfortunately, society's general view of ADHD doesn't begin to encompass the many challenges that it really brings. This makes it even harder to explain the challenges to those around us, leading it to feel more like a personal failing than anything else.

Now imagine if you could learn strategies that would significantly reduce the occurrence of these problems. Instead of happening regularly, maybe they just impact you here and there or during times when you are under a lot of stress. This book will equip you with the practical tools and strategies to improve your executive functioning now and for years to come.

What to Expect

In this book, you'll learn exactly what executive functioning is and the many ways deficits in this area can impact you. You'll gain awareness of specifically how executive dysfunction impacts you as an individual. We all experience it a bit differently, and areas of severity for one person may differ from those of another. You'll learn to recognize the areas in which you are most impacted so that you can prioritize those skills.

You'll learn exercises that you can practice and tips that you can implement to start improving your executive function skills. Some of these things will help immediately, and others that work by changing and developing connections in your brain can take several weeks to a few months to see genuine improvements.

How to Use This Book

This book is meant to be completed in 8 days, but that doesn't mean your practice ends there or that all of your executive functioning issues are resolved in 8 days. It means that in 8 days, you'll already be implementing some strategies to improve your executive functioning immediately, and other skills will improve over time as you continue to practice them.

In each chapter, you'll learn background information about the strategies presented and you'll find relatable stories of people navigating executive functioning deficits and implementing these strategies. When you see, "Here's What You Do", this lets you know that you're about to get step-by-step instructions for how to implement the techniques to help build that executive function skill.

Having a specific timeline for these practices can be helpful. For longer-term improvements, a 90-day commitment to practicing the strategies you'll learn is ideal. Multiple studies have shown brain structure changes associated with improved executive functioning occurred with 8-12 weeks of meditation training (Hepark et al., 2019). Additionally, research results show that it takes 2 months on average to form habits, with some people taking less time and some taking more (Gardner et al., 2012). For these reasons, a 90-day plan offers a reasonable expectation to see some of the lasting changes you'll be working toward.

If you need longer than 8 days to really get through and digest the content in each chapter of this book, that is 100% fine. As you move through the book, you'll be answering prompts, taking assessments, and completing exercises to further your understanding and practice your skills. The importance here is absorbing and implementing the information rather than speeding through it. Take whatever time you need with each exercise. But make sure to keep the momentum going.

Now that you know what to expect in the upcoming chapters, let's get even more clear about what executive functioning means and what exactly EF skills are.

What is Executive Functioning

Executive functioning generally refers to a set of cognitive processes involved with managing ourselves and our actions. It really is like the CEO of a business. This CEO oversees how we manage ourselves and our tasks. In a non-ADHD person, otherwise known as neurotypical, the CEO is experienced. They know how to keep things going smoothly, delegating what should be worked on and when, for how long, and what the overall plan is. This helps the business to run pretty efficiently.

Now let's consider the CEO who runs the show for a person who has ADHD. Your CEO has not quite developed the same skills and might be juggling too many things at once without the ability to prioritize. They're answering the phone, working through a stack of paperwork, taking in new ideas, and promptly forgetting them just as quickly. This CEO is not nearly as efficient as they need to be to face the daily challenges that come their way. And so, the business suffers.

People with ADHD often have varying degrees of executive dysfunction. Each person who struggles with ADHD may not experience the same struggles with the same frequency and severity. But our biological differences from people without ADHD are the reason why someone telling us to try harder or to focus more, doesn't work. Our struggles are not for lack of trying or wanting to do these things well. The problem is that areas and structures within our brains have literally not developed as well as they have in people who don't have ADHD.

How EF Skills Develop

Neurotypical people begin developing their executive functions at birth. They develop these functions in predictable stages from birth through their early 20s. By 25 years of age, they are considered to have a fully developed executive function system.

The typical person with ADHD develops their executive functions at a rate of about 30% behind their non-ADHD peers. As a child, this often means they can be 3-5 years behind their peers in the development of EF. While there are some adults with ADHD who experience EF issues much less than others, many continue to experience executive function deficits throughout adulthood (Adler et al., 2017; Barrett, 2018).

The EF Skills You'll Learn

Experts differ in how they list executive functions. Some list 3 main categories, others list 4, while others list 7 or 8. Ultimately, even when only 3 functions are mentioned, they become umbrella categories for multiple skills. This book will address in detail the 8 executive function skills that people with ADHD struggle with. Remember, you may struggle with some of these more than others. In the next chapter, you'll be able to really narrow down which areas pose the biggest challenge for you and how.

EXECUTIVE FUNCTIONING SKILL #1: **ATTENTION AND FOCUS**

The "attention deficit" part in the name of ADHD sounds like we lack the ability to pay attention. That's not true at all. We just lack the ability to direct our attention to the right thing at the right time and for the necessary duration. So instead of paying attention to what's expected of us or what would be most beneficial at that moment, another stimulus in our environment may have captured our attention. Or we might even be captivated by our own thoughts.

You might be in mid-conversation with someone, and something they say could trigger a thought of your own on a completely different topic. Before you know it, they've been talking to you for the last 20 seconds, and you didn't even realize you were somewhere else in your thoughts.

Or you could be working on paperwork, get distracted by an email, then that email triggers another thought, and before you know it, you're shopping on Amazon, having completely lost your focus on the paperwork you were doing.

Focusing on tasks we're not interested in or seem boring is the most difficult. These can feel nearly impossible to accomplish. If you've ever seen two magnets repel each other, that's what it can feel like our attention is doing when we consider doing a task that we find boring or overwhelming.

Deficits in this area often cause the biggest problems at work and in school. But they can also hinder your relationships with friends, family, colleagues, and essentially anyone you interact with.

If you can't focus and sustain attention, it is nearly impossible to get things done. This means things may take longer than they should, or they might not happen at all. Projects at work remain unfinished, school assignments are late or not turned in at all, and people in your life may feel slighted or disconnected when you are easily distracted while engaging with them.

You'll learn tips and strategies that will improve your ability to maintain focus long-term, as well as things that you can implement that will make it easier to focus now.

EXECUTIVE FUNCTIONING SKILL #2: **WORKING MEMORY**

This is a big one. Working memory is our ability to hold information in our mind and use it to perform a task or to make decisions. Working memory is used during problem-solving, decision-making, and task completion.

Have you ever gotten directions with a series of steps, whether verbal or written, and then had to complete the task? If you have working memory deficits, chances are you often need to refer back to the instructions. Relying on hearing or reading them once is likely to have the task falling apart before you even begin.

I cannot stand it when people try to give me directions. I know they are trying to be helpful, but I always tell them not to worry about it because I won't retain it. Chances are you've lost me by the time we get to the third step because I've already forgotten the first. Working memory deficits can make it pretty difficult to take the information you are receiving and conceptualize it in a way that is useful or retain it long enough to implement it.

Working memory is why you need a list to go food shopping or risk forgetting things you knew were important and thought there was no way you would forget. It's also why you probably need to check the directions repeatedly when you're completing a task that has multiple steps.

Working memory can even impact your ability to follow conversations and retain the context of what is going on. You might find it difficult to engage in large groups where multiple conversations are going on. You might try to follow one and then get distracted by another one, losing what was going on in the first.

With difficulties in this area, you may easily get distracted, misplace important items, and struggle with planning and organizing due to difficulty manipulating the information in your mind. Working memory deficits actually cover many difficulties we see with ADHD.

Working memory deficits can hinder your ability to remember instructions or follow through on commitments. This means that even if you do accomplish your commitments on time, you might make seemingly careless mistakes because you missed steps that were outlined in the original instructions. Struggles with working memory can also lead to clutter in your home. When you have something in your hands and don't automatically know what to do with it, where does it go? Usually, somewhere it doesn't belong. You might even intentionally put it in a very visible place, thinking that this will help you remember it, when in reality, it's just the start of another pileup.

EXECUTIVE FUNCTIONING SKILL #3: **TASK INITIATION**

If you have ever found yourself procrastinating and unable to start a task, even if you know exactly what the first step is, you may struggle with task initiation issues. People with ADHD often struggle to initiate tasks that they don't find interesting or tasks that they feel are complex and will require significant mental effort.

When you struggle with task initiation, you may find yourself engaging in productive procrastination. This might look like the urge to tidy up a random area of your house, check your emails, have a snack, etc. Even if you want to get the task done, your brain struggles with taking that first step.

Difficulty initiating tasks leads to procrastination and feeling stuck. Not only does this affect the outcomes of the task you were supposed to do, but it also keeps you stuck in a cycle of avoidance and self-blame, making your stress and anxiety even worse.

Many strategies can help with this, depending on the reasons that underlie your procrastination. You'll learn to identify what is causing procrastination for you and which strategies will help you start initiating tasks with ease.

EXECUTIVE FUNCTIONING SKILL #4: **TIME MANAGEMENT**

Time blindness is a common phenomenon in people with ADHD. This means that you struggle to judge time accurately. This includes the time you estimate it will take to complete a task and the time you think has passed. Struggles with time management make it harder to allocate the correct amount of time for tasks, resulting in missed deadlines, rushed work, or constantly feeling behind.

Poor time management can result in chronic lateness, missed appointments, and can hinder your ability to prioritize tasks effectively. This puts a strain on both personal and professional relationships. Difficulties with time management are also a big contributor to anxiety symptoms and feeling overwhelmed.

EXECUTIVE FUNCTIONING SKILL #5: **ORGANIZING**

Deficits in this area mean you likely struggle to keep your environment organized. You may have clutter and disorganization in multiple, if not in all areas of your home and workspace. Even if you manage to get an area organized, it can feel impossible to maintain if you don't have specific strategies and systems in place.

Organization issues also include organizing your schedule. Your ability to keep track of appointments and obligations may suffer, especially if you are not keeping an organized planner or agenda somewhere.

You might also struggle to organize when certain tasks make sense to work on in your schedule.

Struggling to organize your tasks, belongings, or information can make it challenging to manage daily life. This leads to more stress, feeling overwhelmed, and failure to meet personal and professional responsibilities.

EXECUTIVE FUNCTIONING SKILL #6: **IMPULSE CONTROL**

Impulse control issues often lead to interpersonal struggles, poor decision-making, financial strain, and even legal issues. Deficits in this area are common in people with ADHD and typically present as making spontaneous decisions without considering the consequences. People who struggle with impulsivity may also interrupt or intrude upon others.

Impulsive decisions may be small, like a purchase that you potentially didn't need. Or they can be big life-altering decisions that you end up regretting. People who struggle with controlling their impulses may be more prone to risk-taking behavior, including substance use.

Struggles with impulse control often lead to questionable decision-making, risky behaviors, and rash reactions. People who have impulse control deficits normally experience the most impacts in their personal lives. Relationships are often impacted, substance abuse can occur, and impulsive spending can lead to significant debt. So, learning to manage impulses can be a crucial skill in improving one's quality of life.

EXECUTIVE FUNCTIONING SKILL #7: **COGNITIVE FLEXIBILITY**

This skill is the ability to take on different perspectives, thoughts, and tasks easily. People with issues in this area will be more likely to find it hard to go with the flow and struggle when plans change suddenly.

They may also have difficulty adapting to new information on a topic they are familiar with. These struggles often look like frustration and resistance when faced with unexpected situations that require cognitive flexibility.

Cognitive rigidity makes it difficult to adapt to new situations, consider alternative perspectives, or engage in creative problem-solving. This deficit leads to frequently increased frustration and difficulty navigating complex social and professional situations.

If you get extremely bothered when plans change, if you find it hard to function when the rules of engagement in a situation you were otherwise familiar with have changed, or if you find it nearly impossible to shift your perspective, this may mean you struggle with cognitive flexibility.

EXECUTIVE FUNCTIONING SKILL #8: **EMOTIONAL REGULATION**

People with ADHD may experience frequent overreactions to situations they experience. Their reactions may come more quickly, last longer, and be more intense than the emotional reactions of people who don't have ADHD. They may even be aware of these intense reactions and want to de-escalate them but find it difficult to rein them back in.

Consequences of emotional dysregulation include mood swings, outbursts or other impulsive behavior, struggling to express emotions appropriately, impaired relationships, and increased risk of comorbid mental health disorders. Both personal and professional functioning can be significantly impacted when a person lacks the ability to regulate their emotions.

Gaining a thorough understanding of the negative impact of executive functioning deficits on your life is the first step to creating lasting change. By acknowledging the challenges you experience and to what extent, you can begin to focus on the targeted strategies and interventions to address those challenges and improve your overall functioning.

Remember that executive functioning skills can be developed and strengthened over time. With practice, patience, and the right strategies, it is possible to overcome these challenges and create a more balanced, organized, and fulfilling life.

This is a large part of why people with ADHD often exhibit outbursts of anger and may commonly be diagnosed with comorbid depression. ADHD makes it difficult to shift one's emotions back into a positive and healthy place, even if it intellectually makes sense to do so.

Breaking down the EF skills in this level of detail should help you to start homing in on the areas that you struggle with the most and identify the impacts on your daily life so that you can start considering which skills may be most crucial for you.

For each skill, you'll learn more about what is going on for the person who struggles with that deficit and several ways to address it. It's important to remember that this is not a one-size fits all approach. While executive dysfunction can impact nearly every area of life for a person who has ADHD, it is important to consider and test out the different strategies presented so that you can determine what really works for you.

YOUR UNIQUE ADHD PROFILE

ADHD is a complex neurodevelopmental condition. It presents in different ways for each person, however, the DSM-5 breaks it down into 3 distinct categories. Understanding your ADHD type can offer valuable insights into your executive functioning strengths and weaknesses, thereby helping you develop personalized strategies that will address your needs.

The three types of ADHD are:

1. Inattentive Type: Characterized by difficulties with attention and focus. These individuals often struggle to maintain concentration on tasks and can struggle with memory and disorganization.
2. Hyperactive-Impulsive Type: Characterized by hyperactivity and impulsivity. Individuals with this type struggle with impulse control, fidgeting, and interrupting others during conversations.
3. Combined Type: Characterized by a combination of inattentive and hyperactive-impulsive symptoms, individuals with this type of ADHD experience challenges related to both attention and impulse control. This is the most common type of ADHD.

Recognizing the unique characteristics of your ADHD type allows you to better understand your strengths and weaknesses and helps you develop personalized strategies to manage your executive functioning challenges. It's crucial to remember that each person with ADHD has a unique cognitive profile, and no two individuals will experience the exact same challenges or successes.

Executive Function Skills Assessment

Now that you have a deeper understanding of the importance of executive functioning and the impact of ADHD on these skills, the next step is to assess your executive functioning abilities. By identifying your specific challenges, you can focus on targeted strategies to address these problems and improve your overall functioning.

This assessment is designed to help you evaluate your current level of difficulty in the eight skill areas of executive functioning. For each question, rate your level of difficulty on a scale of 1-10. 1 should be the items that you never struggle with and 10 represents the items that are always a struggle.

For each section, you'll add up your ratings and take note of the skill sections with the highest scores. These are your biggest problem areas, while the areas with the lowest scores are less impacted by your executive function deficits. Even though you'll utilize this entire book, you'll want to emphasize learning the skills and strategies presented in the areas that scored higher.

Bear in mind that this is not a diagnostic assessment. Rather, it is meant to provide you with a better understanding of your strengths and struggles in executive functioning so that you can focus your ongoing efforts more on those areas.

If you find that you scored high in several areas, that is quite common and just means that you'll benefit more from various sections in this book as you work to improve your overall EF skills. You'd benefit the most from going in order through this book.

Let's Get Started

Please take your time to reflect on each question in this assessment:

EXECUTIVE FUNCTIONING SKILL #1: **ATTENTION AND FOCUS**

_________ 1. Do you have difficulty concentrating on a single task for an extended period?

_________ 2. Do you often catch yourself daydreaming during conversations or lectures?

_________ 3. How frequently do you get distracted by external stimuli, such as noise or movement in your environment?

_________ 4. Do you struggle to refocus on a task after being interrupted?

_________ 5. How often are you unable to prioritize tasks or decide what to work on first?

Total Score: ___/ 50

EXECUTIVE FUNCTIONING SKILL #2: **WORKING MEMORY**

________ ❶ Do you have trouble remembering instructions or steps given to you verbally?

________ ❷ Can you easily hold onto and manipulate information in your mind while problem-solving?

________ ❸ How often do you forget important details or tasks you intended to complete?

________ ❹ Do you struggle to remember the context of a conversation if interrupted?

________ ❺ Do you find it difficult to do relatively simple math equations that require multiple steps without using a calculator or pen and paper? Such as 20% of 350, 16x3, or converting 3 feet 7 inches to inches

Total Score: ____/ 50

EXECUTIVE FUNCTIONING SKILL #3: **TASK INITIATION**

________ ❶ How often do you delay starting tasks, even when you know they have to be done?

________ ❷ Do you find it difficult to start tasks that are boring or complex?

________ ❸ How often do you begin a task and quickly lose motivation or interest?

________ ❹ Do you struggle to break down large tasks into smaller, more manageable parts?

________ ❺ How often do you rely on external motivation or pressure to begin a task?

Total Score: ____/ 50

EXECUTIVE FUNCTIONING SKILL #4: **TIME MANAGEMENT**

_______ ❶ Do you frequently underestimate how long a task will take to complete?

_______ ❷ How often do you find yourself rushing to meet deadlines or finish tasks?

_______ ❸ Do you struggle to create and stick to a daily schedule?

_______ ❹ How often do you procrastinate on tasks or assignments?

_______ ❺ Do you have difficulty allocating the correct time for tasks?

Total Score: ___/ 50

EXECUTIVE FUNCTIONING SKILL #5: **ORGANIZING**

_______ ❶ Do you find it difficult to maintain an organized home or workspace?

_______ ❷ How often do you lose or misplace important items, such as keys, phone, or documents?

_______ ❸ Do you have difficulty organizing and prioritizing tasks or projects?

_______ ❹ How frequently do you struggle to manage your schedule and keep track of appointments?

_______ ❺ Do you find it challenging to create and follow routines?

Total Score: ___/ 50

EXECUTIVE FUNCTIONING SKILL #6: **IMPULSE CONTROL**

________ 1. Do you often make decisions without considering the consequences or taking them seriously?

________ 2. How frequently do you interrupt others during conversations?

________ 3. Do you struggle to resist temptations or distractions when trying to focus?

________ 4. How often do you engage in impulsive behaviors, such as making unplanned purchases or sudden changes in plans?

________ 5. Do you find it difficult to wait your turn or follow the rules in structured settings?

Total Score: ___ / 50

EXECUTIVE FUNCTIONING SKILL #7: **COGNITIVE FLEXIBILITY**

________ 1. Do you struggle to adapt to changes in plans or unexpected situations?

________ 2. How often do you have difficulty switching between tasks or adjusting to new information?

________ 3. Do you find it hard to see a situation or problem from multiple perspectives?

________ 4. How frequently do you become stuck in a certain approach to a task?

________ 5. Do you have difficulty brainstorming new ideas?

Total Score: ___ / 50

EXECUTIVE FUNCTIONING SKILL #8: **EMOTIONAL REGULATION**

________ 1. Do you experience intense emotional reactions that feel overwhelming or difficult to control?

________ 2. How often do you struggle to express your emotions in appropriate ways?

________ 3. Do you find it difficult to bounce back from disappointments or setbacks?

________ 4. How frequently do you have mood swings or sudden changes in your emotional state?

________ 5. Do you struggle to maintain emotional balance in stressful or challenging situations?

Total Score: ___/ 50

Now that you've completed your skills assessment, you are well on your way to improving those areas of executive functioning. This assessment is an essential first step toward understanding your ADHD and developing a personalized plan to overcome your challenges.

Once you've finished answering each question, be sure to add up your scores for each EF skill. This will give you a clear idea of which skills are the most challenging for you. From here, you might prefer to jump ahead and start with the skill you are most impacted by, or you can start in order from Day 1.

Next, we'll move on to Day 1 of the 8 executive functioning skills. Whether you start here or on Day 6, you can start making meaningful changes in your life with reduced stress and overall improvement in your well-being.

DAY 1.

HONING YOUR ATTENTION AND FOCUS

Attention is a multifaceted concept. Selective attention refers to our ability to focus on a specific thing or task while being exposed to other potentially distracting things in our environment. Sustained attention is our ability to pay attention to a thing or a task for a longer duration of time. And focus is the central point of our attention at any given moment. EF deficits impair all of these attention processes and make it difficult to engage in and complete tasks. Deficits in this skill also impact other areas such as planning, problem-solving, and decision-making (Grane et al., 2014).

But you know that if you're really interested in something and in a quiet and calm enough environment, you can probably focus extremely well for an extended period of time. So attention difficulties in people with ADHD seem to change based on our environment and whether we're motivated to complete the task, which is something we rarely feel in control of. (Grane et al., 2014).

Don't Neglect the Obvious

You've likely heard some of the basics that are necessary for optimal functioning, especially if you have ADHD. While their importance cannot be overstated, we won't spend too much time on them here aside from a quick reminder.

If you don't want to exacerbate your ADHD symptoms and you want to make sure you are in the best shape to improve your cognitive deficits, you should be doing the following:

- Getting adequate sleep
- Exercising on a regular basis
- Using calming strategies to manage your stress levels
- Eating a balanced diet that's not too high in sugar and refined carbs

In addition to generally taking care of yourself as outlined above, there are a few tips and strategies we'll focus on for the rest of this section to improve your attention and focus.

Give Your Focus a Workout

Remember that people with ADHD have underdeveloped areas in the brain, which is the reason for their executive functioning deficits. One of these executive function areas that remains a constant struggle for people with ADHD is our attention and focus. If you imagine that your ability to focus is a weak and underdeveloped muscle, what follows is that you need a workout. And not just one. You need a workout routine that has you doing reps, building strength, and staying consistent. When you do that at the gym, you see results. Likewise, when you do it with your brain, you'll see results.

This is where I encourage you to read the full explanation of how this works. Because you'll likely have some assumptions, and what you don't want to do is close yourself off from these potential benefits based on assumptions and past experiences.

Multiple clinical research studies have shown differences in brain function and, specifically, differences in executive function after practicing this exercise consistently. And these changes did not occur after years of practice. They occurred after 8-12 weeks of practice for 3-30 minutes per day (Hepark et al., 2019).

The expectation is not that you would do this perfectly, and of course, there will be times you forget, but if you can make a commitment to try for 90 days, there is significant evidence that you will experience results.

The exercise is mindfulness meditation. This is the practice that gives your brain the workout it needs. When people think of meditation, they don't normally think it falls under the category of a workout. But for your brain, which is very prone to wandering, it is an extremely effective workout.

Zack, a 32-year-old sales rep, had resisted meditation for years. After trying a few sessions here and there, he knew it wasn't for him. He had ADHD and he knew his brain wasn't built for the extended period of Zen that meditation seemed to require. And any time he had tried to meditate, it seemed like the chatter in his brain went into overdrive in rebellion against the whole thing.

Zack's job offered monthly wellness activities for the staff in his office. When these activities occurred, it was the general culture of the office that everyone would participate. Some of the activities were not too bad. A yoga instructor came into the office one day, another day, they were provided a healthy breakfast, and during mental health awareness month, his office manager circulated a 31-day wellness challenge to the whole office. Zack generally appreciated these efforts.

One day, the activity was mindfulness meditation. He was beyond disappointed and immediately started wondering how long they would be required to keep their eyes closed and sit still so he could play along until it was over. It was going to be torture. But first, the woman leading it explained how it worked. As she explained how it worked, she pointed out that the mental action of focusing on a specific thing, like one's breath, noticing every time their thoughts wandered, and gently pulling them back to focus was like building a muscle. She highlighted that every time you practice, you make that muscle stronger. Her explanation seemed a lot more active than Zack thought meditation was. And it actually created a goal and activity for his mind to do during the meditation practice.

Zack decided to give it a try on his own after that session. He downloaded an app that would guide him through mindfulness meditation. He committed to the lowest possible time, which was 3 minutes, and he committed to practicing every morning before his morning coffee. Over time the duration of his practices extended to 15 minutes. After about 3 months, he noticed that when his mind was wandering at work, he was very familiar with using the muscle of noticing it and pulling it back. Whereas before, his wandering thoughts could really interfere with his productivity, now they were small blips that occurred and reined in pretty easily.

Here's What You Do: Mindfulness Meditation

Mindfulness meditation is about bringing nonjudgmental attention to your experiences in the present moment. Judgmental attention sounds like:

- "This isn't working."
- "I keep wandering off."
- "I'm not made for this."
- "There I go again, I don't know why I'm doing this."

Can you hear the judgment in those self-statements?

Non-judgmental attention just means that you label it.

- "Thoughts."
- "Thinking."
- "Planning."
- "Judging." (If you do find yourself accidentally judging.)

Notice the difference? Here you're just using a word to point it out and then pulling your attention back to what you were focusing on. Every time you pull it back, rather than considering it a failure and evidence that you can't do this, I want you to consider it a rep. Weights work to build muscle because they create resistance. A wandering mind during a mindfulness meditation also feels like resistance. But just like you don't judge the weight, don't judge your wandering thoughts. Notice it, expect it, and pull it back. That's a rep.

Over time, you'll notice your mind becomes stronger. You'll be able to focus more easily when you want to and sustain your attention for longer. As I mentioned, mindfulness meditation has actually been shown to improve several areas of executive functioning, including emotional regulation and working memory (Hepark et al., 2019).

Aside from its obvious link to practicing attention and focus, this is your first exercise because it does impact the other executive functions as well. My suggestion is you make a commitment to try it daily for a duration of anywhere from 3-30 minutes for 90 days. If you start at three minutes, try to increase it slightly once the three-minute exercise begins to feel comfortable. Just like in weight training, we need to have some resistance to build our strength. I expect you will miss some days, I expect sometimes you won't feel motivated. Continue to try. Set an alarm. Set a few alarms. Continue to make the effort for 90 days, and if you can gain some consistency in your practice, you will start to see changes.

Now there are multiple apps that can guide you through this kind of practice. One of my favorites is the Balance app at balanceapp.com. But you certainly don't need an app to do it.

Below you'll find a Mindfulness Meditation exercise that you can use along with a simple timer on your phone. You can ask someone to read this for you, or if your e-reader has a read-aloud function, this may be a good place to use it. Again, once you take a look at this exercise, you'll see there are multiple places you can find similar ones available online and even have your phone read one aloud for you.

MINDFULNESS MEDITATION **FOR BEGINNERS WITH ADHD**

Choose a length of time that you will meditate for. If you are unsure, start small. 3 minutes is the perfect place to start.

If you are using a timer on your phone, change it to a gentle sound that you could see bringing you out of a meditation (rather than the jarring sound it might automatically be set to). You can also make your timer alarm start low and gradually increase in volume, but this is just personal preference.

Begin by finding a comfortable seated position. You can sit on a chair or on a cushion on the floor, whichever feels best for you. Keep your back straight but relaxed, and gently rest your hands on your knees or in your lap.

Close your eyes or lower your gaze, and take a few slow, deep breaths. Inhale deeply through your nose, and exhale gently through your mouth. Allow your body and mind to settle into this present moment.

Now, gently bring your attention to your breath. Notice the sensation of the air as it enters your nostrils, fills your lungs, and then leaves your body. Don't try to control your breath; simply observe it as it flows naturally. Continue to observe it. In and out. In your mind, you can say "in" and "out" if you find this helpful.

As you focus on your breath, you may find that your mind begins to wander. This is completely normal. Each time you notice your mind wandering, gently acknowledge the thought by saying in your mind – "thought" or "thinking" and then bring your attention back to your breath. This act of refocusing helps to strengthen your focus skills.

You might think of your thoughts as clouds passing through the sky. As they drift across your mind, acknowledge them without judgment, and then let them continue on their way, always returning your focus to your breath.

If you find it difficult to maintain your focus on the breath, you can use a simple counting technique to help. Each time you exhale, count "one," and continue counting with each exhale until you reach "ten." Once you reach "ten," start again at "one." If you lose count or your mind wanders, simply return to "one" and begin again.

Continue this practice for the length of time that you set at the beginning, focusing on your breath and gently bringing your attention back each time your mind wanders. Remember, every time you refocus, you are strengthening your focus skills.

When you hear the timer go off, slowly start to bring your awareness back to the room. Notice the sounds around you, the feeling of the surface beneath you, and the sensation of your breath. Gently wiggle your fingers and toes, and when you feel ready, slowly open your eyes.

Take a moment to acknowledge the work you have done in this meditation, and remember that each time you practice, you are building your focus and attention skills. If you did your meditation in the morning, you carry this sense of accomplishment with you as you go about the rest of your day.

Let's Talk About Hyperfocus

Have you ever found yourself so absorbed in something that you lost track of time and barely noticed anything happening around you? That's hyperfocus. And generally, it occurs in people with ADHD when they find something interesting or fun. Imagine you're immersed in a video game, painting a picture, or working on a project you're passionate about, you are likely to experience hyperfocus while engaging in these activities.

The same description can be applied to the concept of flow, introduced in 1990 by psychologist Mihaly Csikszentmihalyi in his book, "Flow: The Psychology of Optimal Experience." The concept of flow has gained popularity in recent years as people have recognized the benefits to both their state of mind and their productivity. Evidence suggests that hyperfocus and flow states are actually the same phenomena, just with different names and having been explored in different fields of psychology (Ashinoff & Abu-Akel, 2021).

In the animated movie "Soul," the concept of flow is depicted through the experience of the main character, Joe Gardner, a middle school band teacher, and jazz pianist. In the film, the state of flow is referred to as "being in the zone," which Joe experiences when he's completely immersed in playing the piano.

In these moments, Joe becomes so absorbed in his music that he loses awareness of his surroundings and time. He's fully emerged in the creative process. His mind is entirely focused on what he's doing, and he's feeling joy, satisfaction, and fulfillment.

"Soul" visually highlights the power of flow and how it can elevate a person's experience and allow them to tap into their full potential.

While anyone can experience hyperfocus, research suggests that people with ADHD experience it more often (Ashinoff & Abu-Akel, 2021). Studies have also shown that as the state of hyperfocus is sustained, we use less cognitive effort over time while engaging in that activity (Ashinoff & Abu-Akel, 2021). In other words, we're completely absorbed, enjoying it, and it feels easy because we're so in the zone.

The research on hyperfocus shows that we may not be as attention-impaired as we thought. In fact, we can pay attention excessively if the conditions are right (Ashinoff & Abu-Akel, 2021; Sklar, 2013).

Laura was a software engineer who had recently been promoted to a team lead position. Being the only person that she knew of on her team who struggled with ADHD, she'd had many moments of comparing herself to colleagues who seemed to perform effortlessly. Sometimes she wondered if she was really cut out for such a demanding and detail-oriented job. Earning this promotion meant a lot to her and she didn't want to disappoint.

As team lead, one of her new responsibilities was to solve critical issues that came up in the product. While these issues were not infrequent, their occurrence was impossible to predict and they often coincided with the rollout of new features. This made it even more important to resolve the problem quickly. One day, a major glitch was found in the software a few days before it was supposed to launch for a client.

Laura was under a lot of pressure to address the issue effectively. She was worried that if she didn't, her manager might second-guess her recent promotion. She also saw this as a great chance to show her team what she was capable of. The glitch was complex, and her team was counting on her. She didn't see an option to fail.

Laura buckled down to work on the issue. She looked at it like a puzzle to be solved. She knew that if she strategically went through every line of code, she should be able to find the problem. So she immersed herself in trying to figure it out.

She spent hours at her desk, going through every piece of information. She took quick breaks to refuel but went right back to her task. The rest of the world essentially faded away as she focused on solving this puzzle.

Laura's sense of urgency, and her ability to see this situation as a challenge and an opportunity to impress her boss and her team set the stage for her to hyperfocus on the task.

When she presented the solution to her team, they were surprised that she had solved it in such a short time. It had been less than 24 hrs. Laura felt a huge sense of pride and accomplishment. She had faced her first challenge as team lead, and she had overcome it.

Now in Laura's case, it appears that she was in a state of hyperfocus. But solving software issues and strategically going through code is not something that most people would consider interesting or fun. So, what happened there? We know that our brains effectively turn "off" when things are boring or hard (Milliken, 2016). But we also know the ADHD brain is most active when experiencing something we deem novel, interesting, urgent, frightening, or fun (Barrett, 2018).

There are two concepts at play in Laura's scenario that we'll delve into in our next two exercises.

Laura's perspective

- She saw this as an opportunity to prove herself since she had just been promoted.
- She knew that it was her team's responsibility to address the issue.
- She was worried that if she could not address it, then her manager may regret promoting her.

- The task was time sensitive based on the upcoming launch date for the client.

Gamification of the task

- Laura made this into a puzzle.
- The rules of the game were simple. Go through every line of code, find the problems, and fix them. The inherent reward was the positive response she would get from her colleagues and the avoidance of postponing the client's launch date.
- She had quantifiable progress. She could see what she had reviewed and what was left. This constant progress measurement helped to keep her motivated and on task.
- Once she fixed the glitch, she won the game, and she could take a break.

While there is yet to be a proven handbook on how to trigger hyperfocus at will, there are known factors that contribute to it and effectively set the stage. The remaining exercises and tips in this chapter will target how to create the optimal circumstances for intense focus to occur.

Shaping Your Perspective

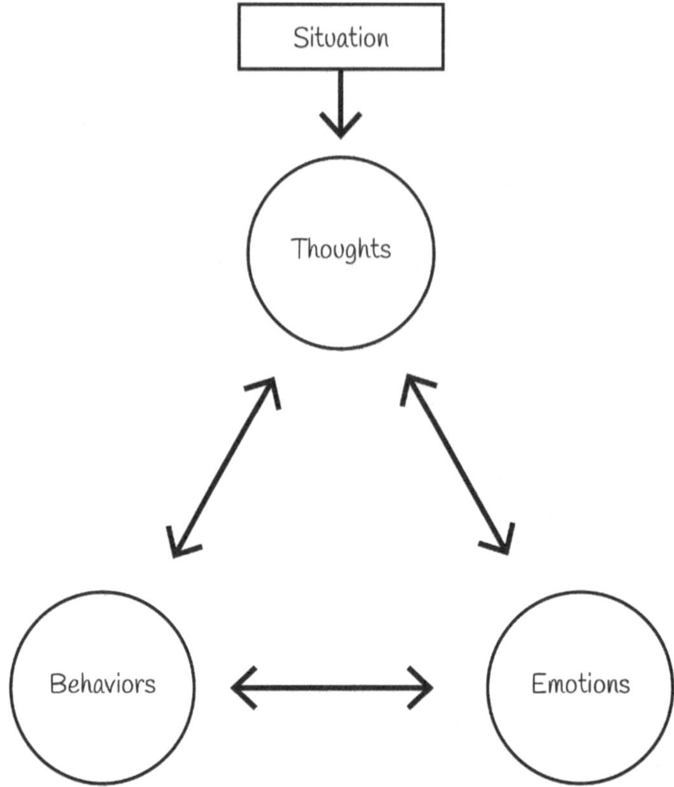

Cognitive Behavioral Therapy (CBT) is one of the most widely used and best-studied forms of psychotherapy. It's based on the Cognitive Behavioral Model, which explains the relationship between our thoughts, feelings, and behaviors. Essentially our thoughts lead to our feelings, which then lead to our behaviors and back around again. Below is the cognitive triangle which visually demonstrates the link between the situations we experience and our thoughts, feelings, and behaviors that follow.

Every situation in our lives triggers this cycle. But sometimes, we have emotions and behaviors that we want to change. This is where cognitive behavioral exercises come in, as you aim to change your thoughts and beliefs with the goal of influencing the feelings and behaviors that result from those thoughts. When we think of something as boring, impossible, or pointless, we will naturally have extreme difficulty paying attention and sustaining any focus on that task. Focusing in this context would likely be difficult for anyone having those thoughts, but even more so for someone with ADHD, when we consider the differences in dopamine, difficulties with impulse control, and additional executive function deficits. Practicing CBT exercises will help you understand why and how shifting your perspective will improve your ability to focus.

LET'S CONSIDER AN EXAMPLE OF THIS:

Michelle and Kathy work in different departments of their job. Each one is tasked with doing the quarterly report for their team. It's due next week. This task goes on rotation throughout the team, so neither of them does it more than once a year. Both Kathy and Michelle happen to have ADHD. (Event)

Kathy thinks – *I don't have time for this. Now I'm going to have to chase everyone down to get their updates. Then I'll have to use that template I hate, and somehow make it look good. Everyone else always makes theirs look nice when they present it. I'm not creative like that. It's going to look awful. I wish they could just skip me.* (Thoughts)

She's feeling overwhelmed, inadequate, and dreading it. (Feelings)

She knows that she has to get started or it won't be done in time, so she sits down with the intention of outlining everything that goes into this report. (Behavior)

When her phone gets a notification about 15 minutes later, Kathy stops to answer it. It's an email from a coworker about something unrelated.

Kathy knows she has work to do, but she thinks *I'll just get this email done so I don't forget to go back to it later.* (Thoughts)

She jumps onto the email and starts responding. It takes her 10 minutes. After she responds, she automatically hits her social media app without even thinking, as if it's just muscle memory when her phone is in her hands. Another 15 minutes pass. (Behaviors)

Kathy realizes she has just been scrolling and the outline for her report is sitting open on her computer just barely started. She thinks, *I really have to get this done* (Thoughts).

Kathy starts working on the outline but is feeling restless with this task. She doesn't want to be doing it and she feels like she doesn't really know what she is doing. (Feelings)

When a colleague comes in to ask for help on something, she figures she'll just *get back to this later when her mind is fresh.* (Thoughts).

She closes the outline and leaves her desk to assist her colleague (Behaviors).

Her week continues like this with her anxiety growing with each day that passes. The day before it's due, she's working on it all day, ignoring all of her normal daily tasks as well as any possible interruptions as she gathers what information she can for the report. She's overlooking details and making mistakes because she's so stressed. She continues working on it at home until she finishes at 9 pm. It's all she has focused on all day, and it's finally done. It's not the best, but at least it's done. (Behavior).

SAME EVENT...

Michelle thinks – *I really have a lot to do this week. This is important, though, because everyone is going to see it. Last quarter they showed some pretty nice ones, which made reviewing them in that meeting less painful. I don't know how they did that, but I should check with Joe and see how he got the font and graphics like that. If Joe can do it, I can figure it out. That would be cool to get really good at these, so next time it comes around, mine will be just as impressive as the others.* (Thoughts)

She's feeling some pressure, hopeful, determined, and at ease with where she's at for today. (Feelings)

The next day Michelle is determined to do well on this. She goes to Joe's office first thing in the morning. She asks him to show her how he made his report look so nice. She's intent on learning how he did it. He shows her Canva and how easy it is. He even gives her some thoughts on diagrams she might add. He also asks if she wants to join the team for lunch as they were planning to go out to a nearby restaurant.

Michelle thinks that would be great, but she wants to take advantage of the time she has to get this report done (Thoughts).

She's feeling determined (Feelings).

She declines lunch, letting him know that she will definitely join them next week (Behavior)

Michelle knows that if she is going to get this done, she'll need to carve out times when she won't be interrupted so that she can be intentional about prioritizing this report (Thoughts).

She feels good about this plan as it makes the whole thing feel much more achievable (Feelings).

Over the next 2 days, she takes advantage of the quiet mornings, having strategically decided to work during these times when there are fewer distractions (Behavior).

She also blocks out time on her calendar each day so that people can't book her for meetings at those times and she'll be free to focus on this report. By intentionally giving herself time blocks to focus on the report throughout the week, she pulls it all together by the time it's due. It ends up looking pretty good. (Behavior).

Try a few for yourself. You can use any event that has recently occurred in your daily life. They can be mundane. You woke up late, your favorite show came out with a new season, your Aunt Lisa called, etc. Identify the thoughts, feelings, and behavior that followed. Try a few of these to get comfortable with creating the connections for yourself.

PRACTICE 1:

Event	Thoughts	Feelings	Behaviors

PRACTICE 2:

Event	Thoughts	Feelings	Behaviors

By now you should be getting a sense of how your thoughts and feelings relate directly to your behaviors. But if your first reaction tends to be more like Kathy, how do we get you closer to thinking like Michelle?

Next, you'll learn about some common thought patterns in people with ADHD that can be pretty unhelpful and how to change them.

Recognizing Your Unhelpful Thoughts

As you've learned, cognitive behavioral exercises typically involve shifting thoughts in order to positively impact feelings and behaviors. When it comes to recognizing the thoughts that need to be shifted there are some very common unhelpful patterns of thinking that people engage in. In therapy, these are called cognitive distortions. While there are many cognitive distortions that one can engage in, there are few that are prevalent among people who have ADHD.

According to Dr. Abigail Levrini, licensed clinical psychologist and ADHD specialist, all adults with ADHD can benefit from CBT exercises. She goes on to explain that there are several unhelpful thought patterns that are most common among people with ADHD (Levrini, 2023).

FILTERING

Imagine you have a mental filter that lets the good things pass through and hangs onto all the bad things. In our example, Kathy saw a lot of negatives about the task ahead of her, whereas Michelle had the same task and didn't focus much on those negatives. Kathy was filtering.

Write about a time when you engaged in filtering. What feelings and behaviors did this lead to?

____

____

____

PREDICTING THE WORST

Otherwise known as catastrophic thinking, this is when your thoughts jump to the worst-case scenario. In this situation, you don't just see it as possible that the worst would happen, you see it as very likely. In Kathy's situation, she saw her report coming out awful as the only possibility. Whereas Michelle saw the possibility of it going okay and started thinking of how she could accomplish it.

Write about a time when you were predicting the worst in a situation. What feelings and behaviors did this lead to?

____

____

____

FORECASTING

Just like the weatherman who tells you if a storm is coming, forecasting is when you predict what will happen in the future. In this context, we are specifically referring to forecasting negative things. And just like the weatherman, you might also be wrong about these things. This can be similar to "predicting the worst," but there are some differences. Forecasting is when you think you already know how something will turn out, and it's not going to be good. Kathy assumed that getting information from her team was going to be a negative experience.

Write about a time when you were forecasting. What feelings and behaviors did this lead to?

____

____

____

MIND READING

This is when you assume you know what someone else is thinking or what their intentions are, without them actually saying it. Kathy didn't engage in this unhelpful thought pattern, but if she did, she might have assumed Michelle was going to try to show her up or that her whole team must be thinking that she doesn't know what she's doing. These would have been examples of mind reading in her situation.

Write about a time when you were mind reading. What feelings and behaviors did this lead to?

____

____

____

BLACK AND WHITE THINKING

This is when our thoughts are very 'all or nothing' with no room for nuances or shades of gray. Kathy thought to herself, *"I don't have time for this."* Even if she is pressed for time, she could re-prioritize something else, or look at her schedule to see how she might fit it in, rather than assuming automatically that there is no time for it. She also sees herself as not creative. She might have the capacity to come up with something creative, but she automatically assumes she cannot do it.

Write about a time when you used black-and-white thinking. What feelings and behaviors did this lead to?

____

____

____

EMOTIONAL REASONING

This is when you believe something to be true based on your feelings about it, rather than actual evidence. Examples of how Kathy may have used emotional reasoning would be "I feel anxious about gathering updates, so it's going to be a disaster." Or "I feel less creative than others, so my report will definitely look worse."

Write about a time when you used emotional reasoning. What feelings and behaviors did this lead to?

____

____

____

When we engage in these types of unhelpful thought patterns, we create a situation in which we are very unlikely to be able to pay attention and focus. If we focus best on situations that we find fun, interesting, or novel. It's very likely that Kathy's focus to complete the task kicked in when she found it urgent and was fearful about not being able to deliver, but if she had been able to recognize and reframe her unhelpful thoughts earlier, she may have been able to hone her focus much sooner.

REFRAMING OUR THOUGHTS

When you find yourself struggling to pay attention to a task or to focus on it, that's a good time to step back and consider how you view this particular task or situation. A good starting point might be to run through the list of unhelpful thought patterns because we know they are common among people with ADHD. If you find that you are engaging in any of them, it would be more helpful to reframe that thought.

Reframing is when we change our perspective on a thing or situation. This doesn't mean we pretend things are amazing if they aren't, but this is where we try to look at the situation from a different angle and see if there are ways in which we might be able to view it as more fun, interesting, or novel.

Unhelpful Thought Pattern	Situation	Unhelpful Thought	Reframed Thought
Mind Reading	Alice is at a family gathering and notices her sister-in-law seems distant.	"She must be upset with me about something."	"It's not necessarily about me. She might be having an off day. I can check in with her or I can focus on enjoying the rest of the evening since we rarely get to do this."
Emotional Reasoning	Grace is nervous about an upcoming presentation at work.	"Since I'm so worried about this, I'm definitely going to mess it up."	"The more worried I am, the worse it will be. Let's see what happens if I can focus on staying calm. They say that helps. This will have to be an experiment to find out."
Predicting the Worst	John was scheduled last minute to meet with a new client.	"I'm not prepared, I'm going to lose this client."	"Likeability is half the battle. The better I engage with this client, the more likely he'll book the next meeting with us. It's fine if I don't know everything. I'll give what information I can and take every opportunity to get to know more about him and what he'd like to accomplish."

In each of these examples, the reframed thought was just a change of perspective. The situation stayed the same, but the person was able to find a different way to look at it that highlighted the fun, interest, or novelty of the situation. Each of these reframed thoughts gave the person a better reason to focus on the situation they were in.

Now it's your turn. You'll start by identifying situations that you are finding difficult to pay attention to or focus on. Then you'll write down what your perspective or thoughts are about this situation. Next, you'll review the list of unhelpful thought patterns and see if any of them apply in this scenario. Recognizing the pattern is often an easier way to see how you might change the thought, but it's not necessary to reframe a thought that is hindering you. If you can recognize the thought pattern, jot it down. You may start to notice which patterns are most prevalent for you and recognize them more quickly in the future. Finally, you'll create a new thought using a perspective that highlights how the situation could be more fun, novel, or interesting. Remember that the new thought has to be believable for it to be helpful for you.

Unhelpful Thought Pattern	Situation	Unhelpful Thought	Reframed Thought

Continue to practice this strategy in the upcoming weeks. Mastering this strategy can take some practice at first, but the more you notice the impact of your thinking and the power that you have to leverage it to your advantage, the easier it will become to set the stage for better focus.

Who Doesn't Like Games?

Gamification is the use of game-like elements in non-game contexts. Dr. Kirsten Milliken is a clinical psychologist and ADHD coach who talks about taking situations and tasks that are not games and turning them into games in our everyday life (Miliken, 2016). She highlights that when we find things hard or boring, our brain essentially turns "off" and that games are a great way to turn it back "on".

As you consider ways to gamify things in your own life, bear in mind that games usually involve clear rules, goals, a certain amount of risk, constant feedback/rewards, challenge, momentum, and fun (Miliken, 2016).

The draw of this concept is pretty simple. People with ADHD love things that are fun or novel. We also love a challenge. Dr. Miliken highlights that sometimes we don't even need to add a reward, because playing the game itself might be rewarding enough. She uses the example of speed as a reward, simply because she finds it fun. Likewise, you might find that challenging yourself and beating your own high scores is fun enough to motivate you to stay on track.

But if rewards are more enticing to you feel free to add them wherever you like. This is where some creativity is involved. Take that as a challenge and have fun with it! Only you can identify what things you like and what things you might be enticed to work for. Try to make your rewards the things that you don't give yourself all the time or the things that you like, but might feel guilty about indulging in. Bear in mind that rewards could be undermined if poor impulse control has you skipping the effort and jumping right to the reward without earning it. Some of us prefer to enjoy the game rather than working toward a reward. You'll need to choose what works best for you.

Take a look at the table below. I've added some of my own examples. Continue to fill out the table with the tasks that you find difficult to focus on or pay attention long enough to do and start gamifying them!

Task	Rules	Fun Game Element	Reward (if needed)
I need to unload and load the dishwasher. But I always get sidetracked and end up doing other things, so it ends up taking forever.	I'm going to aim for a 5-minute max for each part – unloading and loading. I'm to set a timer and then record my time. If I can do it in less than 5 min each, I win. Then next time I have to beat my time to see how low I can get it.	Speed The challenge of beating my own time	
My unread emails are out of control. I need to sort them out and respond to important ones.	I get 1 point for each regular email that's sorted and 2 points for each important email that I sort and respond to. I need to hit 20 points or more.	20 points earns me a reward. Beating my high score either doubles my reward or gets me a better reward.	20 points means I can take a 10 min break to scroll social media without feeling guilty about it. Beating my high score either doubles that time or means I get delivery from my favorite cafe.

Task	Rules	Fun Game Element	Reward (if needed)

This is a concept that you can use daily and use almost anywhere. It's only you that have to know the rules of your own game and be motivated by them. As you work on creating your own, here is a list of some common gamification elements you might use:

- Points system
- Time challenge
- Reaching higher levels
- Competition
- Streaks
- Tracking progress
- Meeting milestones
- Role-playing

As we know, there is an app for everything. There are several apps that can help you gamify your everyday tasks. You might find it easier or more fun to use one of these apps rather than creating and tracking the game yourself. If so, some apps to check out that involve everyday gamification are:

- Habitica
- LifeUp
- Epic to-do List
- Do It Now

Gamification is an excellent way to improve your attention and focus for any tasks that you are not finding motivating enough on their own. The more you practice this strategy, the better at it you will get. As you go, it will feel easier to apply games throughout your daily life to accomplish tasks that you might otherwise have no interest in. Don't be afraid to get creative with this one, and if you need a little help to get started, check out the apps, as new ones are coming out all the time.

Pro-Tips:

While not strategies to practice, implementing the following will help you focus better in the moment, so I recommend you try to incorporate them when possible:

FOCUS BURSTS

Think sprints rather than marathons. You are more likely to sustain your focus for short bursts of time rather than hours. One commonly used strategy is the "Pomodoro Technique".

One example of the Pomodoro Technique is as follows:

1. Choose a task that requires an hour or more to complete.
2. Set a timer for 25 minutes (this is one "Pomodoro").
3. Work on the task until the timer goes off.
4. Take a 5-minute break. (Get up, move around, don't scroll. You need an actual break.)
5. Repeat the cycle by starting another Pomodoro.

After completing four "Pomodoros," take a longer break for about 15-30 minutes.

These time blocks are not set in stone. You should adjust them to fit your needs and the nature of the task. The main point is that you alternate between focus periods and short breaks to maintain your productivity and prevent burnout.

ELIMINATE DISTRACTIONS

We're already prone to distraction, even without things happening in our environment. It will be more helpful to eliminate avoidable distractions when you can.

- Silence the notifications on your phone and computer.
- Let people know you'll be working on a task and ask that they try not to interrupt.
- Be intentional about when and where you choose to work on the task.

USE MUSIC

Music has been shown to improve focus in both children and adults with ADHD (Maucieri, 2016). Different kinds of music work for different people, so experiment with this to find what works best for you. There are also lots of playlists available on YouTube, Spotify, and in a general online search targeted toward people with ADHD. Searches to try include:

- ADHD focus music.
- ADHD study music.
- Binaural beats for ADHD.
- Some genres that have anecdotally been helpful include classical, instrumental, rock, electronic, and lo-fi.

Take some time to try different kinds of music to find what works best for you.

You've learned a lot in one day! Take a break and digest everything you learned. Tomorrow we'll move on to Executive Functioning Skill #2: Working Memory.

DAY 2.

ENHANCING WORKING MEMORY

Our difficulties with working memory show up every day, all day. Deficits in this area can be incredibly frustrating and impact your performance at work, at home, and even in conversations with friends.

Here are some quick examples of what working memory issues look like on a daily basis:

- You walk into the house, put down your keys, that's the last time you saw them, now they're lost.
- You go outside to get the mail, realize there's a bill you need to pay. You plan to address it as soon as you get inside, then the phone rings. The end of the month comes, and that bill never gets paid, and you're not even sure where it went.
- Out to dinner with a group of friends, if you wait to make your point, it's gone. If a side conversation starts, you lose track of the first one. 15 minutes pass and you haven't actually said anything because your attention keeps getting pulled, and you're forgetting what you wanted to say.
- Putting the peanut butter in the fridge and the jelly in the cabinet while thinking about what you'll make for dinner tonight.
- Leaving the house and not remembering whether you locked the door, turned off the lights, or unplugged the iron. Turning around to go back home because you really need to check.

Working memory is the function that allows us to hold onto information long enough to work with it. This means holding onto the details you need while problem-solving or completing a task. Working memory deficits can be a significant challenge in adults with ADHD. We also know that executive function issues are interrelated. Groves et al. (2020) found a significant relationship between inattention, emotional dysregulation, and working memory. They found that severity in one area could predict severity in the other. Considering this relationship, it makes sense that working memory, like attention, is also heavily influenced by nutrition, exercise, sleep, and stress. It is crucial that you are managing these basics if you want to see improvements in your working memory skills.

Additionally, some of the elements you learned yesterday are also helpful for building working memory skills. Mindfulness meditation has been shown to improve working memory over time (Hepark et al., 2019). While gamification improves working memory performance during the actual task that has game elements added (Ninaus et al., 2015).

Improving working memory issues often involves implementing strategies during the moments where you struggle the most. This way, you're giving your working memory some assistance to keep track of the information you need.

Multi-Tasking Versus Monotasking

If you've never heard of monotasking, it's pretty much what it sounds like. One task at a time. As opposed to multitasking, which we are used to doing, and some people may even brag that they do well.

Multitasking makes our working memory issues worse. In reality, we are not doing two or more things at the exact same time. Instead, we switch back and forth between tasks very quickly. This puts more exertion on our working memory and increases the likelihood that we'll forget things related to either task we're engaged in.

Imagine that someone needs to spin 2 wheels for 1000 rotations. That's the task. Both wheels need to be spun 1000 times, and then they're done. The wheels are not close enough to spin them both at the same time by standing in between them, rather, you have to walk (or run or cartwheel) over to the other one and back if you want them both to spin at the same time.

Consider the person who monotasks versus the person who multitasks. The one who monotasks focuses on one wheel at a time. He stays at that wheel, focusing on spinning it until it completes the 1000 rotations, then he goes over to the second wheel. Because he's standing in the same place while doing the task, he notices details if they come up. Sounds the wheel makes, if one is wobbling a little more than the other, etc.

The multitasker gives wheel #1 a good spin or two and then runs over to #2, gives it a few spins, runs back to #1 because it's slowing down, and then back to #2, and so on. Did the multi-tasker finish first? I really don't know. I imagine it was close. But let's look at how the people who did both tasks are doing. When I visualize this, my monotasker is pretty collected, maybe he's breathing a bit quickly from the work he just did, but he's standing up straight, and he's doing okay. My multitasker? He's sweating, panting, leaning on one of the wheels while he tries to catch his breath. He's done. He'll be tired tonight and sore tomorrow. And no, he doesn't recall anything in particular about the wheels. Was he supposed to?

Think of these characters as your brain doing either a task one at a time, or multiple tasks at a time. Although we know that, to an extent, our attention spans are naturally doing some of this back and forth to us throughout our day, why would we intentionally do this to ourselves? It puts that much more strain on our executive functioning, depleting us quicker and ensuring that we barely remember any of the details in the process.

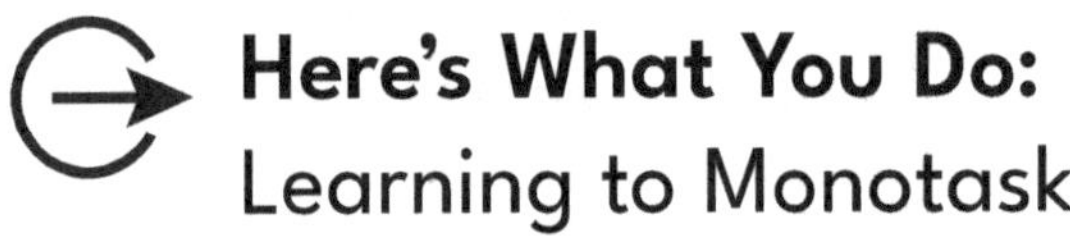

Here's What You Do: Learning to Monotask

If you want to improve your working memory, the first step is reducing the behaviors that put more of a strain on it. Be the monotasker. One task at a time. Even if you naturally wander, make it your anchor that you come back to. This task is your goal until you intentionally decide to move onto something else. This will increase your ability to hold onto information and details compared to the difficulty you'll have trying to retain information while doing multiple things at once.

Monotasking doesn't really come naturally to us though, so here are a few steps you can use to start practicing:

1. Identify the task you'll be doing – if it's a large or multipart task with many parts, break it down:

- A paper or report could be broken down into each section so that you are only focusing on one piece at a time.
- Cleaning a room could be broken into which section of the room you are in or the activity you are doing, such as wiping things down, dusting, or vacuuming.
- Food shopping can be focused on just getting the things on your list - before you start considering extras and what you want to make for dinner that night.

2. Say to yourself: "I'm just doing X right now". This gives you a stronger reminder than just deciding that's what you'll do.

- "I'm just making this graph on quarter 1 revenue right now."
- "I'm just making the bed right now."
- "I'm just going down the list right now."

3. If other things come into your mind that feel important or that you're worried you'll forget – stop to note them down, then go right back.

- Do not engage in another task until you've completed the monotask. Even if it's quick. We both know it's a slippery slope.
- Later in this chapter you'll learn more tips about writing things down to avoid forgetting – but a nearby whiteboard, a post-it that you'll check, or the notepad in your phone (as long as you avoid checking emails) are good options.

4. Take breaks if you find your mind and motivation wandering consistently.

- You're more likely to need a break if the monotask is taking a long time or if you have done a few monotasks back-to-back.
- Set a timer or alarm for your break so that you can get back to the task.

5. Practice consistently.

- This is a strategy that you will get better at with practice.
- You have multiple opportunities on a daily basis to use this strategy.

ADHD and Autopilot

We all have those moments where we're functioning on autopilot. According to the University of Cambridge (2017), a set of areas in the brain considered the "default mode network" (DMN) causes us to switch into autopilot mode while performing tasks that we're familiar with. The DMN helps us perform the task while other areas of the brain are resting. It's overall deemed to be a pretty efficient process that our brain has developed.

You're probably very familiar with autopilot, considering that people with ADHD tend to have overly active DMNs during goal-directed tasks (Sidlauskaite et al., 2016). So, what should be an efficient process can end up being pretty unhelpful for us.

So, in addition to trying to do many things at once, we often forget things because we're doing them on autopilot. We can go through the motions, almost like muscle memory, and have no recollection of them. Most of the time, the door probably was locked, but you didn't notice yourself doing it. And forgetting even a few times is enough to have you turning back when you're really not sure. In these moments, we need a way to draw attention to the thing that we're doing or want to do.

Here's What You Do: Say it Out Loud

Stopping to acknowledge these moments out loud increases your chances of remembering them because you heard yourself say it. The other benefit of doing this is that you stop long enough to focus your attention fully on that thing, even if it's just for a couple of seconds. Without stopping to take notice and say it out loud, there's a good chance you do it quickly while thinking about something else, causing you to lose the information completely.

But how will you remember to say it out loud? And what if you didn't actually do it? Eventually, the goal is that these will become habits, but until then, go grab a Post-it and stick it on the wall next to your door.

Write something like:

- Lock door.
- Unplug iron.
- Pack laptop charger.

Put it at eye level, right next to your door, so you see it as you are leaving. This will signal you to stop for 3 seconds. Now you can either say them out loud if you know you did them, or you'll run and check.

- "Door locked."
- "Iron unplugged."
- "Charger in the bag."

This takes you maybe an extra 5-10 seconds before you leave the house, but also saves you from ever having to drive back home again.

Eventually, these will become habits in your morning, so you'll be giving your working memory a helping hand by stopping to acknowledge what you did.

Take a moment to consider other working memory lapses that impact you daily so that you can create similar systems that can eventually become habitual.

- ________________________________
- ________________________________
- ________________________________

Once you've identified how you'll use this verbal cue for yourself, we'll move on to one of the most common and effective ways of retaining and recalling important information.

Simple, But Effective

While our working memory is certainly a struggle, it doesn't always need to create problems for us. What creates a bigger problem is when we depend too heavily on poor working memory to follow through on important things in our lives. The perception that we just need to try harder or come down on ourselves for not remembering is not helpful.

People with poor vision would have a lot of issues if they relied on their natural eyesight while driving, reading, writing, etc. They would have problems all day long at work and at home. But we don't tell them to squint or look harder. They wear glasses. They use a tool to supplement what their vision can't naturally accomplish.

We need a similar approach when it comes to working memory. There are various tools, resources, and strategies at our disposal that make it so we don't need to hold all of the information in our heads. It's important to consider how we are using these tools on a daily basis. Some of the simplest strategies can be the most helpful.

Here's What You Do: Note-Worthy Moments

Some things just make sense to write down. Although we often don't think to write these down, we might not prioritize writing them, or we do write them and then lose the Post-it we wrote them on. Ultimately these are the things that if we do happen to forget, we'll be kicking ourselves. Either because they were important, they were related to something we wanted to do or something that we committed to someone else. These are what I consider noteworthy moments.

They are recognizable by thoughts that sound like:

- This is important, I'm not going to forget.
- I need to make sure I do this today.
- I can't forget to do that.

Or statements you make to other people that sound like:

- I'll get that to you this week.
- I'll send you X after this call.
- I'll have that done by X.
- Or when someone starts to give you specific instructions

These scenarios may have you nodding your head at this point, knowing exactly what happens next if you don't write those things down. Use the extra spaces below to write down more noteworthy moments that are specific to you.

Thoughts that indicate noteworthy moments:

- ______________________________
- ______________________________
- ______________________________

Statements you make to others that indicate noteworthy moments:

- ______________________________
- ______________________________
- ______________________________

Writing things down is not new advice. But part of the frustration that occurs with this suggestion and why it may not have worked in the past is the struggle to remember which things to write down and then to look back at that note. This brings us to the next point.

You'll Need a Planner

If you have a planner, that's perfect. You'll just need to make sure it's easily accessible to update as needed and to check multiple times per day. The kind of planner you use will depend on your personal preference, however, there are a few aspects that would be helpful to consider when choosing the right planner for you:

- Simplicity – some planners have all the bells and whistles going on. Try to choose one that is clear and easy to navigate. You don't want to look at a page and feel overwhelmed or distracted before you've even written anything.
- Structure – planners that have designated areas for different categories can help with organizing and prioritizing tasks. Time slots throughout the day are also a huge benefit.
- Portability – To make sure it's accessible, a hard copy planner should be small or light enough to bring between work and home. Otherwise, it should be supplemented by a calendar in your phone to refer to it when needed.
- Reminders – if you use a digital planner or calendar, make sure you can set reminders before each task or appointment.
- Ability to sync – if you have a calendar on your phone, it's helpful to be able to pull it up on your computer as well. While not required, since your phone is likely nearby, the more easily accessible your planner is, the more you are likely to use it.

You might choose to have one place to store your schedule and keep track of your tasks, or you might have a few. Don't be afraid to combine different methods to suit your needs.

Beth used to lose track of everything. "I forgot" was a normal part of her vocabulary. She was incredibly frustrated because people took this to mean she didn't care, which couldn't be further from the truth. She started to realize that there were some things that just had to be written down.

She got a planner that she could write in with hourly slots and a weekly view. She could keep track of her appointments and meetings there, as well as any notes to remember or tasks to accomplish. She could bring the planner back and forth between work and home. Even though it came back and forth with her, inevitably, she might be somewhere without her planner and have to remember something or schedule something. So, she started keeping a Google calendar and made sure it matched her written planner. She preferred to write things, but the Google calendar was her backup. She could also color code different types of commitments and set it to give her reminders before each task or appointment, which saved her from forgetting pretty often. Additionally, the notepad on her phone became the place where she could quickly take a note without having to worry about where to put it in her schedule. As long as she reviewed it at the end of her day and assigned it a spot in the planner, it would be addressed.

These changes took some trial and error to figure out the right combination and a bit of time to gain consistency. But the people around her noticed that she was more on top of things. Beth started feeling more confident, realizing she didn't have to constantly apologize for missing things all the time. This had a ripple effect on her overall stress levels, ultimately reducing her stress on a daily basis.

What worked so well in Beth's story was her flexibility to capture information whenever she needed. This helped her stay on top of all her tasks. Both of her planners acted as a backup for one another, allowing her to refer to her schedule throughout the day.

Often our approach and our perception of writing things down hinders us from really making use of this strategy. We might expect it to fail or consider that we've tried before. But if you decided that all of your tasks, appointments, and to-do's would, from now on, be recorded somewhere, you'd be much more likely to check that place repeatedly.

It's important to commit to this strategy and integrate it into your daily life for it to work. If you only consider writing down things you'll forget or just your work appointments, then it's unlikely that this strategy would be much help. There needs to be a mindset shift to think about this as the place where all your plans live. You put them there so that you don't have to rely on your working memory. Your planner is an extension of your working memory. So if it's worth remembering at all, you record it, and then you start to build a habit pretty quickly of going back to find everything you need. What are some recent examples of things that you should have and could have written down but didn't? What were the impacts?

What happened as a result?

____

____

____

____

Things I should have written:

____

____

____

____

Now, when you think about those things that you didn't write, consider why you didn't.

Reasons I didn't write important things down recently:

____

____

____

____

This is where you should really start to recognize a pattern developing. Chances are, your reasons were some variation of what you thought you'd remember, you didn't have access to a place to write it, or you didn't want to stop for a moment to write it. I've been there. A lot. But once I accepted that my working memory doesn't do a great job at capturing some things, I started using my planner as an extension of what I imagined would happen if I had amazing working memory. A place to store the information, access it when I need it, and even be automatically reminded when I'm supposed to do something.

At this point, the times I check my planner are often throughout the day, often after I complete a task. I consider tasks to be milestones in my day. I complete a milestone, then I go see what the next milestone is. But if this feels too much for you in the beginning, and if you have several things to keep track of for one day, try to identify 3-4 times you can consistently look back at your planner.

Try to associate this with other things you do during the day. For example, you could check it right after you brush your teeth so that you know what to expect for the morning. Then you can check it mid-day around lunch. Again before you leave work, make sure you don't miss or forget anything there. Then again, in the evening, make sure you carry over any notes you took during the day and add them to your planner if they are things you need to keep track of.

Identify the times of day that you can check your planner:

❶ ______

❷ ______

❸ ______

❹ ______

Now that you've mastered some of the foundational strategies to improve your working memory, we'll explore and leverage some more complex techniques that you've actually used for years to enhance your retention and recall.

Mnemonics Have Been Helping You For Years

These are memory aids or techniques designed to enhance your memory recall. They help us organize and retain information by creating associations or patterns that make it easier to remember. Mnemonics can be in the form of acronyms, visualization techniques, rhymes, or any other method that helps make information more memorable. The ultimate goal is simplifying the process of retrieving information from your memory.

I guarantee you know a few mnemonics. Remember PEMDAS?

Parentheses
Exponent
Multiply
Divide
Add
Subtract

I wouldn't have passed 8th-grade algebra without that one.

How about the rainbow? Do you know the order of the colors? If you said ROY G. BIV, that's another mnemonic. **R**ed, **O**range, **Y**ellow, **G**reen, **B**lue, **I**ndigo, **V**iolet.

Chances are, the way you learned the alphabet is also a mnemonic. If I asked you what letter comes before R or after G, you might sing that part of the alphabet in your head quickly. Both the tune and the grouping of the letters are mnemonics. I'll bet you group them like this:

ABCD EFG HIJK LMNOP QRS TUV WX YandZ

That's how we were taught to sing them, so if any of us quickly needed to recall the order, that's how we would do it, with the tune and grouping we learned.

THIS EXAMPLE OF A TIME I USED **ASSOCIATION COMES TO MIND**

I met a woman named Jacklyn a few years ago. Now, I'm terrible at remembering names. But I had known one other, Jacklyn, and she was an adorable kid I had met years prior. So, to remember this woman's name, I imagined them playing together. I created a visual of them at the park on the swings. The next time I saw this woman, I remembered the visual, and I knew her name was Jacklyn.

Some people lean toward creating acronyms, others create rhymes, and others paint a visual in their minds or create an association. If you are new to creating mnemonics yourself, it may take a little practice in the beginning to apply it, but soon you'll find that it's a great way to remember things you don't want to forget. All of these techniques make storing and retrieving information quicker and easier. In the situation with Jacklyn, I wouldn't have been able to write that one down and go retrieve it when I happened to see her again. So here, the mnemonic was perfect.

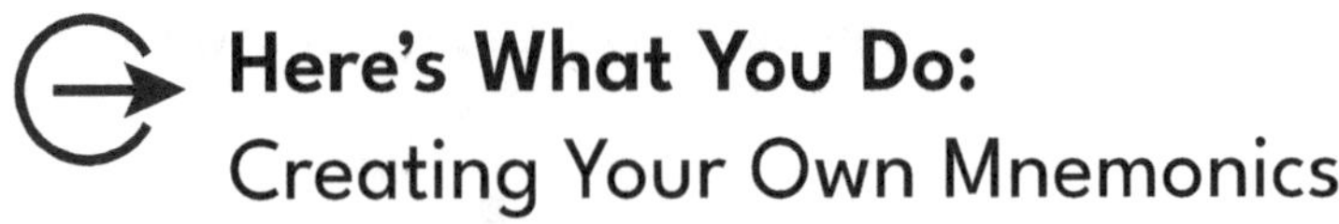

Here's What You Do: Creating Your Own Mnemonics

The beauty of mnemonics is that they can be personalized to your own way of thinking. I use acronyms the most. You might prefer a song, a rhyme, a mental picture, or a short story. The key is creating ones that work for you and learning to apply them in your everyday life.

Try developing a few mnemonics of your own here:

Let's say you need to remember 4 specific items to grab from the store next time you go. How can you use a mnemonic to recall?

Or what if you have a presentation where you need to explain a process that is a series of steps? Imagine a process that you use and how you might create a mnemonic to remember it if you needed to explain it to a crowd.

Think of someone you met recently. If you're bad with names like I am, how might you remember theirs?

Try to get some practice with mnemonics in the upcoming days or weeks so you get more experience with integrating them into real-life situations.

While working memory training programs do exist, research demonstrates mixed results on whether the improvements last beyond the actual training and whether they can be generalized to other daily tasks.

However, as we mentioned on Day 1, mindfulness meditation is one exercise that has demonstrated lasting improvements in several areas of executive functioning, including working memory.

With that said, if you want immediate changes in how your working memory impacts you on a daily basis, the strategies in this chapter can quickly get you on track so that you don't miss any more appointments or forget to follow through on things you committed to.

Take a break, you learned a lot today! Tomorrow we'll delve into the problems of procrastination as we discuss how to improve your task initiation skills on Day 3.

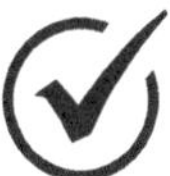

Pro Tips for Working Memory

- Monotasking beats multitasking every time.
- Saying it out loud can pull you out of autopilot for a moment, making you more likely to remember.
- If you know it's important, even if it's simple, write it down.
- Use a planner and get used to checking it regularly.
- You've been using mnemonics since you were a kid. Try making your own.

DAY 3.

MASTERING TASK INITIATION

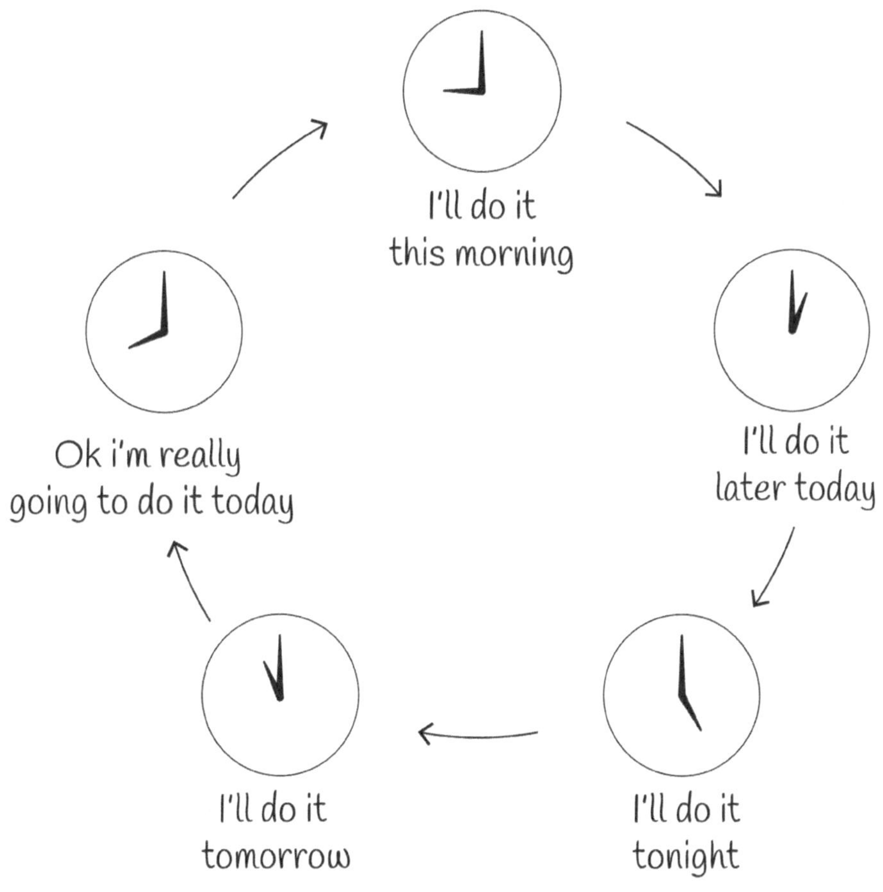
The Procrastination Cycle
I'll do it
this morning
I'll do it
later today
I'll do it
tonight
I'll do it
tomorrow
Ok i'm really
going to do it today

The relationship between ADHD and task initiation is multifaceted. Many of our symptoms coincide with our difficulty beginning tasks that we find boring, overwhelming, or otherwise unenjoyable in some way. Struggles with motivation, focus, prioritization, planning, organizing, and managing our time all feed into our tendency to procrastinate. Ultimately procrastination is extremely common in people with ADHD. Our thoughts and feelings play a significant role in our difficulty initiating tasks. Several common examples of this are:

- We feel overwhelmed by how big the task seems.
- We may struggle to identify where to start.
- The task doesn't feel rewarding enough / low motivation.
- Negative emotions are getting in our way.
- You're not accurately gauging how long it will take you.
- Perfectionism.

Additionally, people with ADHD most commonly use the maladaptive escape/avoidance coping skill (Torrente et al., 2014). This is when we engage in behaviors that help us to escape or avoid beginning the task that we are procrastinating on at that moment. We can be pretty creative in how we do this. Our efforts to escape or avoid tasks can look like the following:

- Excessive distraction with other things that we prefer to do – essentially just escaping into things we find more enjoyable: TV, video games, social media, etc.
- Overplanning. We can convince ourselves that we need to spend all this time pre-planning before we can start the task. This might involve researching, outlining, listing steps, etc. These things feel like we're doing something productive, but often they're just a placeholder for really jumping into the task.
- Taking excessive breaks to engage in other 'important' things like checking our email, paying a bill, or suddenly needing to follow up on something else we knew we needed to do.
- Rationalizing in some way, the need to start this task later, although later always seems to get pushed back.

This is a coping skill because it is our way of dealing with the discomfort associated with starting the task, but it's considered maladaptive because it doesn't serve us well and ultimately causes more harm than good. Considering our difficulty with emotional regulation and recognizing that the thoughts and feelings associated with our avoidance are uncomfortable, it makes sense that our automatic response is to escape or avoid the task for as long as possible.

During our periods of escape or avoidance, we're likely to engage in productive procrastination, which feels better. This means that we are engaging in constructive but lower-priority tasks rather than doing the higher-priority task that triggered our avoidance (Ramsay, 2017).

The Role of Perfectionism in ADHD

Among people with ADHD, the most common reason identified for procrastination is perfectionism (Ramsay, 2017). This is not to say that it is always the case, and there are certainly other times that any of the above reasons may come into play – but it is worth considering whether perfectionism plays a role for you.

Ramsay (2017) differentiates between two types of perfectionism. 'Back end' perfectionism is the most common view of what perfectionism looks like. This is the person who appears almost obsessive and struggles to complete a task because they get stuck in the process of trying to make sure everything is flawless. However, 'front end' perfectionism is what is more commonly seen in people with ADHD. This is when we defer starting the task at all because we need the circumstances to be just right, which includes being in what we perceive to be the 'right mood' before we can even start the task (Ramsay, 2017).

Miles had a long history of front-end perfectionism that almost always made it feel impossible to get started. He felt that under the perfect conditions and the right mindset, he could do truly exceptional work. Convinced that he needed to wait for inspiration to strike or gather all the right information before he could start, he often postponed initiating his tasks. Unfortunately, this usually resulted in starting his work with barely any time left, not because the perfect moment had miraculously arrived, but because time had run out.

When he was tasked with organizing an event at work, his thoughts were no different. He could see the perfect event in his mind. But there was a lot of pressure involved in this event. There would be a lot of important people depending on the outcome of his work. His actions and how he chose to handle this would be directly responsible for the experience that his leadership and colleagues would have. Miles knew his patterns pretty well and he realized that he couldn't afford to strive for perfection in this situation. If he did, he would be risking everything falling apart. He decided that 'good enough' was better than rushed. He would start and do his best with what he had. He took the first step of talking to some colleagues to gather ideas. That night he made a list of the calls he would need to make the next day. The next morning he started reaching out to vendors and speakers.

Miles moved quickly to keep up his momentum. With each step he took, the event started falling into place. There were a few hiccups and problems along the way, but he had the time to address them rather than scrambling at the last minute.

The event finally took place. It wasn't perfect in his mind, but people gave him good feedback. They had a good experience, and the minor issues and setbacks that occurred were barely noticeable to anyone else. For the first time, Miles was not completely drained at the end of an event. He realized that in accepting imperfection and facing tasks directly, he was not only more efficient, but he also produced work that he was happier with, and so were the people around him.

Ultimately our need and expectation for perfection are unrealistic and extremely unhelpful. If you struggle with front-end perfectionism, you'll need to recognize and challenge these tendencies head-on, while being both realistic and compassionate toward yourself.

Here's What You Do: Accepting Imperfection and Jumping In

Consider the last big task you procrastinated on because you felt like circumstances needed to be just right or because you had such high expectations for the outcome that you couldn't quite get started. Answer the following questions:

1. What was the task?

2. What time frame were you allotted to work on it?

3. What were the expectations that you had for it which made it difficult to start?

4. By the time you really started, how much time did you leave yourself?

5. What compelled you to start when you finally did? Were conditions ideal?

6. How did it turn out?

7. Could it have been better with more time? If so, how?

Chances are that your responses to these questions have played out again and again with many tasks over time. This is a pattern that you know well, but likely haven't taken the time to truly break down and acknowledge. Seeing how this habit works directly against the perfect outcomes that you want can provide the motivation you need to jump in even when it's not the 'right time' yet.

Truthfully, by the time we finally start on a task, it's often not because the stars finally aligned and the timing is right. It's usually because we are down to the wire, and we have no choice. So we make it work. But in the course of 'making it work', we often realize that we could have done a much better job if we gave ourselves more time.

The next time you find yourself procrastinating due to perfectionistic expectations, consider what happened the last time you engaged in this pattern. Then:

1. Define a set of *realistic* outcomes. Visualize what they look like.
2. Commit to doing a run-through – a first draft – that you'll have the freedom to go back and fix because you'll still have time.
3. Acknowledge this isn't going to be perfect either way. But it has the chance to be better the sooner you start.

Your Patterns Matter

Whether perfectionism is the sole reason for your procrastination or whether you have several different reasons depending on the situation, it can be helpful to have a better understanding of your patterns if you want to change them.

We have patterns in the things we do. The way that we think is fairly consistent across different areas of our lives and it continues to influence our behaviors in similar ways. If I tend to avoid things that seem difficult or complicated, I'm just as likely to procrastinate on starting a report as I am in reorganizing my closet. Too big, not fun, I don't want to do it. Avoidance kicks in whether I'm at work or at home.

Understanding our own behaviors in various situations helps us to start recognizing the patterns. This way we are more likely to predict how we'll respond or at least have a stronger awareness of what is happening and why. If I struggle with task initiation, I might rationalize reasons not to start now and tell myself I'll start at a later time. If I didn't have a strong awareness of my patterns, I might actually believe that and then buy the next excuse to push it off again – all the way up until the deadline. But by now, I can see it a mile away, which has changed my approach to certain tasks so that I can avoid this pattern as much as possible.

Here's What You Do:
Identify Your Patterns

In the following table, under the first column labeled 'Task I Procrastinated On', list 10 things you procrastinated on. These can be the things you procrastinated on most recently, or they can be some of the biggest things you've procrastinated on that caused the most trouble in your life.

Next, going through this list one by one, complete the second column labeled 'Why I Didn't Start Sooner', filling out what you think is the primary reason you didn't start sooner. If you need help here, consider our initial list of common reasons that task initiation is a struggle. Your reasons don't have to be on this list, but they are likely to be something along these lines:

- We feel overwhelmed by how big the task seems.
- We may struggle to identify where to start.
- The task doesn't feel rewarding enough / low motivation.
- Negative emotions are getting in our way.
- You're not accurately gauging how long it will take you.
- Perfectionism.

Our primary goal here is to understand the pattern so that you can start to change it. Ultimately you should start to see one or two reasons for procrastination emerge as repeat offenders on your list.

Finally, in the third column labeled 'What if I had started sooner?', detail explicitly what could have gone better if you had given yourself more time.

Task I Procrastinated On	Why I Didn't Start Sooner	What if I had started sooner?
Creating the slides for a presentation at work	Front-end perfectionism - I wasn't in the mood, I knew I could do it, but the timing was just never right – until I had no other choice	• I would have had time to make the visuals nicer. • It would have been more detailed. • I would have felt better about it. • I wouldn't have been as stressed the night before and the day of the presentation.

How CBT Applies

CBT is one of the most effective evidence-based strategies for addressing ADHD symptoms. If we consider that escape-avoidance is our primary coping mechanism, then that's the piece of the puzzle that needs to be addressed to improve our issues with task initiation.

Escape and avoidance are two distinct but very closely related behaviors that we often use to deal with discomfort. Hence the name of the coping mechanism combines the two. To escape means we try to find a way out, while to avoid refers to our attempts to not be involved in the first place. By reframing tasks in ways that help us view them as more approachable, we can increase acceptance of discomfort and ultimately our willingness to engage, thereby reducing the need to cope through escape-avoidance.

As you move forward with digging into your patterns, you'll start to get a better sense of how the skills you'll be developing are essentially various ways to make tasks feel more approachable by breaking down and targeting the specific aspects that are holding you back.

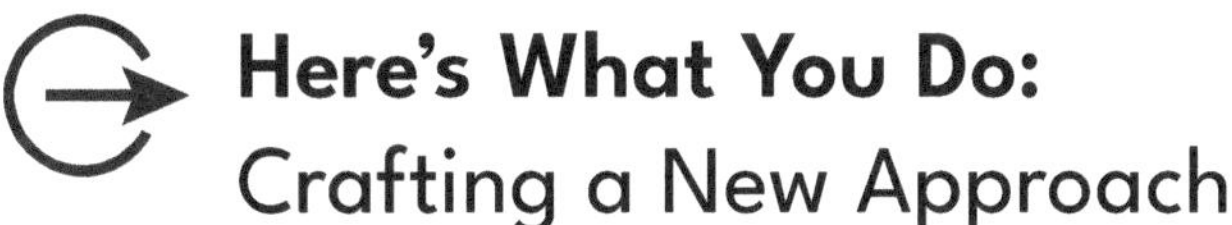

Here's What You Do: Crafting a New Approach

Much like we did on Day 1, we need to explore alternative perspectives and approaches to address the patterns that are preventing us from getting started.

Take a look at the chart below. On the left, you'll see the common reasons we don't start tasks. On the right, you'll see alternative approaches. As you look through these alternative approaches, notice that they involve changing your perspective and your thought process in that moment. Additionally, a common theme is breaking things down into really small achievable parts. Breaking things down makes them less daunting and also makes getting through them more rewarding because each part that's completed feels like an accomplishment and propels you forward. An important thing to remember with this chart and these kinds of alternative approaches is that we're always just aiming for the next move. We're not committing to the entire task or to something that feels impossible, it's always just the next move and re-evaluating from there.

If....	Then...
I'm struggling with front-end perfectionism. • I'm not in the mood. • The timing doesn't feel right. • I can do it really well, just not right now.	I don't have to do a lot right now, but I can get something out of the way. • I can choose the theme for my slides. When that's done.... • I'll draft the titles for my slides – they might change, but at least I'll get an idea of the layout. When that's done... • Maybe I'll throw on a couple of bullet points that I know could go in those slides.
Feeling overwhelmed because the task is too big.	• I'm not even going to do it right now. • I'm just going to start writing out the steps involved so that I can see them laid out in front of me. When that's done... • I can just do step 1. When that's done... • I'll get out my planner and schedule step 2 – it doesn't have to be now, I can do step 2 tomorrow morning and I can just block off 30 min... if it takes longer, I can either finish it then or do another 30 min later in the day.

If....	**Then...**
I don't know where to start – I can't do anything if I don't even know what to start with.	• I'll just gather some information. • I'll google how people do this. • I'll check out "How To" articles, I'll search it on YouTube, I can even ask a colleague what their process was. When that's done... • I'll start writing my steps.
Low motivation, it's not rewarding or enjoyable at all.	Since I'm going to have to do this, I'll try not to let it be torture. • I can put on music while I do it. • I can use the Pomodoro technique and do short focus bursts of time. 4 Pomodoros and I'm done for the day. • I can call up Emma and see if she has work to do as well, maybe we can meet at Starbucks and work on our stuff together.
It's not going to take me that long – I'll get it done in 2hrs the night before, which will be fine.	We know how this goes by now. If it wasn't a problem, it wouldn't be on this list. • If it's only going to take 2 hours, let me get the first hour out of the way ASAP. • Then I'll have a better idea of whether my estimate was right. • If I was wrong – I'm lucky I started and checked, now I can make a plan to move forward. • If I was right – I'm halfway done! I'll put a reminder on my calendar to do the other hour tomorrow, and I don't have to deal with this anymore.

Negative emotions: • I'm terrible at these things. • I hate these kinds of projects. • I'm not going to be able to do it. • Everyone else is so good at these, I have no idea what I'm doing. • Etc.	• I learned about unhelpful thoughts yesterday – is that what's happening here? • If I wanted to feel more hopeful or positive about this, how could I look at it?

As you can see in this table, the battle really is in getting yourself started. To do this, we have to move you from a state of paralysis to a state of feeling like the task is approachable. Consider the table above and create your own below, using the reasons in your "Why I didn't Start Sooner" column and building small plans for how to address them. Use examples of things that you are procrastinating on right now or have procrastinated on recently. Filling in charts is a great start, but if we want these concepts to stick, these need to be things that you can start taking action on almost immediately.

Why I Didn't Start Sooner	What I can do now / next time this comes up

These tasks may seem extremely simple, but that's a good thing. They're not hard and they can be applied to anything that you are procrastinating on. A major reason that they work is because we rarely stop to assess our automatic thoughts or reactions. Instead, we just go with them. This process helps us to slow down and examine what we are doing and why. Then we are prompted to be more deliberate with how to proceed once we've acknowledged where we're at. A simple, yet incredibly powerful skill to build.

What To Do First?

Up to now, these exercises have helped to uncover your patterns in detail and offered you compelling ways to visualize better outcomes if you begin tasks sooner. But committing to initiating a task sooner doesn't necessarily answer the question of 'how'. Prioritization is an important part of effectively accomplishing the things that we set out to do.

We often struggle to prioritize our tasks. I briefly mentioned productive procrastination earlier. This is a common way we get away with avoiding tasks we don't want to do, while still feeling productive. This helps us reduce the anxiety or guilt that might come with avoidance since we're still doing something. But in reality, when we do this, our priorities are out of whack.

There's a simple way to fix this. Again, it involves slowing down enough to take notice. The importance of a planner and writing things down has already been mentioned. Next, if you have an important task that needs to be accomplished or that you know you're likely to avoid until the last minute, you'll need to start prioritizing the activities in your day.

Here's What You Do: Effectively Prioritize Your Day

Up to now, we've covered the importance of breaking things into smaller parts and writing them down. Now you'll take a look at the list of things on your to-do list and prioritize them. The most important thing should have an "A" next to it, the next most important thing will have a "B", then a "C", and so on.

Now establish the rules for yourself. Perhaps "A" tasks must always be accomplished or worked on. Perhaps "B" tasks are addressed almost always. "C" tasks you try to get to often, but it depends on the time you have. "D" tasks would be nice to get done, but only if you have free time, and so on.

Priority	Task
C	Sort emails
A	Pay electric bill
B	Work on presentation
D	Read the next book in my queue
A	Schedule doctor appt

If this was my to-do list, in no particular order, I would label each thing in order of priority, then I would address the A's first. Acknowledging their order of importance makes it harder to work on non-priority tasks and still feel good about it. Since we can be very reward oriented, structuring our to-do list, as shown above, gives us a simple way to feel accomplished for doing the 'right' tasks first rather than the 'wrong' ones.

Recognizing that people with ADHD are often visual learners (Levrini, 2023), if you prefer to use colors instead of letters, you can do that as well. You'll just need to stick to a color-coding system that is easily identifiable. For example:

- A = Red (urgent)
- B = Orange (still important but less urgent)
- C = Yellow (should get it done after red and orange if time allows)
- D = Green (would be nice to get this done)

Whatever system you come up with, stay consistent with it so that it becomes automatic when you look at your list to quickly understand which thing should be prioritized next in your day. Additionally, stay flexible. A green today, may be a yellow tomorrow if it doesn't get done. Or if your boss calls, she might give you information that moves a yellow to a red. Being able to adapt is crucial to staying on top of priorities as they may potentially change throughout the week or day.

Give it a try with your current to-do list. Once you have finished, consider whether you would have naturally done your tasks in that order, or if you might have done them according to what you felt like or what was convenient at that moment. Creating this type of list is another way to draw attention to the nuances of our own behaviors and build a simple strategy to improve them.

Priority	Task

Understanding and challenging your patterns, visualizing different outcomes, risking imperfection, and prioritizing your tasks are all effective strategies to get unstuck when you need to get started. Take a look at the Pro Tips below as you prepare to face procrastination head-on.

Pro Tips for Task Initiation:

- You need a planner or calendar to schedule your tasks.
- To-do lists are a must.
- Prioritizing your lists can curb productive procrastination.
- Challenge the thoughts that keep you stuck in procrastination mode.
- When in doubt, aim to make it smaller and more approachable (we gravitate toward quick wins).
- Don't underestimate the power of rewards and fun, incorporate them whenever possible.

DAY 4.

APPLYING TIME MANAGEMENT

If you're no stranger to time management struggles, then the exercises in this chapter will help you slow down where it matters and get in control of your time and the things you need to accomplish. Having ADHD means we can be affected by time management issues in a few different ways:

- We lose track of time.
- We misjudge the amount of time that's passed.
- We get distracted during tasks, inadvertently cutting into the time that we set aside to accomplish them.
- We underestimate the time that something will take us to complete.

- We commit to too many tasks, stretching our available time too thin to accomplish it all.

It's easy to see how struggling with time management can have serious impacts on many areas of our lives if we don't develop strategies to get on top of it.

Part of time management includes prioritizing your tasks which you learned yesterday. Recognizing which tasks are more important than others and which ones need to be addressed first is a necessary step to ensure you allow enough time for each important task.

When you consider the above list of our struggles with time, each one represents either a struggle with our perception of the time that we are currently spending on something or a struggle with making future estimations of time. When we lose track of time, misjudge the time that has passed, and get distracted during the time we allotted to complete a task, these are all examples that we are not accurately tracking the time we are currently spending on a task or interest. And when we commit to too many things or underestimate the amount of time we'll need to finish something, this is our inability to estimate future time.

Considering that everyone with ADHD doesn't have the exact same issues with time management, you'll need to create a strategy that works for you. But starting with some of the basic requirements for anyone to manage their time well, we know that you'll need to have a good sense of how long tasks might take, a decent control of distractions and things that might waste your time, and the ability to discern what you can reasonably commit to doing in the space of any given day or week.

When Our Perception is Off

According to Ptacek et al. (2019), people with ADHD have a legitimate impairment in the perception of time. This means that inherently we have difficulty gauging the time that has passed. Luckily, we don't have to rely on our perceptions to track and gauge time. This is an example of an area in which we need to use the tools and resources at our disposal to help us achieve success.

- Use visual timers.
- Depending on the task, TV shows or music playlists can also keep time for you.
- Set alarms even when you don't think you'll need them.
- Create a list of common activities or tasks you engage in and how long they take you.
- Identify your biggest distractions and eliminate as many as possible when working on a task you need to complete. This includes phone, emails, and people that are likely to disturb you during the task.

If you consistently struggle to accomplish tasks in a reasonable amount of time, it could be helpful to intentionally time yourself so that you know how long it takes for you to get it done. For this one round of completing that task, you'll be mindful that you are being timed and, therefore, more likely to stay on target. Consider this an experiment to find out how much time you really need to complete the task.

Nikki always struggled to get regular household tasks done in a reasonable timeframe. She felt like these tasks took forever, and in fact, she did end up losing a good portion of her day when she set out to clean a few things around the house. For example, she would start doing the dishes, then get distracted by a notification on her phone, then remember she needed to send an email, then see some papers on the counter she wanted to organize, and before she knew it, she was doing everything else while the dishwasher just stayed open. In this way doing the dishes could take her upwards of 45 minutes. So her avoidance of doing the dishes because she knew it would take forever was not entirely wrong. But during the actual task, she was losing track of time and getting distracted by other things, making her overall time management worse.

One day, she decided to see how much time she actually needed to do the dishes. She guessed about 20 minutes. She set a timer on her phone and put it on the windowsill above her sink so she could see it the entire time. As soon as she started the timer, she started unloading the dishwasher. She didn't intentionally speed through it, but she aimed to be efficient, knowing that the timer was going. She unloaded the entire dishwasher, put the dishes away, loaded the dishwasher, washed the pot that was in the sink, and wiped down the area. As soon as she finished, she hit the timer button to stop it. 9 minutes and 36 seconds. She concluded that in the future, it should take her about 10 minutes to do the dishes.

Knowing this, she now sets her timer to count down from 10 minutes to keep her on task. The goal is not to rush herself but stay within a reasonable timeframe that she knows she can complete this task in. Once in a while, it goes over depending on how much is in the sink, and sometimes she goes faster. Ultimately, she always aims to stay around 10 minutes and no longer has 45-minute distracted dishwasher sessions.

This worked for Nikki because it created awareness of the time she actually needed, it set up a future expectation that was reasonable for her, and there is an added accountability and gamification element when a timer is counting down, whether she uses this to race against the clock and beat her best time (some tasks could be fun to do this with) or whether she uses this countdown to periodically check during a task to make sure she's staying on track (such as working on a report).

Here's What You Do: Keeping Track

In this exercise, you'll time yourself for tasks you often need to accomplish but that you tend to misjudge the amount of time needed. First, create the list of tasks that you want to time, then if you can do any of them today, get them done with the goal of figuring out how much time they should generally take you. Then mark that time down. This will be what you set your future timer to count down from.

The table below already has some examples of things you may want to time that you frequently misjudge. But you can do this for any task that you have to do on a recurring basis and that you struggle to manage or gauge. If you assume a report will take you 2 hours, and you find out that without rushing and going at a normal pace, it actually takes you 5, then that's going to benefit you to keep in mind for future times when you need to complete that report. Likewise, if you are consistently late to meet up with friends, you may want to time how long it takes you to get ready.

Task	How long it really takes
Daily email checking and responding	
Completing the monthly report at work	
Balancing your monthly budget	
Folding the laundry from one load	
Getting ready to leave for work	
Getting ready for an outing with friends or a date	
Reading a chapter	

Creating Focus Bursts

Bear in mind that when it comes to things that take more than 30 min or an hour, you'll benefit from building in breaks to keep your productivity and momentum going. Strategies like the Pomodoro technique or any other breakdown where you alternate focus bursts with short breaks.

For a little background, "pomodoro" is the Italian word for 'tomato'. A man named Francesco Cirillo developed this time management technique in the late 80's using his tomato-shaped kitchen timer. So when you imagine your "Pomodoros", it's really your 25-minute timer.

This is a common strategy used by people with and without ADHD to stay focused and improve productivity. It works especially well for us when we have longer tasks to do. By periods of focus alternated with breaks, we improve our ability to pay attention during the focus times, and we also keep track of time with a set number of 'Pomodoros' or focus bursts.

Here's What You Do: The Pomodoro Technique

The typical Pomodoro Technique consists of 4 sets of 25 minutes focus periods with 5 min breaks in between. So it looks like this:

1. Engage in the task for 25 minutes.
2. Take a 5-minute break.
3. Engage in the task for 25 minutes.
4. Take a 5-minute break.
5. Engage in the task for 25 minutes.
6. Take a 5-minute break.
7. Engage in the task for 25 minutes.

What works about this strategy is the ability to break a longer task up into shorter tasks and give yourself short breaks in between. The breaks should be long enough to give you a moment to move around, maybe grab a drink of water, and take your eyes off the task. But the breaks shouldn't be so long that you run the risk of becoming engaged in something else, thereby killing your momentum. If the exact 25/5 minute ratio doesn't work for you that's okay. You might experiment to find what works for you. Your strategy might also differ depending on the project you have. You might prefer to break it up into sections rather than periods of time.

Before You Know it, an Hour is Gone

While the breaks in the Pomodoro technique are meant to be short, we know it can take about 2 seconds for our attention to shift to something else, and we can come back up an hour later, realizing that we've just wasted a lot of time. So even if you have nice short established breaks, let's take a moment to consider the distractions that could throw you off track.

For many people scrolling social media is a good example of this. Another common time trap is shopping online. However, it's not always something obvious. Depending on our particular interests, it could be something that we would hyperfocus on, whereas another person might not even find it interesting. If I decided to crochet for just 15 minutes, it would unlikely be 15 minutes because it's the kind of thing that makes me want to keep going, and I could easily continue for an hour or two before I pry myself away from it to get back to being productive.

We don't need to avoid our time traps, we just need to know when we can engage in them and when we should save them for later. Try not to engage in a time trap when you're in the middle of a task. Breaks are good and healthy, but taking a break to engage in a time trap is setting yourself up to throw off the schedule you had planned.

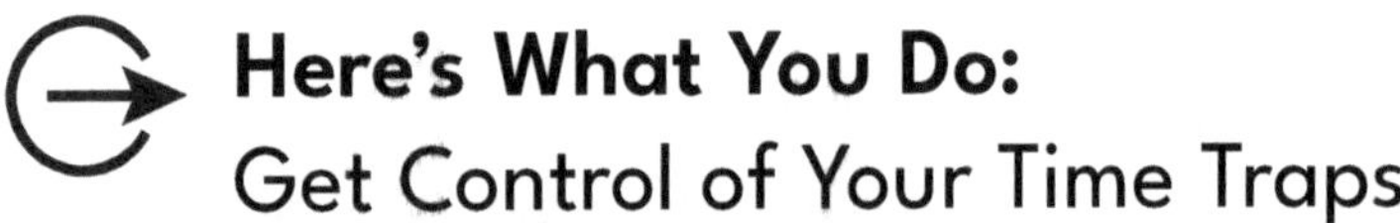

Here's What You Do: Get Control of Your Time Traps

Take a moment to list 5 of your biggest time traps here – these things can be rewards at the end of the day or at a time when you don't have other things to get to, but try to avoid getting involved in any of these when you still have more tasks to get to. If you must engage, for example, you need to make a purchase or respond to someone on LinkedIn, set a time limit before you start so that when the timer goes off, you're done.

My biggest time traps are:

1. ______________________________
2. ______________________________
3. ______________________________
4. ______________________________
5. ______________________________

This list can be good to keep visually near your desk or your workspace as a reminder of the things you don't want to engage in when you are trying to be productive. With the visual reminder, you'll be more likely to catch yourself and be more mindful that engaging in these things is a known time waster.

The Importance of Planning

Since you've gotten a better understanding of the time that's passing, how to stay on track when you set a specified time for a task, and also how to manage your distractions, we need to acknowledge that none of these will be much help without making sure that you haven't overcommitted yourself. We are notorious for taking on too much. Through a combination of our interest in multiple things, potential people-pleasing tendencies, and our difficulty estimating how long a new task might take us, we can easily find ourselves with way more on our plate than any person could reasonably expect to finish. This is where planning comes in.

We all have those days when there is way too much to do and not enough time to do it. Sometimes our perfectionist tendencies feed into this. Ultimately overcommitting almost always leads to feeling overwhelmed and puts us on the fast track to burnout. And let's not forget the obvious, if we don't have enough time to accomplish things, they don't end up getting done.

What we want to do is create a plan that lays out how much time can be devoted to a particular task. That way, the expectations are clear from the beginning. This involves a few strategies:

- Remember your planner? Any time you commit to a task, it needs to go in your planner. Assign it to a specific day/time or multiple, if needed. This way, when there is no more room to accept new tasks, it will be visually clear that your time is accounted for.
- Take stock of your commitments on a weekly basis. Choose a time each week that you can look at the week ahead and make sure that everything can still go ahead as planned. If you see something that needs to be shifted, this should give you some advanced time to take care of it.
- Always always always overestimate how much time a task will take you if you are unsure and have not completed this exact task before. Our time estimation skills are pretty poor. You'll be glad you gave yourself some wiggle room.

Steve had been struggling to stay on top of things at work. His email was something that he often pushed off till later, then avoided altogether. He would only respond to what was absolutely necessary. So then, he had about 450 unread emails that he needed to go through. But he didn't have the space in his schedule to address all of it in one day, nor did he want to. That felt incredibly daunting, and he had a lot of other things on his to-do list.

So, to start tackling his email, Steve looked at his schedule that day and decided he could give 20 minutes to his email. For 20 minutes, he started going through them, sorting, responding, and archiving. Then, the next day, he took a look at his schedule and saw he could give it another 30 min. He proceeded this way and cleared his email by the end of the week.

When it comes to your daily tasks, if you have a lot planned for that day, it's important to not allow a task to take significantly longer than the time you blocked off for it. But sometimes, we struggle to start something if we think we won't be able to complete it. Plan ahead to just make a dent in certain tasks if they are likely to take much longer than you have for that day. Then make sure other spaces are blocked off throughout your week to continue chipping away at it.

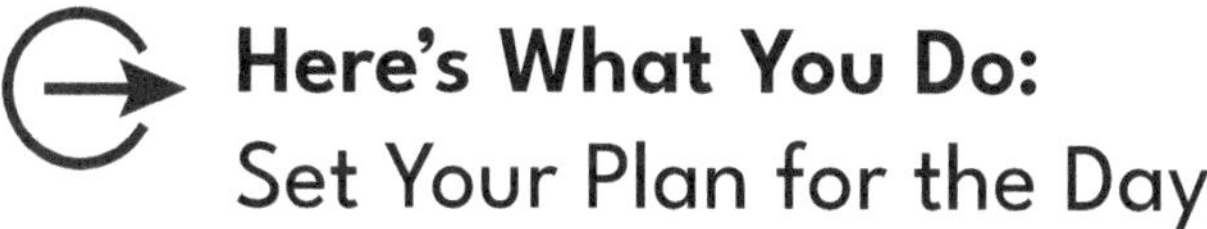

Here's What You Do: Set Your Plan for the Day

When you know something will take a large amount of time and the idea of tackling it feels impossible with the rest of your schedule, not only is this a task initiation issue, but it's also a time management problem. If the task does not have to be completed right away, but you find that you're avoiding it because you can't see how to integrate it into the rest of the tasks on your plate, set a specified amount of time you can devote to it each day, fitting it around the rest of your schedule. Then set the timer, and when it goes off, you're done for the day.

Are there any tasks that you know you can't complete all at once but that you need to start tackling? List them here:

Task: ____________ Start date: ____________ Time allotted: ____________

Task: ____________ Start date: ____________ Time allotted: ____________

Task: ____________ Start date: ____________ Time allotted: ____________

Next to each task you listed here – decide if you'll start it today or tomorrow. If you're reading this in bed, I imagine you'll start tomorrow. But if it's earlier in the day and you technically have the ability to give the task even 5 or 10 minutes, then start today. Waiting to begin just increases the chances that you won't get to it at all until you've barely got any time left.

Once you have identified which tasks you'll do, when you'll start, and how much time you'll give them, make a point to put them in your planner at the days and times where they should go. If you're not yet used to using your planner in this way, this is a good opportunity to begin practicing. As you move through completing these tasks, stick to the times you set, use a timer, and continue doing this until your task is completed.

Keep in mind that reading about these exercises without implementing them will be about as helpful as reading a recipe and never buying the ingredients. Sure, it was entertaining for a moment, but you'll miss the chance to experience it for yourself and add it to your own culinary repertoire. Wherever possible, try to engage in these tasks immediately and look for more opportunities to practice them throughout your week. This will help you generalize the skills beyond just this moment and naturally identify where these skills make sense in your normal routine.

Take a moment and reflect on what you've learned and how you'll begin to implement it. Get ready for tomorrow, which is Day 5! You're about to be more than halfway through, and you learn all about how to manage your impulses.

Pro Tips for Time Management

- Don't rely on your perception. Learn how long tasks really take you.
- Use the Pomodoro technique for tasks that are an hour or longer.
- Manage your time wasters.
- Break large tasks into pieces and block off time for them each day.

DAY 5.

ENACTING ESSENTIAL ORGANIZATION SKILLS

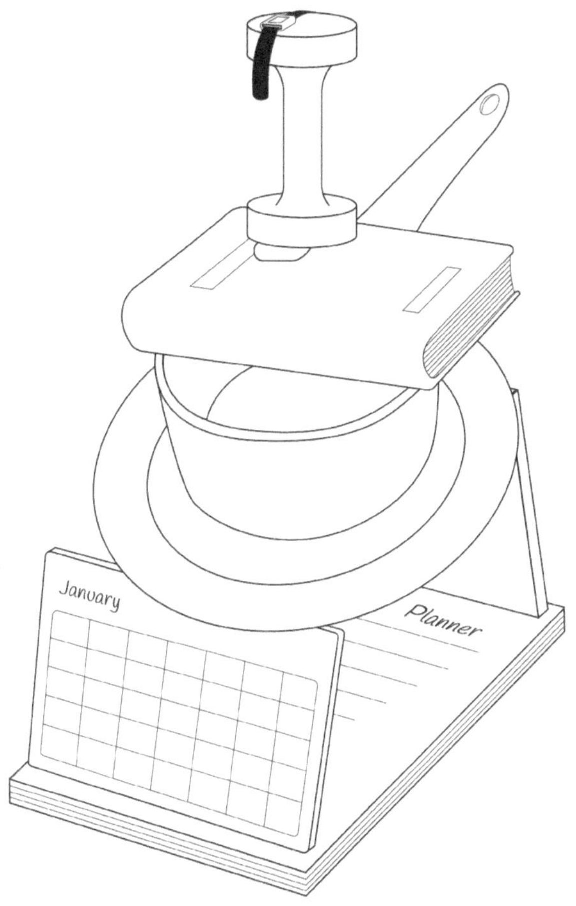

We can be extremely sensitive to visual distractions in the same way that we are distracted by any other stimulus in our environment, so we function best in an environment that looks neat and structured as opposed to chaotic and cluttered (Betker, 2017).

So, although we love the feeling of being in an organized room and can feel calmer and more collected when our space is put together, our difficulties with executive dysfunction don't make organization skills our strong suit.

We often put things down and forget about them, or don't feel inclined to take the extra time that would be needed to figure out where something should go. On top of that, the thought of organizing or re-organizing a space that has gotten cluttered or messy can feel so overwhelming that we'd rather ignore that area altogether until we absolutely have to go digging for something we need.

Difficulties getting motivated without urgency or an immediate reward, combined with our tendency to avoid or escape tasks that feel unpleasant, mean we tend to struggle in this area more than the average person.

Sharice came into therapy asking for help with her "willpower." She described herself as "naturally lazy" and shared that she always had difficulty doing things around the house that she knew she was supposed to do, and she wanted to learn how to be more disciplined. She described waiting until she ran out of clean clothing to do her laundry – which always resulted in having to do multiple loads to get all of the dirty laundry done. She also described how her house was usually in a state of clutter and she found it incredibly overwhelming to clean even the simplest of things. For example, if there were crumbs on the floor in the corner of the kitchen, she couldn't just sweep up those crumbs. Her mind would jump to how she should then just sweep and mop the whole floor and that if she was going to do that, she should probably wipe down the counters and table first. So, suddenly that one thing on the kitchen floor became something that would take much more time and energy than she was ready or able to commit to at that moment. It became easier to leave the crumbs there for now, since she didn't have time to do the whole kitchen. The problem was, it would soon be forgotten, and she wouldn't return to clean it until either someone was coming over or until the kitchen got so bad that she felt she had no choice but to clean it.

In her initial session, Sharice reported being diagnosed with ADHD as a kid, but she assumed she had grown out of it and hadn't thought much about it since.

It wasn't until she started looking at her behaviors through the lens of ADHD and executive function deficits that she began to understand how the right strategies could make organization more doable for her. She found that with a few changes, she could get her space decluttered, she could maintain organization, and most importantly, she could stop thinking of herself as a lazy person who just lacked discipline.

Ultimately, Sharice had not needed more "willpower" or "discipline", nor was she "naturally lazy." Sharice had executive function deficits that made keeping the space around her organized incredibly difficult. Even though she wanted it to be neat and orderly, her thoughts about the actions she would have to take to achieve that made it feel so overwhelming and unpleasant that she would continue to avoid it, as many people with ADHD tend to do when faced with these uncomfortable feelings.

What she needed was a set of strategies and tools that directly addressed her executive dysfunction issues and the barriers that were causing her difficulty in those moments of avoidance, forgetfulness, or not knowing how to organize her space.

Organization Essentials

When it comes to organization struggles, it's not only that the task feels daunting, but it's also that we often don't know where to start. How to organize a particular space may not be clear to us. Executive dysfunction, including difficulties with working memory, can make planning and conceptualizing a space difficult, because this involves keeping the information in our mind long enough to effectively form a fleshed-out idea.

To achieve and maintain organization, you'll need a few things. You'll need to get rid of the clutter. This is the messiness or piles of things that are currently sitting on top of the spaces that you want to organize. This needs to go so that you have the space and clarity on the items that are there rather than piles of things that don't make sense taking up surface space everywhere.

In addressing your organizational needs, you're going to start with the space that is most important in your life, which is your home. Once you have a clear idea of how to establish and maintain organization in this space, you'll be able to generalize the skills that you have learned and apply them to other spaces in your life.

First, you'll need to create some ground rules for yourself. Some general things that become the norm of how you keep your household. This includes creating homes for important items so that you can confidently find them every time you need them. It also entails having a few very basic rules that you'll stick to as a general standard in your home, and then finding the places in your normal routine where you can start to include organizational behaviors.

The Role of Habit Building

When it comes to creating organization in your environment, the good thing is, the needs can get pretty predictable. The rooms in your home stay the same and by now, you are familiar with the messes that can pile up and the spaces that may need attention in your environment. Therefore, you'll want to create some ground rules and emphasize building some specific habits to make staying organized easier.

The problem is that building habits doesn't come easy to us. If you have ADHD, you are more likely to struggle with maintaining a routine or being consistent (Carr-Fanning, 2020). Our need for immediate rewards, low tolerance for uncomfortable feelings, low impulse control, and general forgetfulness can add up to being anything but consistent with something like organization.

So despite understanding that a routine would be incredibly helpful in this area, it's likely been something that has escaped you up to this point if you've not had the right tools and strategies to get there.

We want to create habits in two ways. First, you'll need to identify set places in your home for your most important items. These are the things that if you lose them, it will stop you in your tracks, and you'll need to tear apart the house until you find them so that you can continue with your day. How many times have you needed to leave the house and:

- Couldn't find your keys,
- Forgot where you left your purse or wallet,
- Your phone or laptop was about to die and you had no idea where you left the charger,
- Or you needed an important document which you're sure you put somewhere safe, but don't recall exactly where that is.

These are the important items in our household that need forever homes. This way you can get into the habit of putting them back there and finding them there when you need.

Habit stacking is another essential component of building habits. This strategy will be used as you identify organizational behaviors that need to occur on a regular basis. These things can include:

- Making the bed.
- Loading and unloading the dishwasher.
- Taking out the garbage.
- Decluttering.

If these things need to happen on a regular basis, do you have a set time of day or part in your routine when you get them done? If the answer is no, habit stacking may be beneficial for you. This strategy refers to identifying the things that you already do regularly as part of your normal routine. These things can have nothing to do with organization at all. Habit stacking means that you'll identify these random daily habits, and intentionally associate a new behavior that you want to build into a habit with one of your existing habits.

For example, if you feed your cat every evening around 6, this can now also be the time that you unload and load the dishwasher. Now those two things go together. You know you are going to feed the cat, so if you pair this with doing the dishes, you now can expect to do the dishes every day at 6. Habit stacking does take some practice, but it is a much more effective way to build new habits rather than assigning them to isolated places in your schedule, which you are more likely to forget or avoid.

Now that you have a concept of the types of habits you'll need to build, let's give it a try.

Here's What You Do: Building Organizational Habits

Based on the importance of finding forever homes for your most important items, you'll list those items here and assign them to a place in your home that makes the most sense.

Choose a spot that might be associated with where you are likely to use that item and consider the first place you think of if you had to look for that item right now. Remember that if after a week or two, this spot is really not working for you, you can choose another spot.

When trying to find a spot that made sense for my keys, I started with a basket on my kitchen counter. That wasn't great, so I switched to a spot on the shelf in the hallway. Still not great. Ultimately, I got a set of key hooks, placed them close to the door, and this works perfectly because it's visible and right in my path when I'm leaving the house or coming back in. While changing spots every week defeats the purpose of finding a forever home for these items, it is important to be intentional about the areas you choose so that you can find what works.

In the table below, I've listed what might be important items for you. Feel free to add your own to the list and disregard ones that don't apply to you. Then on the right, you'll identify a particular space for these items.

Important Item	Forever Home for this Item
Keys	
Wallet / Purse	
Important Time Sensitive Documents	
Laptop Charger / Phone Charger	

Remember this list does not have to be extensive, it just has to capture the necessities.

In the next part of our habit-building exercise, you'll begin to identify normal habits in your daily routine that might be good for habit-stacking some of your new organizational actions. You may already have an idea of what some of these actions are, and others, you may establish as you move through this chapter. When you identify a new action that you want to form into a habit that happens on a daily basis, come back to this page and add it to one of the existing habits on your list. So right now, you'll fill out the left column of existing habits with as many daily habits as you can think of, and on the right, you might start to place habits you need to build, and you'll return to that side of the list as you finish the rest of this chapter.

Some examples of existing daily habits that you might choose to use for habit stacking are:

- Brushing your teeth.
- Having your morning coffee.
- Feeding a pet.
- Getting dressed for the day.
- Taking a shower.
- Getting home from work.
- Turning off the lights for the evening.

While filling out this table, if you decide to pair brushing your teeth (existing habit) with wiping down your bathroom counters and mirror (new habit that you want to start doing daily), then you'll put brushing your teeth on the left, and in that same row you'll add 'wiping down bathroom counters and mirror.' This now indicates that you are stacking the new habit onto that existing habit, and they'll be done immediately after one another. As soon as you finish brushing your teeth, you start wiping down the counter and mirrors because those two things now go together.

Existing Habit	New Habit

The Importance of Decluttering

It's going to be impossible to organize if you have a layer of clutter in the way. So the first thing you'll need to do is declutter.

Clutter is a problem for most people with ADHD. We often just put things down as we go. We lose track of where things are supposed to go. We get so busy that we never find the time to come back and organize that area, so eventually, a collection of random things develops and continues to attract more random things. Before you know it, you have no clue what's in that pile, but it definitely doesn't look good like that, and you've most certainly taken it apart a few times when you've been searching for something.

These areas of clutter have to go. So here, you'll learn how to get rid of your existing clutter and how to maintain it by decluttering on a regular basis.

Here's What You Do: Decluttering Crash Course

1. Choose a spot.

You're going to choose one spot at a time. Not the whole house, not a whole room, just one spot.

- The corner of your kitchen counter,
- The top of your dresser,
- The ottoman in your living room,
- The junk shelf in your hallway.

This spot is wherever you find a collection of random things that doesn't make sense being where it is.

2. Grab 2–3 garbage bags.

   You'll need these bags for garbage, donations, and if you recycle, you'll have a bag for recyclables. Mark the bags accordingly.

3. Start sorting.

Start pulling things out of the pile of clutter and placing them either into one of the bags or begin creating separate piles for different categories of things. It can be easiest to grab the largest items first.

Ultimately, whether it's office supplies, paperwork, shirts, books, etc., you'll start separating the things you pull from the pile based on their category or function.

- If you haven't used it in a year, it's ready to donate.
- If you haven't used it and you can't donate it for some reason – whether it's personalized or not in great condition, toss it.
- If it hasn't been used, but "you never know when you'll need it", Get. Rid. Of. It. This one is way too common among people with ADHD. We're not doing ourselves any favors by holding onto things "just in case" when they haven't been used in a year.

So you'll start to have your bags filling up and your piles forming.

4. Move quickly,

How many times have you started to organize an area, just to be distracted by the items in that area and then you spend more time looking at or playing with that item while the mess just sits there. Then so much time passes that you'll have to stop and get back to the task another time altogether.

This is why you are aiming to move quickly. Sorting – that's all you're doing. Looking at things only long enough to put them in a bag or pile. Keep it moving.

5. Music helps.

Upbeat or workout music will help you move at a good pace and will be more likely to keep you engaged in the task.

6. Time to address the sorted piles.

Once the clutter pile is gone, get rid of the bags (garbage in the bin, donations in your trunk ready to go to Goodwill or another drop off location), and now you'll start working on your piles.

Start with the easiest ones first. Begin putting things where they go. There's a good chance that you won't actually have an established spot for many of the things in that pile, which contributes to the clutter in the first place.

If items don't have a spot where you know they belong, do your best to identify the room and area of that room they should be in. Consider their function – where, when, and how you use that item. Remember this is about decluttering, not getting perfectly organized.

Aim for speed and keep it moving. Organization will come later. This does not mean toss miscellaneous items onto your bed. This just means put them down in the spot that seems most appropriate, neatly enough so that you're not just creating a new clutter pile somewhere else.

7. Continuing throughout the house.

Because you chose a small spot to begin with, it shouldn't take you more than half an hour to move through the pile. Take a look at your planner and block off a half hour each day, or more than that if you want to achieve more in one day to declutter spaces around your home.

The goal is to get through it all. So if that takes a week or two, that's totally fine, as long as you keep up the momentum.

8. Maintaining.

Once you've decluttered your home, you'll choose an existing habit from your habit stacking table and assign 15 minutes of decluttering daily. For example, if your existing habit on the left is 'changing into comfortable clothes after work', you can add '15 minute declutter' to that same row on the right. This now means that right after you change into comfortable clothes after work, you start your daily 15 minutes of decluttering.

During these 15 minutes you'll do a walkthrough of the rooms in your house and pick up anything that seems to be out of place or that has the potential to turn into a clutter pile. By doing this daily, you may not even need the whole 15 minutes, but it keeps you on top of things that get out of place.

9. Progress, Not Perfection.

Some spots will accumulate again. That is okay. Use the steps you've learned to address them. Set aside half an hour and move through that pile. It's not about being perfect and never ever creating clutter again. It's about being realistic, allowing yourself to be human, and learning to declutter and stay fairly neat and organized on a regular basis.

10. Minimalists are on to something.

You might not need an overflowing closet full of clothes, or all of those decorative items on your mantel. 3 umbrellas might be a bit much. The same goes for the 4 throw pillows on your sofa. We often have more than we need, which further contributes to clutter. So even if you've used all 3 umbrellas to match your outfits each time you went out this year, consider whether you really need that many. Consider which items throughout your home could afford to have a more minimalist approach to reduce your overall clutter.

Shortly after I had moved into my first-ever apartment, my best friend, Emma came over. We had grown up together, she did not have ADHD. When she saw how I'd arranged my kitchen cabinets, she asked me, "What's going on there?".

Now, I knew I had struggled to figure out where to put things, but I figured that was probably because I just didn't have enough cabinet space. You make do with the space you have, and things were put away, so that was good enough. She looked at it again and said, "It just doesn't make sense."

What the heck did that mean? Sure, I hadn't quite figured out the best spots for everything yet, and it didn't look perfect, but "make sense"? Was there a kitchen organization chart I had missed somewhere? She started showing me how the places where I had chosen to put things were not the most efficient and that, visually, it was all over the place.

I had canned goods in a few different places because they didn't all fit on the shelf I initially chose. I had breakfast pantry items intermingled with dinner pantry items, and olive oil was in one cabinet, while vegetable oil was in another. These had gotten separated because the vegetable oil was too tall to fit on the same shelf where I placed the olive oil, but Emma emphasized that restructuring all of this would be much more efficient and look better.

So I asked her to fix it. It didn't take her long, and it seemed like she actually did have that kitchen organizational chart in her head. She started pulling everything out, moved all the canned goods to a bottom shelf where they could all fit, and lined them up by type so that multiples went further back in the same column and visually I could see every type of food that was there. She placed taller boxes and bottles toward the back and kept them categorized based on the type and how it was most likely to be used. For example, baking staples were together, breakfast foods were together, kinds of pasta were together, etc.

When I tried, I felt like I was lacking the ability to see what "made sense" in terms of organization. I had ended up taking things out multiple times, putting them somewhere else, still not feeling great about it, but glad that everything was away. I imagined that as long as I got used to where things were, it was okay that it didn't look like the 'after' version in a home organization reality show. Nobody else would be using my kitchen anyway, so it was fine.

I had difficulty organizing this space in my head. So I had muddled my way through it, trying to establish some sense of categorization, trying to picture how other people's cabinets were set up, and ultimately just putting things in places where they would physically fit. What had ultimately been an annoying and frustrating task to me, seemed simple and intuitive to her.

But once she fixed it, I realized she was totally right. The way she set it up looked good! It looked like a normal kitchen, rather than the chaotic situation I had going before. To Emma, these changes just "made sense."

Looking back at this, there are some general strategies that would have helped me get there on my own. Even though it didn't come as naturally for me as it did for Emma, I still could have saved myself some frustration along the way and gotten a better outcome.

Getting Organized – It Starts at Home

Just like the improvements Emma made to my kitchen, organizing your space entails putting things in places that make sense with similar things often grouped together, where they can be most useful, and in a way that is visually appealing.

As you start really integrating these organizational skills into your daily life, you'll get a better sense of how you might apply them in the other spaces that you may want to have organized, such as your car or your workspace. But for now, we'll be keeping our focus on the home.

We touched on having a few general rules to abide by earlier in this chapter. Now that you've decluttered, we can add to that. Since you've likely gotten most of your clutter-prone surfaces clear, we'll need to keep them that way.

Floors and surfaces (tables, counters, couches, and anywhere else that you can randomly put things down) should stay clear unless they are meant for storage. For example, a bookshelf is a surface that should have books on it, but it shouldn't be a landing space for things that you don't have another place to put at that moment.

- As a side note, you *are* going to put random things down where they don't go. Expect that to happen, and don't beat yourself up about it. But having the general standard that your floors stay clear, and things don't randomly land on surfaces, will reduce your daily maintenance and keep your rooms looking less overwhelming.

Before we jump into your step-by-step organization plan, let's bring back some important components from earlier. You'll again be breaking things down into smaller parts to make them more manageable. Using time blocks will be helpful here as well. This means looking at your schedule and seeing where you might be able to devote a half hour or an hour to organizing. If you need to start with smaller blocks of time to get going, that works too. Remember that the biggest investment is upfront when getting organized. This may look like a bunch of 10-minute sessions, several half-hour sessions, or a couple of half days devoted to getting organized. After that, maintenance will take less time. But you'll also have learned the strategies you need to achieve organization because it is likely that there will be times in the future when you need to use these strategies again.

Don't forget, these tasks are a great opportunity to listen to your favorite music, or podcast, or to catch up with a friend by phone or video.

Once you've got these basics down, it's time to get organized!

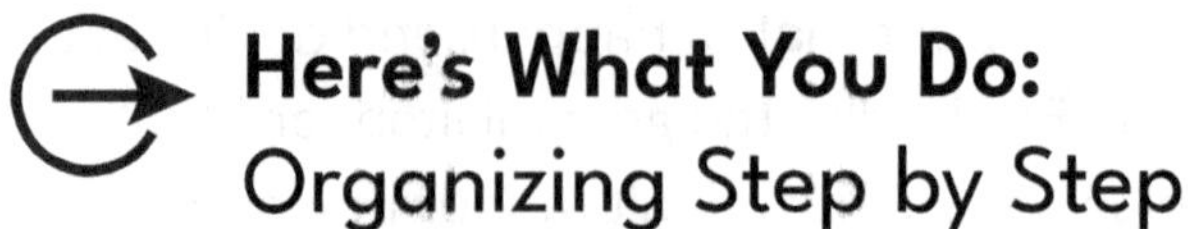

Here's What You Do:
Organizing Step by Step

STEP 1:
CHOOSE A STARTING POINT

Start with the high-traffic rooms. These are the places that get used the most.

- Living room
- Kitchen
- Hallways
- Bathroom
- Home office
- Then you'll move onto the low-traffic areas.
- Closets
- Basement/Attic
- Guest room
- Formal dining room
- Patio

Starting with your high-traffic areas, give you the most opportunity to see and feel the outcomes of your accomplishments. This is rewarding and encourages you to keep it going much more than spending time organizing an area where you don't even spend time every day.

Once you've chosen a room, quick wins feed our need for immediate gratification and are more likely to keep us going. With that in mind, choose your quickest win first. This is the spot in the room that needs the least amount of work. Whether that's straightening up your bookshelf, arranging the board games more neatly, or organizing your office supplies.

Once that's done, choose your next quickest win, and so on.

Ultimately, if the room is altogether so disorganized that finding a quick win isn't possible, then choose one spot to start in and move around the room clockwise.

To give you a sense of the size of the spots you'll be working on, you shouldn't have to walk to access different areas of the spot. It should generally all be accessible when sitting, kneeling, or standing in the same place.

STEP 2:
DECIDE WHAT STAYS

It's very likely that you'll have things in each room that have no business being in that room. So, if you left a book in the kitchen because that's where you were last reading it, then it goes back to the bookshelf or to your reading area.

You'll consider larger items, like furniture, as well as smaller objects when deciding what stays and what needs to go.

If smaller items need to be moved elsewhere, have a bin handy where you can put them for now and distribute them correctly later.

STEP 3:
MAKE IT MAKE SENSE

If the item is in the correct room, it now needs to be in the right spot. When choosing the right spot, consider what the item is, so that you can keep similar items together, and make sure the space you choose aligns with the item's function and frequency of use.

Objects should be in relatively close proximity to where you'll be when you need them. They should also be more easily accessible the more frequently they are used. On the other hand, something that is used once a month, can be stored away as long as you know where it is.

Once you've decided to store things together in one place, keep the similar items together, and also the larger or heavier items go toward the bottom or in the back. This way you can still easily see and get to the smaller items.

Things that are meant to be displayed should be arranged intentionally whether that's by type, genre, color, alphabetically, etc. If it doesn't need to be out and visible, consider storing things in a basket, bin, or drawer. Even if things are arranged well, a room can look messy if there are too many small things visible at a glance. If it can be put away, without sacrificing accessibility, the room will look neater overall.

Finally, get a label maker. As you decide where things go, out of sight – out of mind can cause more difficulty for us in remembering that things do actually have a place to go, or remembering where to find them. Once you give items a home, make a label for that spot, so that you know what's in that drawer, bin, basket, etc.

STEP 4:
MAINTENANCE

In addition to decluttering, you may want to add daily organizing. You can add another 10-15 min if needed to your decluttering routine daily to make sure that you take the time to organize things that may have gotten messy. Ultimately, if you are maintaining daily, it's unlikely you'll need a full half hour to declutter and organize, but it's worth blocking it out.

Do a run-through, decluttering first, then go back and organize the specific areas that need it. If your home tends to get very disorganized on a regular basis and the daily maintenance isn't enough to keep it at bay, consider a longer time block once per week. For example, you might set aside 1hr every week to more effectively organize the areas that need it.

Using these strategies, you can achieve a clutter free and organized house and maintain it with a maximum of 30 minutes per day and 1 hour per week.

Progress, Not Perfection

By now, you've gained specific strategies to help you achieve and maintain organization. While the specific steps offered are constructed to help you achieve your goals while facing executive dysfunction difficulties, it is also crucial to practice self-compassion.

Nothing will have you throwing in the towel faster than beating yourself up or telling yourself that you just can't do it. Learning how to organize and keep things that way is not an overnight process. It will take some time, but with practice, you'll get there.

Try to acknowledge your accomplishments daily, and cut yourself some slack when you slip up, recognizing that you can always get back up and try again.

Another thing to be mindful of is that not every person with ADHD, executive dysfunction, and difficulties with organization struggles in exactly the same way. Look for opportunities to adapt strategies to meet your needs. If something isn't working, think about why and how it could be better. Don't be afraid to experiment as you figure out what works for you.

Lastly, like with any other strategy in this book, expect slip-ups. They are going to happen. They don't mean you can't be successful. Progress is still occurring even when there are slip-ups in between. Perfectionism is often a blocker for us and it stops us from taking action. Instead, focus on making progress, little by little.

Pro Tips for Getting and Staying Organized with ADHD

- Build solid habits by establishing 'forever homes' for important items.
- Use habit stacking to leverage existing habits to help you create new habits.
- Declutter first
    1. Choose a spot.
    2. Grab your garbage bags (donate / toss).
    3. Start sorting.
    4. Keep up the momentum.
    5. Use music.
    6. Maintain with 15 min a day.
- Get organized
    1. Start in high-traffic rooms and aim for quick wins first.
    2. Decide what stays in that room, set aside what needs to go and distribute those things later.
    3. Be intentional about where and how things are arranged. Consider type, function, and frequency of use. Label storage spaces.
    4. Maintain in 15 min per day and 1hr weekly as needed.
- Practice self-compassion.
- It's about progress, not perfection.
- You are unique. Make it work for you.

DAY 6.

TAKING COMMAND WITH IMPULSE CONTROL

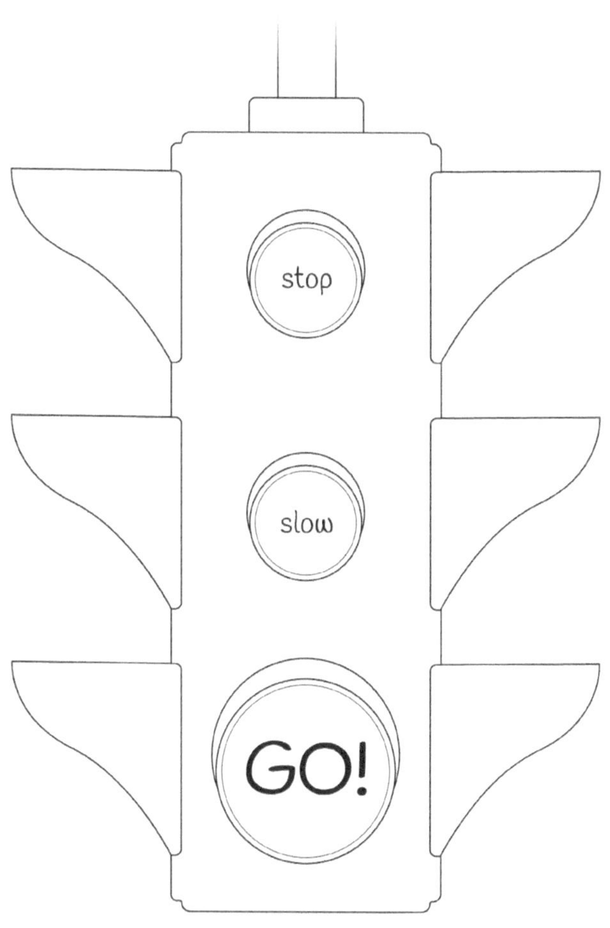

Impulsivity is essentially doing things without thinking ahead (Ramsay, 2021). The concept of thinking ahead refers to planning and considering potential outcomes or consequences. When we act without planning or consideration for potential outcomes and consequences, this can have significant negative impacts on our daily life.

Not every person with ADHD and executive function deficits will struggle with impulsivity. But many do. If your impulsive behaviors are negatively impacting your relationships, career, health, or any other part of your life, then this may be an important chapter for you.

The impacts of impulsivity are often underestimated. It's not just interrupting others or deciding to take a spontaneous trip. Severe impacts from impulsivity can include the following and more:

- Impulsive purchases beyond one's financial means, resulting in debt.
- Engaging in risky behaviors such as reckless behaviors or substance use.
- Confrontations and escalated conflicts.
- Skipping important responsibilities.
- Quitting a job without having a plan.
- Giving an automatic "yes" or "no" to requests, leads us to be overextended or to be perceived as oppositional.

In addition to difficulty planning ahead, impulsivity is also associated with dopamine chasing. This is when we engage in behaviors or activities that give us a quick dopamine boost. In other words, we get immediate gratification without thinking of the potential consequences or long-term impacts of the behavior. Impulsive purchases, unhealthy food choices, or excessive social media use are all examples of dopamine chasing.

Additionally, impulsivity can amplify the responses associated with our emotional regulation difficulties. So not only will we feel an intense emotional reaction, but we may also be driven to act impulsively in response to our extreme emotions. This is less about the dopamine boost and more about our inability to self-regulate.

The opposite of impulsivity is impulse control, otherwise known as response inhibition. This is when we resist or interrupt our initial response to a stimulus or situation. This may look like waiting for our turn to speak even though we want to jump in with our thoughts right away, not purchasing the thing we have in our online shopping cart because we know that we really don't need it, and the cost is way out of our budget for this month, not immediately sending that angry email to your boss letting her know that you quit as soon as she assigns you yet another project despite how busy you are. Response inhibition is when you can hold off on doing those things in favor of more careful consideration before taking action.

Therefore, the work here is in learning to intentionally plan ahead and to avoid or manage risk.

Your Self-Concept Matters

As with anything that we are new to learning and practicing, we can count on messing up at one point or another. But with practice, we can significantly reduce the frequency and level of risk as well as better manage how we handle slip-ups. However, he emphasizes that we need to first get rid of the thought that we have "no control" over our impulsive behaviors.

While control may be difficult, the most unhelpful thing you could do is characterize yourself as someone who just cannot manage it. This self-concept would lead anyone to be highly unsuccessful in their efforts to change this behavior, if they made any efforts at all.

Jeremy worked at an outlet store selling high-end skincare and cosmetics. It was a fast-paced role, and the days were never the same. There was a lot of work to be done, but Jeremy considered himself one of the hardest workers on that team. Additionally, Jeremy had good relationships with many of the customers he interacted with.

One day, Jeremy had a particularly difficult customer. Jeremy had also been under stress in his personal life lately, so he was feeling spread pretty thin. This customer seemed impossible to satisfy. They were finding fault with everything Jeremy suggested and they seemed to want something that didn't exist. So at the height of his stress at that moment, Jeremy decided he was done with this conversation.

"You're totally right, I don't think there is anything here for you. Please find somewhere else to make your purchase since we don't seem to be cutting it for you." As he said this he walked away and left the customer standing there.

Understandably, the customer complained. Jeremy's boss approached him about 15 minutes later. She asked Jeremy to take the rest of the day off and suggested they meet the following morning to discuss how they would move forward to avoid this happening again.

Jeremy was embarrassed and angry that his boss didn't see his side of things. Jeremy was a top performer. This customer was in the wrong. Jeremy didn't think twice when he said, "Don't worry about it, I won't be back." He walked out and didn't answer the phone call that came from his boss the next day.

While Jeremy hadn't been thinking of quitting, he had been feeling frustrated with a lot of things in his personal life, and he did have a history of making snap decisions like this when he was especially stressed. But in his mind, it was all because of one customer. He struggled to see how it wasn't the interaction with the customer at all, but actually, his impulsive behavior that had ultimately cost him this job. And he had made this decision without considering whether he was financially ready or recognizing that this could ruin his chance at getting a reference from the place where he had invested 3 years of hard work.

Jeremy might have benefitted from a strategy that was taught to me by a former client. During a session, where the topic of discussion that day was impulse control, a client shared that he had often struggled with saying things that would get him into trouble. He shared that what helped him was learning to ask 3 questions to decide whether or not to say something that was on his mind.

1. Does it need to be said?
2. Does it need to be said by me?
3. Does it need to be said by me right now?

I later researched and discovered that the person who came up with these 3 steps was Craig Ferguson, comedian and late-night show host, who has long been open about his own struggles with mental health and substance use.

The client who shared this said that this strategy had really resonated with him because he often struggled with impulsively saying things that he would later regret. He made it a point to memorize these 3 steps and apply them in both social and professional situations where he would have otherwise said something and wished he hadn't.

He gave the example of when he was recently out to dinner with some friends. He shared that when he and his friends went out, they usually split the bill evenly at the end of the night. But they had one friend who always insisted on asking for their own separate bill to pay for only what they had. They weren't technically in the wrong for doing this, but this client knew it rubbed everyone in their friend group the wrong way. So during their most recent dinner out, when the bill came, this client looked over to that friend and thought he might throw a sarcastic comment about him asking for his separate check again.

But because it felt like a quick decision, he decided to run it through the three questions in his head.

1. Does it need to be said?
   Yes. Someone should say it because everyone just talks about it behind his back and resents him for it.

2. Does it need to be said by me?
   Probably not. It's not something he's doing just to me, and anyone else could say something as well. If I'm the only one who feels the need to say something in this moment, maybe I should hold off.

3. Does it need to be said by me right now?
   I would be doing it now to shame him into doing the right thing. It would definitely embarrass him and if nobody else says anything to back me up, this could get awkward.

He decided this does need to be addressed, but that he could probably find a better way to address it.

By using this technique, he avoided an embarrassing moment and the possibility of straining his relationship with his friend. Ultimately, his awareness of his impulsivity, is what allowed him to implement this technique when he needed it.

So how do you become more aware of your impulses?"

Awareness is Key

Building awareness in this context means identifying the scenarios that lead to the most impulsivity in our lives. He suggests that by having a better understanding of these scenarios, we can create plans to respond in healthier ways. Dr. Crystal Lee (2021) also emphasizes recognizing one's 'weak spots' to be better prepared and more equipped to navigate moments and triggers that increase the likelihood of impulsive behavior.

There are many strategies that can be used to mitigate impulsivity, but without first understanding when you are most at risk, it can be hard to establish an effective game plan.

Here's What You Do: Identifying Risky Situations and Triggers

Here are some examples of situations that may escalate the risk of impulsivity.

- Social gatherings
- Work meetings
- During holiday sales
- When approaching important deadlines

Can you think of events, places, or situations that tend to increase your own impulsivity? If you consider the list above, these are common things we all encounter, but to someone with impulse control issues, these can present significant difficulties.

What are the events or situations that have led to some impulsive behaviors on your part?

Consider your own history. List 5 situations in which you are more prone to impulsive behavior and share an example of what impulsive behavior occurred and why it was problematic.

❶ Situation:

What happened? Why was this problematic?

❷ Situation:

What happened? Why was this problematic?

❸ Situation:

What happened? Why was this problematic?

❹ Situation:

What happened? Why was this problematic?

5 Situation:

What happened? Why was this problematic?

____

____

____

____

In addition to situations, we can also have personal factors that increase our likelihood of behaving impulsively. Personal factors can include feelings, thoughts, behaviors, etc. Whereas the situations listed above are external factors that originate from something outside of yourself, personal factors start with you. They are in your own mind, or a result of your own choices. Some examples include:

- Anger
- Boredom
- Alcohol use
- Loneliness

Think back to times when you were impulsive. Do certain feelings or behaviors usually precede your impulsivity?

Now just like in the exercise above, list 5 personal factors that have been associated with impulsive behavior and describe what happened.

Understanding your emotional response to these personal factors is another crucial aspect of managing your impulsivity. As you complete the exercise below, try to identify what emotion was associated with the personal factor you experienced.

Common emotions might include:

- Anger
- Frustration
- Excitement
- Fear

- Joy
- Sadness
- Surprise
- Disappointment
- Embarrassment

Remember you could have experienced an emotion that is not on this list, and it's possible to experience more than one emotion at a time.

After you identify the emotion, you'll be asked to rate the intensity of it. This will help you get a better idea of how different personal factors impact you and how the intensity of your emotions may influence your impulsivity.

❶ Personal Factor: ____________________

What emotion(s) did you experience at this time? ____________________

Rate the intensity of the emotion(s) on a scale of 1-10 where 1 = barely felt it and 10 = the most intense I've ever experienced. ____________________

What happened? Why was this problematic?

____

____

____

____

❷ Personal Factor: ______________________________

What emotion(s) did you experience at this time? ______________________________

Rate the intensity of the emotion(s) on a scale of 1-10 where 1 = barely felt it and 10 = the most intense I've ever experienced. ______________________________

What happened? Why was this problematic?

____

____

____

____

❸ Personal Factor: ______________________________

What emotion(s) did you experience at this time? ______________________________

Rate the intensity of the emotion(s) on a scale of 1-10 where 1 = barely felt it and 10 = the most intense I've ever experienced. ______________________________

What happened? Why was this problematic?

____

____

____

____

④ Personal Factor: ______________________

What emotion(s) did you experience at this time? ______________________

Rate the intensity of the emotion(s) on a scale of 1-10 where 1 = barely felt it and 10 = the most intense I've ever experienced. ______________________

What happened? Why was this problematic?

____

____

____

____

⑤ Personal Factor: ______________________

What emotion(s) did you experience at this time? ______________________

Rate the intensity of the emotion(s) on a scale of 1-10 where 1 = barely felt it and 10 = the most intense I've ever experienced. ______________________

What happened? Why was this problematic?

____

____

____

____

Now, having acknowledged that these are higher risk scenarios, you'll want to establish some game plans for reducing those risks during these times. As you start to create a more detailed picture of the situations that lead to impulsivity, you'll be able to consider the array of potential game plans to mitigate the frequency and severity of these actions. Later in this section, we'll take a closer look at how to create your own game plan to improve your impulse control.

Impulse Control Tactics

When practicing new skills to improve your impulse control, it's important to recognize that change does not happen quickly. It takes some time and practice to figure out which strategies are most effective for you and which strategies are most effective for which situations and triggers. Throughout this process, self-compassion, acknowledging the normalcy of setbacks, and using these setbacks as opportunities to learn more about yourself and your needs, is crucial (Lee, 2021; Ramsay, 2021).

The following strategies can help you better manage impulse control and mitigate the risks associated with these behaviors.

DELAY

This strategy involves pausing before making decisions or taking action. It's about creating a buffer between the impulse and the action, giving yourself the chance to think things through. Ways to do this include:

- Implementing a 24-hour rule for decisions that do not need to be made immediately.
- Practicing the phrase "let me check and get back to you" before you give a confirmation.
- Stepping away and allowing yourself to de-escalate rather than responding during high stress – (i.e., elevated heartbeat, tense muscles, or other physical cues of stress are not the best time to respond)

CREATE OBSTACLES

This means adding extra steps or barriers between you and an impulsive action. Some examples of this may be:

- Keeping your credit card in a drawer rather than saving it on shopping sites or keeping it in your wallet.
- Not keeping unhealthy snacks in your home.
- Keeping alcohol in a locked liquor cabinet and storing the key somewhere that takes some effort to get to. (This strategy applies to impulsive alcohol use rather than alcohol addiction.)

REMOVE TRIGGERS

This involves identifying and eliminating the things in your environment that cause impulsive behaviors, when possible.

- If you know that poor sleep almost always leads you to be impulsive, then focusing on improving your sleep routine is key.
- If having shopping apps that send your coupons or make purchasing quick and easy contribute to your spending, consider deleting those apps and only using your computer to make these purchases.
- If going to certain places triggers impulsive behavior, avoid those places if possible, and if not possible to avoid them, try to bring a supportive person with you.

SURROUND YOURSELF WITH THE RIGHT PEOPLE

- If certain people you interact with are negative influences, limit your engagement with them or be strategic about how and when you spend time with them.
- Surround yourself with people who understand your struggles with impulsivity and are supportive of your efforts to manage it.

HAVE CONTINGENCY PLANS.

This strategy involves having a plan B in case your first plan is derailed by an impulsive decision and having a backup plan in mind.

- If you cannot avoid a person or place that usually triggers you, explore what other barriers you could put in place to slow down your typical impulsive responses.
- If you tend to overspend regardless of your budget, you might want to keep a completely separate savings account with limited ability to withdraw without going to the bank or having to call.

EMOTIONAL MANAGEMENT SKILLS

These are also an integral part of mitigating impulsive behavior, as impulsivity commonly follows extreme emotions. For a more detailed exploration and exercises to manage emotional responses, please see Day 8.

Here's What You Do:
Create a Game Plan

Having acknowledged your higher-risk scenarios, and after learning common strategies to manage impulse control, it's time to establish a game plan.

The following table has some examples that may or may not be high-risk scenarios for you to engage in impulsive behavior. Include your own examples in the rest of the chart and your corresponding risks and game plans.

Situation or Personal Factor	Potential Risks	Game Plan
Alcohol Use	I probably won't filter as well and I could say something that would annoy or upset people.	I'm going to pace myself at one drink per hour and drink water in between so that I can stay in better control of my behavior.
Anger	I could overreact and say or do something I'll regret.	I'm going to give myself 24hrs before I say anything to the person or take any action in response to the situation that is making me angry.
Social Gatherings	I could interrupt others or easily overshare things that I shouldn't.	I'm going to intentionally let people get to the end of their sentences before I jump in, and I'm going to try to match their level of openness.
Holiday Sales	I spend more than I can afford or buy things that I don't need and likely won't use.	Knowing that the holiday sales are coming up, I'm going to write out my bills and my expected income for this month so that I know exactly how much I can spend frivolously. I'm also going to lock my credit card in my file cabinet.

Once you have this list, keep it somewhere you can easily go back to it. Keep a copy on your phone and somewhere visible in your home so that you are frequently reminded of your high-risk scenarios, potential consequences, and game plans.

Feeling Your Success

If considering the negative consequences of an action isn't doing it for you, Barkley (2021) suggests envisioning being successful in whatever your goal would be in that particular situation. He encourages us to really imagine and allow ourselves to feel the emotions associated with the positive outcome. From there, rather than avoiding certain actions, we should be aiming for specific kinds of behavior that end up working against what our impulsive actions might have been.

The power of this strategy is in the detailed imagery and exploration of positive emotions.

You can apply this to the scenarios that you have already identified as risks for impulsive behavior. Whereas you previously created a game plan to mitigate behavior, you'll now create a vision to experience positive outcomes and identify the behaviors that would be necessary to achieve success.

Nora had always had a somewhat rocky relationship with her sister Isabel. Nora's impulsive behavior often led to spontaneous outbursts when they disagreed. Nora almost always regretted these outbursts because she really wanted to have a close relationship with her sister. She just felt passionate when it came to the discussions and disagreements they would have.

One day, Isabel asked Nora to be the maid of honor at her wedding. Nora was happily surprised. She accepted immediately, but almost just as quickly, she began to worry about how they would navigate wedding planning. The maid of honor had a large role in planning aspects leading up to and in the wedding. She knew these interactions were likely to be tense, and she didn't want to risk damaging their relationship or negatively impacting Isabel's wedding experience in any way.

Nora decided to adopt a new strategy. Rather than telling herself repeatedly not to have an outburst and trying to reign herself in, she instead visualized having fun and meaningful conversations with her sister as they planned her wedding together. She visualized making memories that the two of them would cherish for years. She imagined this process bringing them even closer and Isabel later being able to do the same for Nora when her own wedding was being planned. She played out potential disagreements in her mind and imagined handling them in a way that she could be proud of, which would really show her maturity and consideration for Isabel on her big day. She felt peace, hope, and a genuine sense of accomplishment at her own growth in the process.

Nora zoned in on what actions she would have to take to reach this goal. She would need to prioritize Isabel's preferences and feelings. She would need to actively listen and show that she cared and understood. She would need to tactfully share her own view if it differed from her sisters with the continued underlying goal of working together to create the best experience for Isabel and closeness for them both. She would need to recognize and breathe through moments of frustration or step away at times if needed.

As the process moved forward, during every conversation with Isabel about bridesmaid dresses, or seating arrangements, she would recall her detailed visualization. It was like she had been in these situations before, and she could recall how she would have navigated it and feel her motivation for taking that approach.

Of course, there were times when Nora found herself wanting to say or do something to get her point across, and in the most difficult times, she did ask Isabel for a time out during those conversations. Isabel did notice the difference in their interaction and pointed it out to Nora. She saw that it was a major difference, and she thanked her. Nora had taken the opportunity to strengthen their bond as she had hoped. And despite having moments where she could have lost it, she was proud of herself for maintaining control.

Detailed imagery and connecting to the emotions associated with that imagery can be a powerful tool and motivator for behavior change. Let's take a moment to consider how you might apply this strategy in your own life.

Here's What You Do: Immerse Yourself in Your Success

Consider the scenarios that have been difficult for you. The following prompts will have you complete a journal writing exercise to coincide with fully immersing yourself in your own success.

Start with a situation where you want or need to practice impulse control. Write about your ultimate goal in this situation. What does a totally successful outcome look like? Give details. Really picture what might happen. What would you do? How might others react?

Next, as you are envisioning being successful, consider what emotions are coming up for you. What does reaching this goal feel like? How does it make you feel about yourself and your potential for the future? How does it change your perception of yourself or how you think others might see you?

Now, we'll consider the actions that you would need to take to make this successful outcome a reality. What would come first, next, and so on. Imagine potential barriers or difficult moments. How might you navigate them in order to be successful? What things will you need to remember? How will you remind yourself?

Stick With It

Impulse control can be a struggle for lots of people, but it can be especially difficult for someone with executive function deficits related to ADHD. As you have learned, the expectation is not that you will never engage in another impulsive action. This would be unrealistic. But it is very attainable to start practicing the strategies you have learned here and significantly reduce the frequency and severity of your impulsive behaviors.

By learning to home in on the situations and personal factors that put you at the greatest risk for impulsivity and by establishing personalized game plans to address these situations before you get into them, you will put yourself in a better position to more carefully consider the actions you want to take. This makes you more likely to improve relationships, mitigate financial struggles, and better your professional reputation.

If you are like many people that don't do well with focusing on what they should not do, you may benefit from focusing on the best possible outcome in extreme detail so that you can immediately picture it in your mind when needed and tie it to strong emotions that motivate you to succeed.

Pro Tips for Impulse Control

- It takes practice. You will slip up, but it will get better.
- Know your triggers so that you can be prepared.
- Explore and experiment with various game plans to mitigate your impulsive behaviors.
- When strong emotions are tied to vivid imagery, these can be a powerful motivating influence. Use this to encourage your own success with impulse control.

DAY 7.

DEVELOPING FLEXIBLE THINKING

2 faces or a cup?

Flexible thinking, also known as cognitive flexibility, is our ability to shift our thinking and adapt to new situations, rules, or demands. This involves the ability to see things from other perspectives, tolerate change, problem-solve creatively, and think 'outside the box.' If you've ever heard the saying 'go with the flow', this is also based on our ability to think flexibly.

The opposite of cognitive flexibility is cognitive rigidity. You experience this when you are stubbornly attached to a particular thought, plan, or perspective. Sudden changes in plans might lead to significant stress and frustration, conflicts, difficulty engaging, or withdrawal altogether from the situation.

How Flexible Are You?

Let's take a moment to reflect on your cognitive flexibility. The following activity will help you explore your reactions in situations that call for cognitive flexibility.

For each of the following sentences, fill in the blank with how you typically feel or react. Try not to overthink your responses, as your first answer will often be a good indication of what happens.

There are no right or wrong answers here. Remember to answer with what you think happens, rather than how you believe you *should* respond. The goal of this activity is to gain deeper insight into your thought processes and patterns.

1 When an unexpected change occurs in my schedule, I usually

---

2 When someone disagrees with me, I typically

3	When faced with an unfamiliar task at work, I usually	
4	If I have to switch tasks unexpectedly, I tend to	
5	When my usual way of doing things isn't working, I	
6	If I make a mistake, my initial reaction is to	
7	If my plans suddenly change, I feel	
8	When I receive feedback that I disagree with, I usually	
9	If someone suggests a new approach to a task that I'm familiar with, I tend to	
10	When presented with a new perspective that challenges my current beliefs, my first response is to	

Now let's dive a bit deeper into your responses to start looking for patterns in your reactions and to consider the effectiveness of those patterns in your daily life.

LOOK FOR PATTERNS

Take a moment to review your answers to the completed questions above. Try to notice any recurring themes or patterns.

Use the spaces provided to answer the following questions that will guide your reflection:

1. Were there any responses that indicated your reactions were based on feeling stressed, confused, frustrated, or some other kind of discomfort? Are there specific types of scenarios that seem to cause these reactions?

____

____

____

____

2. Are there instances where you notice sticking with your initial plan or thought even when circumstances change? Identify these moments and consider why you might be responding this way.

____

____

____

____

3. Are there situations where you have found it hard to consider or appreciate different perspectives from your own? Reflect on why this might be challenging in those situations.

____

____

____

____

EVALUATE EFFECTIVENESS

Now you'll start to think about the impacts of these responses. Reflect on the following questions and write your thoughts in the spaces provided.

1. For each response you noted, consider if it helped navigate the situation effectively or if it added to your stress. Write down your thoughts here.

2. Reflect on how your responses impacted your relationships with others involved in the situation. Did your reactions enhance your interactions? Did they lead to misunderstanding? Record your reflections below.

3. Did your responses help you to reach your desired outcomes in those situations? Do you feel your reactions helped you progress or hindered you? Share your thoughts below.

As you develop your awareness of your own patterns and the impacts of your responses, you'll become more aware of your specific situations in which you may want to cultivate more cognitive flexibility.

Why Does Cognitive Flexibility Matter?

Difficulties with cognitive flexibility can cause stress and difficulty coping with:

- Changes in procedures at work.
- Last minute changes in social plans.
- Detours or delays in your normal commute.
- General disruptions in your schedule, normal routine, or expected plans.
- Changes in group or social dynamics.
- Adapting to new software or technology.
- Working on a team where cooperating with multiple personalities and perspectives is expected.

Learning to think more flexibly will help you to be more adaptable, which means more effective in these changing situations. It will also reduce your overall feelings of stress and being overwhelmed when life throws you curveballs. Unexpected changes are a normal part of life and the more we can go with the flow, the more successful we'll be at work, home, in our social lives, and everywhere in between.

Sarah struggled with ADHD, which in many ways led her to be spontaneous and impulsive. But in her own way, she was a creature of habit. She liked having her own structure and preferred it when things went according to plan. If they went differently, she liked to be ready for that or in control of it, rather than it just happening to her.

Sarah realized that her rigidity was causing issues in several areas. At work, her team, which had previously just been herself and a colleague, had expanded to 5. Her supervisor was working on establishing new processes for things that Sarah had developed her own consistent way of doing. She was struggling with resistance and resentment toward these new processes and these new colleagues. Whereas she used to know what she was doing, now, she felt like she didn't know anything. She was even thinking about looking for other jobs because it all just felt like too much.

Additionally, her partner whom she did not live with was trying to be more "helpful" lately. He was cleaning up and organizing things that she had not asked him to and putting things in places she would not normally put them. This had stressed her out to the point of arguments a few times. He said that he couldn't understand why she was so mad at him when he was only trying to help.

Sarah knew that the issue was her own ability to cope with these shifts in her daily life. Although she had urges to leave her job and tell her partner to just stop trying to be helpful, she knew that this was something she needed to work on.

She started with small changes. She wanted to try different ways of doing things to get more comfortable adapting to change. She thought about ways she could start intentionally experiencing changes in situations in her life that she wouldn't normally want to change.

She tried things like ordering a different type of latte in the morning, taking a different route to work, she even tried approaching a task that was normally part of her job and doing it in a way that one of her colleagues did. She knew they did it differently, but never felt any reason to change her own approach. This time she intentionally wanted to try it someone else's way. She tried to hold onto the intention of better understanding this approach and considering what they liked about it, rather than judging it and shutting it down the way she had in the past.

Sarah continued looking for opportunities to strengthen her flexibility. She noticed moments when she would automatically want to revert to her way of doing something and she used that as her signal to be open to someone else's way of doing it. She was realistic with herself in that she still might prefer her own way, but she would try to stay open-minded to learn more about the other person's approach.

Through intentionally practicing these small changes, Sarah got better at handling change in her life and considering other people's perspectives became easier. She still had a way she preferred to do things, but she no longer felt the changes at work were terrible enough to leave her job, and she learned to consider her partner's perspective. She didn't stop getting annoyed overnight, but she didn't allow this particular issue to cause arguments between them anymore as she practiced appreciating the reason that he was doing these things. As she got better at this, she also noticed she felt less stressed overall, which was a personal benefit that made her efforts worth it.

Here's What You Do:
Try Different Experiences

Sarah's approach to improving her cognitive flexibility is actually suggested by professionals who work with individuals seeking to improve their own cognitive flexibility. The idea is that by leaning into our rigidity, we only continue to reinforce it. But by routinely changing things and opening ourselves to new experiences, we can improve our cognitive flexibility the same way we build a muscle, and we can begin to intentionally build our comfortability with change, better adapt, and improve our cognitive flexibility (Cummins, 2022).

To implement this strategy, you'll need to start looking for opportunities to change your own routines and add new experiences that you otherwise might not have wanted to do. Look for things that you can do differently in your daily life, similar to Sarah's choices.

As you explore ways to change your routine and add new experiences, consider areas of your life that have become automatic or strictly habitual. Some possibilities can include the following:

- If you always cook the same types of meals, try adding a new recipe or substituting ingredients to change it up.
- If your workouts are typically the same, you can add a change here. If you usually run, you can try replacing a day or two with yoga. If you typically workout alone, you can consider adding a once a week workout class.
- If you often watch the same types of shows or read the same genre of books, try something different that you wouldn't normally watch or read. This could be a good opportunity to try something that's been suggested by friends or family.
- If you normally go to the same place for coffee or lunch, you could try a different spot.
- If a colleague or supervisor previously suggested approaching a task in a way that you were not receptive to, this is a good reason to try it.

You can also consider changes that come at you unexpectedly and practice leaning into them with the intention to understand and strengthen your cognitive flexibility muscles.

Over the next week, record 2 situations each day where you practiced cognitive flexibility. Try creating different experiences for yourself as well as giving yourself credit for adapting to and embracing changes that come your way.

This is also an opportunity to use your planner. You can enter the experiences that you plan to try in the days and times that it makes sense to do them. This way you will be more likely to follow through.

Next to these efforts, rate how you think you did each day. If it was absolutely awful and you resisted it the whole way, give yourself a 1, but if you did great and you think you'll be a flexible thinking pro in no time, give yourself a 10. Ratings can fall anywhere in between and are meant to help you reflect on your progress.

Day 1.		How did I do?	
Day 2.		How did I do?	
Day 3.		How did I do?	
Day 4.		How did I do?	
Day 5.		How did I do?	
Day 6.		How did I do?	
Day 7.		How did I do?	

Cognitive flexibility is not something that improves overnight, but experts are pretty united on the fact that it takes practice and that it can improve with continued effort. So continue adding opportunities to increase your flexible thinking every day, and you'll begin to feel the positive results in both your personal and professional life.

Being intentional about building cognitive flexibility is one way to do it, but as you'll see in the next section, there are also some efforts that you can make that may be a bit more indirect and potentially more fun.

Play Video Games

It has long been observed that certain types of video games, particularly action-oriented, fast-paced, first-person games can enhance information processing and logical comprehension. In 2013 a group of researchers tested whether real time strategy gaming could improve higher cognitive processes and specifically whether they could improve cognitive flexibility (Glass et al., 2013). The outcomes highlighted positive implications for people with ADHD and executive functioning deficits and confirmed that cognitive flexibility is trainable and that engaging in real time strategy games can improve flexible thinking (Glass et al., 2013).

The researchers found that these games worked to improve cognitive flexibility because they required the person playing them to manage multiple sources of information at one time, to rapidly switch between tasks, and to maintain information for extended periods, and to remember and use information about events that were occurring off screen at that time. This all resulted in essentially a complex exercise where the players used what the researchers referred to as "fast thinking."

So what does this mean for you? In real life, we often have to operate in ways that require us to rapidly switch from one task to another, to manage multiple pieces of information at once, and to remember things that are not in front of us to incorporate into our quick decision making. The relevance here for someone with ADHD is that these types of games can give us a place to practice and train these skills.

If you enjoy video games but have not played in a while, or if you generally have not tried video games because perhaps you feel they are not productive or are more of a teenage pastime, the reality is that they can be a great way to improve your cognitive flexibility skills. If this is an area you struggle with, you may want to consider giving them a try and incorporating them into your routine on a regular basis.

The benefits in these cognitive processes were seen from playing Real Time Strategy games. This is a subgenre of strategy games that allows all players to play simultaneously instead of taking turns.

There are always new games coming out, but the following list of Real Time Strategy games can give you a good place to start:

- Age of Empires
- Command and Conquer
- Northgard
- Homeworld

- Starcraft
- Lord of the Rings
- Dune
- Company of Heroes

Consider your relationship with video games. Maybe you're already an avid player, or maybe you just learned the best reason to give it a try. Moving forward we'll consider your self-talk and how you can be more open to change when it comes your way. And even if you're not a big video game fan, you can still take something from this. While the research presented here focused on the use of video games to train cognitive flexibility skills, it also proved that these skills are trainable when we actively and intensely use them. Activities like sports, particularly team sports, or other puzzle or brain training related games can be beneficial as well. So consider engaging more in activities that require you to juggle a lot of information at once, switch your focus quickly, and make fast decisions to give your own cognitive flexibility a workout.

Positive versus Negative Self Talk

When you experience a change that you didn't expect, it likely sets off a series of thoughts in your head. Your inner voice might be screaming that this is just not going to work, and throwing a fit about why people always do things like this.

These are examples of self-talk. When we tell ourselves that we just can't learn a new way, or that our whole day is ruined, or that we may as well throw in the towel because we can't handle this change, these are all examples of negative self-talk.

Positive self-talk would involve being more open to the potential good things that can come from these situations. Telling yourself that you might have something to learn here, or that this might give you a better opportunity to connect with or understand your peers.

Positive and encouraging self-talk doesn't just happen. Often the way we talk to ourselves is a learned behavior. By learned behavior, this means we picked it up along the way and that we can learn new ways.

I have a friend, we'll call her Tanya. She has ADHD and she tends to be very rigid in her automatic responses. If something is planned a certain way, she expects it to go that way. When something throws off her plans or interferes with her expectation of how things are going to go, she has trouble managing her frustration. This has often led to verbal conflicts or disengaging completely from the situation.

One day I was on the phone with Tanya, while she was waiting for documents related to a work visa while she was traveling. She had gone to the local government office to complete some part of the process, she had been meticulous about making sure she had done everything correctly. On this day, she was told that actually she needed to provide further information. She had taken considerable effort to get everything she needed, and at the eleventh hour she was being told she had needed to provide something else and that this was a normal request in the process.

Her first response was to get angry and to ask why she wasn't informed of that before. She felt it was their fault, because if they had told her, she would not be in this predicament. So she called me to pass some time after making some calls and waiting to see if she could get the supporting documents faxed over. While explaining the story to me she gave me the facts and then said, "But it's fine because it's just another opportunity to practice patience and tolerance. The universe is giving me lots of those lately, so I'm going to practice."

At first, I laughed, thinking she was being sarcastic. But she meant it. She said that she was trying to not let herself get so affected when things didn't go a certain way and that she was now trying to see these moments as lessons that she could learn from. Although I could still hear the tightness in her voice and the frustration at the whole ordeal, she was genuinely trying to turn her response around by changing her self-talk.

To this day, this has become one of her sayings. I remember it whenever I find myself in similar situations. I think, Tanya would be saying this was an opportunity to learn right now. She went from being someone who I saw as rigid and easily frustrated to someone who exemplified tolerating change and learning from it while still being totally human.

Here's What You Do: Looking for the Opportunity

Whether you call it positive self-talk, finding the silver lining, or seeing the opportunity, essentially, we are looking for the positive spin on a situation that you otherwise might not have chosen.

Consider 5 times that you can recall an unexpected change or shift in the way things were done that led to negative thoughts and feelings for you. Consider how leaning into this change might have benefited you. Explore these in the sections below.

- First Column: Describe the unexpected change you experienced.
- Second Column: What was your reaction.
- Third Column: What benefits could have resulted from leaning into or embracing the change? These can include:
    - How others perceived or interacted with you.
    - What you learned.
    - How you felt.
    - Your level of stress.

Unexpected change that led to negative thoughts/ feelings	My reaction	Potential benefits from embracing the change

Time to Start Training

Flexible thinking is a challenge for many of us who struggle with executive function difficulties in the context of ADHD. However, unlike some of the other skills deficits that need to be supplemented with external support, this particular skill can be trained and learned. It can be built like a muscle over time. This gives us the opportunity to take back control of the ways it has been hindering us in our personal and professional lives. The strategies that you learned today are a perfect starting point to improve your cognitive flexibility.

- Cognitive flexibility can impact all areas of our lives.
- Flexible thinking is something that can be improved with practice and training.
- Video games are an excellent evidence-based way to improve your cognitive flexibility.
- By intentionally experiencing new things, exposing yourself to changes in your normal routine, and leaning into the change that come your way, you'll become more adaptable.

- Self-talk plays a big role in your acceptance of change and your reactions when things change quickly.
- Positive self talk can help you remain calm and seek the opportunity when unexpected change happens.

DAY 8.

STRENGTHENING YOUR EMOTIONAL REGULATION

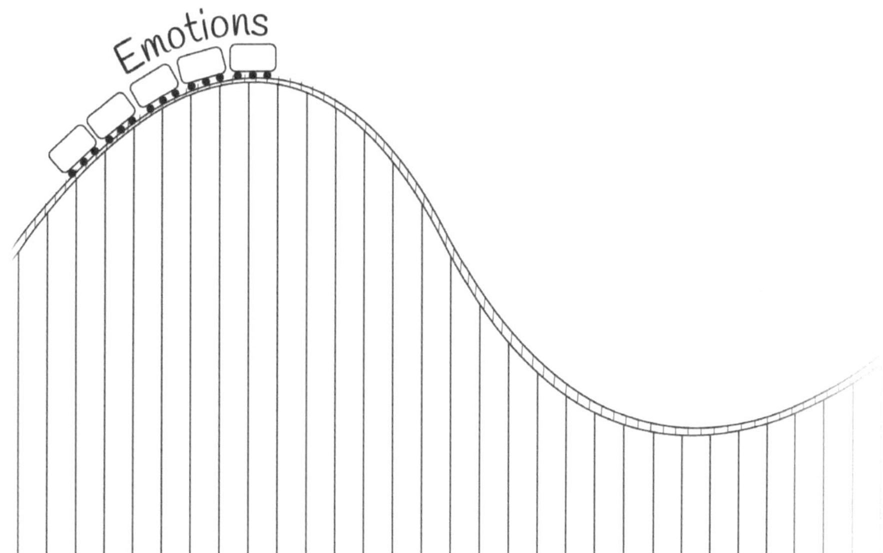

Emotional regulation can be one of the hardest skills to build when it comes to executive dysfunction. People with ADHD experience emotions more intensely than the average person (Brown, 2022). Essentially our brains have difficulty differentiating between minor issues and major ones, which often leads to overreactions and difficulty responding rationally.

According to Jonathan Hassall (2022), an ADHD and executive function coach, explains that people with ADHD can often generate beliefs, ideas, and feelings that can feel genuine yet have nothing to do with what happened. Emotional regulation issues are often interpreted by others as impulse control issues because of their connection to impulsive behavior. However, emotional regulation is different from impulse control. While our strong emotional reactions can certainly lead to impulsive behavior, they are not the same thing.

To look at this more closely, whenever anyone experiences something their brain automatically attempts to understand how they should respond to it by associating it with a past experience. This is our brain's first quick pass at understanding the situation and it's our best guess at that moment. Next, in a neurotypical person, self-regulation and emotional attention will kick in to consider the details, predict future possibilities and consider how to possibly intervene. All of this quiets the initial emotional response and allows the brain to fine tune its emotional reaction to be more appropriate to the situation. So essentially, the initial reaction is paused while the details and potential options are explored using the attention network in the brain. Externally, this allows the person to stop reacting and choose how they want to feel or act in response to the situation.

With ADHD and executive dysfunction, our difficulty is in that pause and attention happening at the right time and to the extent necessary to shift our immediate response. So, we often get stuck ruminating in that immediate reaction, making it feel like we have no control over how we're feeling in that moment.

The real issue occurs in that moment where the average person is able to pause, think, and override their initial response. Hassall (2022) points out that this is the moment where we can find the opportunity for change.

Self-Soothing Strategies

As we've discussed, our difficulties with emotional regulation can involve intense feelings and reactions to situations and triggers. Heightened emotions involve more activity in the amygdala which has an inverse relationship with areas of the prefrontal cortex responsible for logical thinking (Kim et al., 2016). This means that when we are feeling extreme emotions, we literally will have much more difficulty thinking clearly through situations.

This means that before we can consider a situation in detail or what our options might be for navigating it, we need to first calm our emotions so that our logical thought processes have more opportunity to get involved.

This is why understanding how to self-soothe is crucial. Self-soothing is about calming our heightened emotions when we need it. There are many strategies that can help with self-soothing, but not all of them will work for everyone. And not all of them can be implemented in every situation. This is why it's important for you to consider keeping a list on hand or adopting a few main ones that can be your "go to" strategies when you need them.

Not only does self-soothing open the door to appropriately handling a situation, but it also saves us from potentially embarrassing outbursts in professional or other public situations where we might really need to keep our cool.

Self-soothing also can involve grounding techniques. This is a strategy that involves bringing your focus back to physical sensations or your physical environment and taking it off your internal thoughts and feelings (Eddins, 2020).

Let's take a look at some of these grounding and self-soothing strategies so that you can consider which ones you might like to try:

GROUNDING TECHNIQUES **FOR STRESS MANAGEMENT**

When you practice a grounding technique, you are intentionally focusing on some aspect of the physical world around you or your physical experience. This helps calm you by moving your focus away from your intense thoughts and feelings. It's about letting those thoughts and feelings go for the moment to de-escalate and allow yourself to feel calmer. These techniques often engage one or more of your 5 senses.

- 5-4-3-2-1 technique
    - From wherever you are sitting or standing, focus on your surroundings and your physical experience. Name 5 things you can see, 4 things you can touch, 3 things you can hear, 2 things you can smell, and 1 thing you can taste.
- 3-4-5 breathing
    - Breathe in for 3 seconds, hold for 4 seconds, breathe out for 5 seconds. Repeat until you notice your body feeling calmer (your heart rate is slowed down, and your muscles are more relaxed).
- Hold an ice cube in your hands. You can move it around. Pay attention to the sensation.
- Place a cool washcloth over your face.
- Run cold water over your hands.
- Press your heels into the floor, taking note of the sensations.

PROGRESSIVE MUSCLE RELAXATION

This strategy helps to focus your mind, gives you physical sensations to focus on, and helps to overall relax your body. A relaxed body can help lead to a relaxed mind.

You can find many guides for progressive muscle relaxation exercises online. But essentially, they will involve the same components.

- You'll tense and relax each muscle group in your body, one muscle group at a time.
- You can start from the top of your body and work your way down or start from the bottom and work your way up.

- Muscle groups include:

    - The muscles in your forehead by raising your eyebrows or pulling them together.
    - Squeezing your eyes shut.
    - Your neck and shoulders, pulling your shoulders up to your ears.
    - Your biceps.
    - Your lower arms.
    - Squeezing your hands into a fist.
    - Tensing your abdomen.
    - Your quadriceps.
    - Etc.

- You don't have to perfectly attend to every single muscle. The overall goal is to tense the muscles throughout your body, one section at a time.
- Hold for 5 seconds.
- Then relax those muscles completely. As you relax them, say the word "relax."
- Pay attention to the sensations associated with the relaxation.
- Once you've gone through your entire body, notice how relaxed both your mind and body feel.

GENERAL SELF-SOOTHING STRATEGIES

- Enjoy a warm drink – cocoa, tea, coffee.

    - Focus on the sensations, smells, and taste as you drink it.

- Wrap yourself in a weighted blanket.
- Take a warm shower or bath.
- Burn candles or essential oils.

    - Lavender, vanilla, or any other scent you find relaxing.

- Listen to calming music for 10 minutes.
- Play with your pet for 10 minutes.
- Engage in activities with repeated motions like biking, swimming, knitting, etc.
- Put on music you can dance to (and dance).
- Use imagery.

    - Imagine a completely serene environment or a place that brings you peace and joy – imagine all of the details that your 5 senses would experience. Close your eyes and fully engage in the visualization.

- Use self-soothing phrases.

    - I'm safe.
    - It's okay.
    - Just Breathe.

Your self-soothing strategies can involve anything on this list or anything else that brings you joy or peace, even if it's not on this list.

Janel was in her 2nd week at a new job working at a customer service call center. There had been a lot of information to pick up quickly and she felt like she just kept messing up. The person training her was pretty patient overall, but at times she felt like she was even annoying them.

She could feel herself getting increasingly stressed and anxious. The customers were generally not happy by the time she spoke with them. After accidentally disconnecting a call, Janel reached a point where she felt ready to walk out. The feelings were rising, her face felt flushed, and she knew the tears were going to flow any second. She was fighting the urge to grab her bag and tell her trainer that this just wasn't for her.

She took a moment and decided to calmly leave the room. She told her trainer she was going to the bathroom. Janel had seen an enclosed balcony on the floor where their office was. It seemed like a place where employees could sit outside or have lunch. She needed to breathe. She went straight there and was relieved to see no one was there. She sat at the table that was directly under the sun and faced away from the building so that she was just looking out at the trees and other buildings. She closed her eyes and started to focus on her breathing. She continued to breathe slowly until the tightness in her throat went away, and she could feel her body relax.

She decided she would go back in and talk to her trainer. When she went back to the office, she told her trainer that she had just felt a bit overwhelmed, but that she was hopeful that she would catch on soon and she was going to stick with it. She asked if there was something else that she could work on right now so that she was still being productive but could step away from the phones for a bit. Her training was understanding and confirmed that they actually did have a lot of data that needed to be entered into the system. Janel was glad for the break and beyond that, she was glad she hadn't walked out.

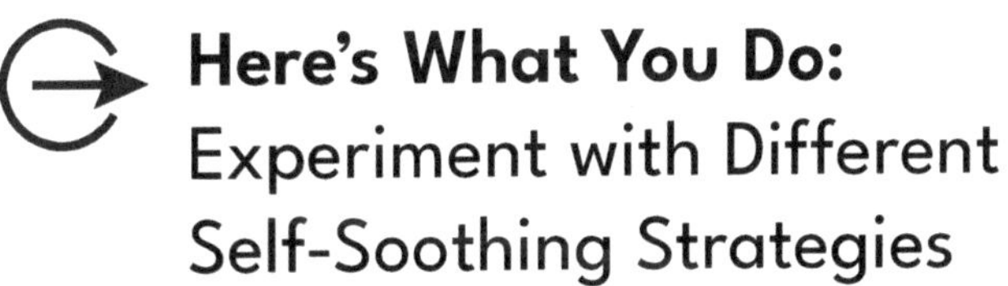

Here's What You Do: Experiment with Different Self-Soothing Strategies

Identify 3 self-soothing strategies you would like to try. Make sure that at least 1 or 2 can be done in places that you normally go outside of your home, such as work or the subway.

Now put these strategies in the notepad on your phone so that you can remember them wherever you are.

Take a moment to open up your planner and identify when you might be able to practice at least one of these strategies each day – even if you are not feeling overwhelmed. It's also a good idea to set some reminders or alerts on your phone if you're not using a calendar app that already does this. Try changing up the strategies you practice throughout the week.

Of course, use them if you do find yourself with heightened emotions, but this particular practice is outside of that. To get good at strategies like this, it's best to learn how to use them even when you are not feeling overly emotional. During these normal practices, take note of how you are feeling before and after. 1 = completely Zen and 10 = ready to explode.

For example – if my phone alarm goes off, telling me it's time to do my daily practice, I will first pause and assess how I'm feeling. Maybe I'm irritated and I'm at a 6. Then I will practice my strategy. When I'm done practicing, I'll take note of how calm I feel. Maybe after my strategy, I'm at a 3. Try strategies more than once, as the first time you do them, you're often focusing on getting it right, rather than really immersing yourself in feeling more relaxed.

You'll record these practices for a week below so that you can start to get an understanding of how different strategies are affecting you.

EXAMPLE DAY 1.

Pre-rating:	6	Strategy:	Progressive Muscle Relaxation	Post Rating:	3

Now record a full week here. After that, you can continue your own experimentation or tracking, or simply keep a reminder of strategies you want to try and practice them so that you are experienced with them when overwhelming emotions occur.

Day 1:

Pre-rating:		Strategy:		Post Rating:	

Day 2:

Pre-rating:		Strategy:		Post Rating:	

Day 3:

Pre-rating:		Strategy:		Post Rating:	

Day 4:

Pre-rating:		Strategy:		Post Rating:	

Day 5:

Pre-rating:		Strategy:		Post Rating:	

Day 6:

Pre-rating:		Strategy:		Post Rating:	

Day 7:

Pre-rating:		Strategy:		Post Rating:	

Now that you've learned how to de-escalate your emotions, let's move onto how to respond in healthier ways.

SOLVE

Hassall (2022) offers the SOLVE acronym as a solution to help stop the immediate reaction and rumination and move forward with more intention.

When you find yourself stuck in negative immediate reactions to something, he suggests that first you:

STOP

You might move to another room. If you're pacing, you sit down and breathe. Essentially, you're setting the stage, by changing your physical responses first.

OBJECTIVE LIST

Here, you list everything you know about the situation. Avoid putting any assumptions on this list. Only consider what you know to be factually true. This can help you recognize the extent to which your assumptions are influencing you.

VERBALIZE

Verbally state a solution to the issue at that moment. That solution might be seeking out further information or it might be taking action. State what the solution is and when you'll implement it.

EXIT

Move on to your next task. Shift your attention to focus on something other than what you were doing at the moment that you were triggered. If you need to return to it, that is okay. Just break away from it temporarily so that you can give yourself an opportunity to reset before you come back to it.

Hassall (2022) confirms what we already know, that our emotionally reactive thoughts are likely to feel like they resurface on their own. This is where he suggests repeating the process. Through repetition, we will be able to move through the process more quickly and with more emotional control each time.

Here's What You Do: SOLVE a Recent Issue

Consider a recent issue in which your emotional reaction led to feelings and behaviors that you wish could have been more calm or more appropriate.

Write down how you could have applied each aspect of SOLVE in that situation. Think back to what you were doing, and how you were behaving, and visualize each aspect of SOLVE. Fill in the blanks below with what that strategy would have looked like in action.

STOP

OBJECTIVE LIST

VERBALIZE

EXIT

Now keep the acronym of SOLVE nearby, including what each step means. I would suggest putting it in your phone somewhere that's easy to find and pull up if needed. The only way to get better at this strategy is by using it. So now that you've practiced mentally, you'll need to put that practice into action the next time you are emotionally dysregulated.

External Reminders

Strategies like self-soothing and SOLVE can be incredibly helpful – if you use them.

Often our difficulties are not related to a lack of skill or knowledge, but our difficulty implementing those strategies when we need them. This is where it helps to externalize your motivation (Cummins, 2023). Essentially, it's not always enough to remember what we need to do. But we also need to remember why we wanted to do it.

You can have a post-it on your desk that says SOLVE, but that's reminding you what to do, not why you need to do it. When you're overwhelmed by an emotional avalanche, it's unlikely that you'll be able to slow down long enough to consider the importance of regulating yourself.

The main difference here is the 'what' versus the 'why.' While it is important to know 'what' to do, you may have experienced that it's often not enough. Therefore, an additional reminder of the 'why', can increase your chances of using the skills you've learned.

Justin and his partner recently moved in together after 2 years of dating. They had previously lived about 30 minutes apart and had to be strategic about their time together as they navigated busy work schedules.

Justin hadn't realized how their distance and time apart often mitigated his strong emotional reactions. He was motivated to handle things more carefully, not wanting to ruin their limited time together or leave things on a bad note.

Moving in together removed those buffers and changed this dynamic, bringing Justin's emotional regulation difficulties front and center.

Justin and his partner now needed to navigate daily life decisions together. Topics that any couple would need to discuss to some extent, like home organization, division of household chores, and managing finances, became battlegrounds. Justin often viewed his partner's requests or suggestions as condescending and critical. He would assume his partner must regret moving in together.

Emotionally reacting to his assumptions, Justin would be filled with hurt, fear, and anger. He would shut down or say things like, "It's fine, we only have 10 months to go on this lease, and then you can have your perfect life back."

These reactions were often out of proportion to the actual issue at hand. His partner began to feel like he had to walk on eggshells or avoid difficult conversations altogether. This started to create distance and disconnection.

Justin often felt ashamed and guilty about his behavior. He knew how to take a step back and respond more rationally but never remembered to try to use those steps in the moment.

He decided to create a vision board that included pictures of some of his happiest moments with his partner. He added visual depictions of their goals, which included a trip to Italy they had talked about since they started dating, an intimate beach wedding, and one day buying a house together.

As he took the time to print and arrange these pictures on the vision board, he envisioned the kind of relationship he'd want to have as they worked toward these goals together.

He imagined himself moving through conversations in a more positive way that didn't involve frustration or withdrawal. Instead, he pictured calm discussions, closeness, and connection.

Justin hung the vision board in their bedroom. He used both the mental images he had created and the vision board itself to remind him of the dynamic he wanted with his partner and the bigger goals they had in life together. This memory and visual cue started to serve as a reminder for Justin to use the strategies he knew would help him navigate difficult conversations more effectively.

Here's What You Do:
Use Visual Cues to Remember

Consider a situation that often triggers strong emotional reactions for you. Write that situation on the line below.

Think about why you want to control your emotions in these moments.

List those reasons below:

- ______________________________
- ______________________________
- ______________________________
- ______________________________
- ______________________________
- ______________________________
- ______________________________

Now identify two different ways you could create an external/visual cue for why you want to manage your emotions in these moments. These could include anything from pictures, post-its, symbols, etc. Anything that you can see that will help you to remember the importance of why you want to use emotional regulation strategies.

1 ______________________________

2 ______________________________

Try implementing one or both of these visual cues this week to start getting a sense of how visual reminders can help you remember to step back and regulate in the moment.

Using Imagery

We've previously touched on how imagery can help us remember things. Notice in Justin's situation, he also envisioned the future goals and relationship that he had with his partner. As he was making his vision board, he was visualizing how he would interact with his partner to work toward achieving those goals together.

Imagery is also something that you can use in this way to bolster your ability to remember the importance of using emotional regulation strategies. In addition to your visual cues, consider in detail how you want to think, feel, and behave throughout your day or in a certain context. For Justin, it was in the context of his relationship. For you, it might be something else.

Combine vivid imagery with creating your external motivator so that you have an experience in mind when you see that visual cue.

Persistence Pays Off

While emotional regulation can be a challenging skill to build, I would argue that it's one of the most important. If we're in a state of heightened emotional distress this flows out into everything we do. We'll be less likely to focus or be flexible, less likely to remember details, and much more likely to be impulsive.

If you struggle with emotional dysregulation, it might feel like there is no way you'll ever get in control of your emotional responses. But you absolutely can overcome this issue and improve this skill.

Your particular approach to building this skill is unique to you, but here are some suggestions as you get started:

- Try one strategy at a time.
    - Try it a few times when you're not emotionally dysregulated and also when you are to see if it helps you.
- Choose the strategies that you like the best.
    - A strategy won't work if you don't feel comfortable using it.
    - If you looked at the suggestions in this chapter and a few jumped out at you, those are the ones to start with.
- If after several tries, you don't feel like this strategy is working for you at all, then feel free to move on and try another.

- On the other hand, if you do feel like it is helping you to feel relaxed and calmer, even a little bit, then continue to work on increasing your mastery over that strategy enough to use it more automatically when you are escalated.
- Once you feel like you can successfully use a strategy when you are emotionally dysregulated and it feels like it comes fairly easy to you, then consider this one of the ones you can pull out when needed and aim to learn another.
- It's a good idea to generally have 3-5 strategies that work well for you. So, continue to work on practicing and testing strategies until you can identify those 3-5 strategies. Anything beyond that is totally up to you, and more ways to self-regulate are always a bonus.

With time, experimenting with the many different strategies you've learned here, and continued practice, you'll be able to better manage your emotions on a regular basis.

Pro Tips for Emotional Regulation

- Emotional regulation can be challenging, but it can be improved with practice.
- Practice self-soothing to de-escalate extreme emotions.
- Use the SOLVE strategy to navigate a situation when you are experiencing emotional dysregulation.

    - Stop – stop what you are doing in that moment.
    - Objective List – list the facts.
    - Verbalize – verbally state a solution and when you'll implement it.
    - Exit – Do something else so that you can reset before you go back to your previous activity.

- We often don't lack knowledge or skills, but we do lack the follow-through.

    - Use external reminders or visual cues to remind yourself why you find it important to use the strategies you are learning.

- Use imagery to go with your visual cues.
- Keep at it, this skill can be built with consistency.

CONCLUSION

Now that you've learned all about the extent to which ADHD executive dysfunction can impact you and the strategies you can use to improve your executive functioning skills, it's time to put what you've learned into practice.

Ideally, you've already been applying some of the skills in this book as you progressed through each day. Just like any new skill, these strategies take practice. The techniques covered in this book have been carefully chosen to improve your executive functioning skills. Depending on the executive functioning area, some strategies will supplement what you are already doing, offering immediate improvement each time you apply them. While others offer ways to train your brain over time to improve those skills.

Acceptance and Self-Compassion

When it comes to accommodating your needs related to ADHD, one of the biggest barriers that I've seen is when we expect ourselves to just do better, and feel shame when we think we don't measure up. This is where acceptance and self-compassion can play a strong role as you aim to improve your executive functioning skills.

Our brains work differently. That's not a bad thing. We think fast, we can be extremely creative, and we can focus with intensity for a longer period of time than the average person when we're in a hyperfocus state.

Sometimes we can do ourselves a disservice when we put neurotypical expectations on our behavior and functioning. This can happen when we feel like we should be able to succeed by doing things in the same way that everyone else does. Truthfully everyone is unique in their needs, perspectives, and the way they accomplish things. Accepting your unique traits is the first step to strengthening the areas that you want to improve.

Practicing self-compassion means understanding that consistency is a challenge for us and perfection is not a reality for anyone. We are going to mess up. Even when we know the strategy to do better, sometimes we won't apply it the way we should or the way we planned to. That's okay. When this occurs, we need to treat ourselves with kindness and understanding.

What leads to improvement is continued effort. So, if you miss a day or a few days, or if you try and it doesn't quite go how you wanted, that is completely okay. The most important thing is that you try again. Mistakes can be great teachers. You'll learn and adjust as you go, getting better each time. We're all works in progress.

Next Steps

So now that you've completed your 8 days, what next?

We've established the fact that continued practice is crucial. But how you go about that practice is completely up to you. You might choose a strategy for each executive functioning skill and aim to practice each of those until they become familiar and comfortable before you move on to other strategies. Or you might choose to focus on your top one or two executive functioning areas in which you struggle the most and work on mastering those before you continue to actively practicing others.

Try not to put a time limit on mastering each skill. Aim for consistency and practice until you reach a point of familiarity and comfortability. At that point, the skill or strategy should be well integrated into your daily functioning without you having to put too much intention behind it. When that happens, move on bringing the next strategy or set of strategies to that same level of comfortability, Ultimately, we want the things you've learned here to become habits. So, the goal for each skill is that you'll have developed some great habits to address and improve each area of executive functioning.

Your Next Month

Here is an example of a plan that you can create to keep working on building these skills. You can fill this one out and keep a copy somewhere visible in your home, or you can create your own variation. It will be important to keep it somewhere visible and easily accessible to prevent it from going out of sight, out of mind.

Remember that you can practice as many or as few strategies as you want each week. The plan below shows one month with 2 skills and 2 strategies for each skill each week. The most important thing is that you do what works for you. Expecting yourself to adopt 7 new skills in one week, may be a tall order. Practicing 2 or 3 may be more realistic. Even practicing one until mastery can be a great option.

Another suggestion is that you can fill each week out as you go, deciding whether to continue previous strategies or to add new strategies based on your progress and how easy they have become for you.

MONTH: _

WEEK 1

EF Skill Area I Will Work On: ________

Why is working on this
area important to me? ________

The Strategy I Will Implement is: ________

When Will I Practice this Strategy: ________

Where Will I Practice this Strategy: ________

How Will I remember to use this strategy: ________

Potential Barriers that may get in my way: ________

How I plan to address or overcome those barriers: ________

EF Skill Area I Will Work On: ________

Why is working on this area important to me? ________

The Strategy I Will Implement is:

When Will I Practice this Strategy: ________

Where Will I Practice this Strategy: ________

How Will I remember to use this strategy: ________

Potential Barriers that may get in my way: ________

How I plan to address or
overcome those barriers: ________

WEEK 2

EF Skill Area I Will Work On: ________

Why is working on this area important to me? ________

The Strategy I Will Implement is: ________

When Will I Practice this Strategy: ________

Where Will I Practice this Strategy: ________

How Will I remember to use this strategy: ________

Potential Barriers that may get in my way: ________

How I plan to address or overcome those barriers: ________

EF Skill Area I Will Work On: ________

Why is working on this area important to me? ________

The Strategy I Will Implement is: ________

When Will I Practice this Strategy: ________

Where Will I Practice this Strategy: ________

How Will I remember to use this strategy: ________

Potential Barriers that may get in my way: ________

How I plan to address or overcome those barriers: ________

WEEK 3

EF Skill Area I Will Work On: ________

Why is working on this area important to me? ________

The Strategy I Will Implement is: ________

When Will I Practice this Strategy: ________

Where Will I Practice this Strategy: ________

How Will I remember to use this strategy: ________

Potential Barriers that may get in my way: ________

How I plan to address or overcome those barriers: ________

EF Skill Area I Will Work On: ________

Why is working on this area important to me? ________

The Strategy I Will Implement is: ________

When Will I Practice this Strategy: ________

Where Will I Practice this Strategy: ________

How Will I remember to use this strategy: ________

Potential Barriers that may get in my way: ________

How I plan to address or overcome those barriers: ________

WEEK 4

EF Skill Area I Will Work On: ________

Why is working on this area important to me? ________

The Strategy I Will Implement is: ________

When Will I Practice this Strategy: ________

Where Will I Practice this Strategy: ________

How Will I remember to use this strategy: ________

Potential Barriers that may get in my way: ________

How I plan to address or overcome those barriers: ________

EF Skill Area I Will Work On: ________

Why is working on this area important to me? ________

The Strategy I Will Implement is: ________

When Will I Practice this Strategy: ________

Where Will I Practice this Strategy: ________

How Will I remember to use this strategy: ________

Potential Barriers that may get in my way: ________

How I plan to address or overcome those barriers: ________

Remember to be Flexible

The plan you created can change to meet your needs. You may have started out with one approach and decided that you need to change your focus or the number of strategies you are working on or even which particular strategies you are using for a skill.

Try not to change only out of boredom, as the real reason you are practicing is to build habits and gain mastery. However, if you realize that certain strategies or plans really just don't suit you, that is when it can be a good idea to change it up.

Resources

While this book offers evidence-based strategies grounded in scientific research to help improve your executive functioning skills, it is still not a replacement for professional therapy or coaching. There are also other resources that can add to your growing understanding of ADHD and how to best manage it that may not have been covered in this book due to the more exclusive focus on executive functioning.

CHADD

Children and Adults with Attention-Deficit/Hyperactivity Disorder (CHADD) is a nationwide non-profit organization that was founded in 1987 and now has individual chapters across the United States. CHADD has a wealth of information and support resources including directories, connection to online communities, and treatment centers.

PSYCHOLOGY TODAY

This is an online organization that offers a wealth of information and resources related to mental health and behavior science. They have US and international directories to help you connect with mental health professionals in multiple countries around the world.

ADDITUDE

This resource has been available and growing for the past 25 years. They offer a massive library of content and connection to ADHD support and specialists around the world.

Embrace Your Success

No matter where you are in your journey of managing your executive functioning skills, these struggles do get better. When you are in the thick of it, it can feel like executive functioning deficits impact your entire life. But the strategies you have learned here have made a difference in the lives of many others and they can make a difference in your life too.

Celebrate your successes along the way, big and small, and remember that your continued efforts will make a difference. Commit to taking steps forward each day and you'll find that these changes create positive ripples into all other areas of your life.

Thank You

I appreciate you purchasing this book and taking the time to read it. I sincerely hope it has been valuable for you, and that the information inside it has made a positive different in your life.

Before you leave, I'd like to ask you a small favor. Can you please consider reviewing this book on the platform? Leaving a review is an easy and incredibly effective way to support independent authors like me, so we can keep working. It also lets other people discover this resource so it can hopefully have a positive impact for them as well.

Lastly, and most importantly, hearing your feedback helps me write books that can make an even bigger difference in your life, and the lives of every reader. I would deeply appreciate hearing what you have to say. You can scan the QR code below to leave a review.

Thank you.

REFERENCES

Adler, L. A., Faraone, S. V., Spencer, T. J., Berglund, P., Alperin, S., & Kessler, R. C. (2017). The structure of adult ADHD. *International Journal of Methods in Psychiatric Research, 26*(1), e1555. https://doi.org/10.1002/mpr.1555

Ashinoff, B. K., & Abu-Akel, A. (2021). Hyperfocus: The Forgotten Frontier of Attention. *Psychological research, 85*(1), 1–19. https://doi.org/10.1007/s00426-019-01245-8

Barkley, R. (2021, July 20). *How to Hit Pause on ADHD Impulsivity*. ADDitude. https://www.additudemag.com/adhd-impulse-control-social-spending/

Barrett, K. K. (2018). ADHD and the Case for Support through Collegiate Age: Understanding the Lifecycle of Developmental Delays in Executive Function for ADHD and its Impact on Goal Setting. *Journal of Childhood & Developmental Disorders*, https://childhood-developmental-disorders.imedpub.com/adhd-and-the-case-for-support-through-collegiate-age-understanding-the-lifecycle-of-developmental-delays-in-executive-function-for.pdf

Betker, C. (2017, November 17). *Environmental strategies for managing attention deficit hyperactivity disorder*. Journal of Childhood & Developmental Disorders. https://childhood-developmental-disorders.imedpub.com/environmental-strategies-for-managing-attention-deficit-hyperactivity-disorder.php?aid=21065

Brown, T. E. (2022, September 21). 7 truths about ADHD and intense emotions. ADDitude. https://www.additudemag.com/adhd-emotional-regulation-video/

Csikszentmihalyi, M. (1990). Flow: The psychology of optimal experience. Harper & Row. https://www.researchgate.net/publication/224927532_Flow_The_Psychology_of_Optimal_Experience

Cummins, M. (2022, October 14). Notetaking strategies for ADHD adults. Marla Cummins: ADHD Coach and Productivity Consultant. https://marlacummins.com/adhd-notetaking/#:~:text=Notetaking%20is%20an%20essential%20skill%20for%20ADHD%20adults.,later%20when%20you%20need%20it

Cummins, M. (2023, April 3). 2 Little Known Strategies ADHD Adults Need to Manage Emotions. Marla Cummins. https://marlacummins.com/adhd-emotions/

Diamond A. (2013). Executive functions. *Annual Review of Psychology, 64*, 135–168. https://doi.org/10.1146/annurev-psych-113011-143750

Diamond, A., & Ling, D. S. (2016). Conclusions About Interventions, Programs, and Approaches for Improving Executive Functions that Appear Justified and Those That, Despite Much Hype, Do Not. *Developmental Cognitive Neuroscience*, 18, 34-48. https://doi.org/10.1016/j.dcn.2015.11.005

Eddins, R. (2020, April 1). Grounding Techniques & Self-Soothing for Emotional Regulation. Eddins Counseling Group. https://eddinscounseling.com/grounding-techniques-self-soothing-emotional-regulation/

Fischer M, Barkley RA, Smallish L, Fletcher K. Hyperactive children as young adults: driving abilities, safe driving behavior, and adverse driving outcomes. Accid Anal Prev. 2007 Jan;39(1):94-105. doi: 10.1016/j.aap.2006.06.008. Epub 2006 Aug 17. PMID: 16919226.

Gardner, B., Lally, P., & Wardle, J. (2012). Making Health Habitual: The Psychology of 'Habit-Formation' and General Practice. *The British Journal of General Practice: The Journal of the Royal College of General Practitioners, 62*(605), 664–666. https://doi.org/10.3399/bjgp12X659466

Glass, B. D., Maddox, W. T., & Love, B. C. (2013). Real-Time Strategy Game Training: Emergence of a Cognitive Flexibility Trait. PLOS ONE, 8(8). https://doi.org/10.1371/journal.pone.0070350

Grane VA, Endestad T, Pinto AF, Solbakk A-K (2014) Attentional Control and Subjective Executive Function in Treatment-Naive Adults with Attention Deficit Hyperactivity Disorder. PLoS ONE 9(12): e115227. https://doi.org/10.1371/journal.pone.0115227

Groves, N. B., Kofler, M. J., Wells, E. L., Day, T. N., & Chan, E. S. M. (2020). An Examination of Relations Among Working Memory, ADHD Symptoms, and Emotion Regulation. *Journal of abnormal child psychology, 48*(4), 525–537. https://doi.org/10.1007/s10802-019-00612-8

Hassall, J. (2022, May 24). Adult ADHD and Emotions. CHADD. https://chadd.org/attention-article/adult-adhd-and-emotions/

Hepark, S., Janssen, L., de Vries, A., Schoenberg, P. L. A., Donders, R., Kan, C. C., & Speckens, A. E. M. (2019). The Efficacy of Adapted MBCT on Core Symptoms and Executive Functioning in Adults With ADHD: A Preliminary Randomized Controlled Trial. *Journal of Attention Disorders, 23*(4), 351–362. https://doi-org.library.capella.edu/10.1177/1087054715613587

Holst, Y., & Thorell, L. B. (2018). Adult Executive Functioning Inventory (ADEXI): Validity, Reliability, and Relations to ADHD. *International Journal of Methods in Psychiatric Research, 27*(1), e1567. https://doi.org/10.1002/mpr.1567

Hölzel, B. K., Lazar, S. W., Gard, T., Schuman-Olivier, Z., Vago, D. R., & Ott, U. (2011). How Does Mindfulness Meditation Work? Proposing Mechanisms of Action From a Conceptual and Neural Perspective. *Perspectives on Psychological Science, 6*(6), 537–559. https://doi.org/10.1177/1745691611419671

Keng SL, Smoski MJ, Robins CJ. Effects of mindfulness on psychological health: a review of empirical studies. Clin Psychol Rev. 2011 Aug;31(6):1041-56. https://doi.org/10.1016/j.cpr.2011.04.006

Kim, M. J., Brown, A. C., Mattek, A. M., Chavez, S. J., Taylor, J. M., Palmer, A. L., Wu, Yu-Chien, & Whalen, P. J. (2016, November 3). The Inverse Relationship Between the Microstructural Variability of Amygdala-Prefrontal Pathways and Trait Anxiety is Moderated by Sex. Frontiers in Systems Neuroscience. https://www.frontiersin.org/articles/10.3389/fnsys.2016.00093/full

Lee, C. I. (2021, June 17). *10 Strategies for Managing ADHD & Impulsivity in Adults – Dr. Crystal Lee.* LA Concierge Psychologist. https://laconciergepsychologist.com/blog/10-strategies-managing-adhd-impulsivity/

Leroy, S. (2009). Why is it so Hard to do my Work? The Challenge of Attention Residue when Switching between Work Tasks. *Organizational Behavior and Human Decision Processes, 109*(2), 168-181. https://doi.org/10.1016/j.obhdp.2009.04.002

Levrini, A. (2023). *Succeeding with adult ADHD: Daily strategies to help you achieve your goals and manage your life* (2nd ed.). American Psychological Association. https://doi.org/10.1037/0000329-000

Maucieri, L. (2016, January 3). Music for your ADHD Ears. *Psychology Today*. https://www.psychologytoday.com/us/blog/the-distracted-couple/201601/music-your-adhd-ears

Milliken, K. (2016). *Gamify Anything.* Children and Adults with Attention-Deficit/Hyperactivity Disorder (CHADD). Retrieved May 6, 2023, from https://chadd.org/wp-content/uploads/2018/06/ATTN_06_16_Gamify.pdf

Mitchell, J. T., McIntyre, E. M., English, J. S., Dennis, M. F., Beckham, J. C., & Kollins, S. H. (2017). A Pilot Trial of Mindfulness Meditation Training for ADHD in Adulthood: Impact on Core Symptoms, Executive Functioning, and Emotion Dysregulation. *Journal of Attention Disorders, 21*(13), 1105–1120. https://doi.org/10.1177/1087054713513328

Nakamura, J., & Csikszentmihalyi, M. (2009). Flow Theory and Research. In C. R. Snyder, & S. J. Lopez (Eds.), Oxford Handbook of Positive Psychology (pp. 195-206). Oxford, MS: Oxford University Press.

https://doi.org/10.1093/oxfordhb/9780195187243.013.0018

Ninaus, Manuel & Pereira, Gonçalo & Stefitz, René & Prada, Rui & Paiva, Ana & Neuper, Christa & Wood, Guilherme. (2015). Game Elements Improve Performance in a Working Memory Training Task. *International Journal of Serious Games.* https://doi.org/10.17083/ijsg.v2i1.60

Ptacek, R., Weissenberger, S., Braaten, E., Klicperova-Baker, M., Goetz, M., Raboch, J., Vnukova, M., & Stefano, G. B. (2019). Clinical Implications of the Perception of Time in Attention Deficit Hyperactivity Disorder (ADHD): A Review. Medical Science Monitor: International Medical Journal of Experimental and Clinical Research, 25, 3918–3924. https://doi.org/10.12659/MSM.914225

Ramsay, J. R. (2017). The Relevance of Cognitive Distortions in the Psychosocial Treatment of Adult ADHD. Professional Psychology, Research and Practice, 48(1), 62-69. https://doi.org/10.1037/pro0000101

Ramsay, J. R. (2020). Cognitive Interventions Adapted to Adult ADHD. Rethinking Adult ADHD (pp. 63-85). American Psychological Association. https://doi.org/10.1037/0000158-005

Ramsay, J. R. (2020). Is There a Cognitive Theme to the Thoughts and Beliefs of Adults with ADHD? *The ADHD Report, 28*(7), 8-12.

Ramsay, R. (2021, July 21). *Adult ADHD and impulsivity*. Psychology Today. https://www.psychologytoday.com/us/blog/rethinking-adult-adhd/202107/adult-adhd-and-impulsivity

Shapiro, S. (2016, January 20). *Adult ADHD and Work: Improving Executive Function*. Psychology Today. Retrieved May 5, 2023, from https://www.psychologytoday.com/us/blog/the-best-strategies-for-managing-adult-adhd/201601/adult-adhd-and-work-improving-executive

Sidlauskaite, J., Sonuga-Barke, E., Roeyers, H., & Wiersema, J. R. (2016). Default Mode Network Abormalities During State Switching in

Attention Deficit Hyperactivity Disorder. *Psychological medicine, 46*(3), 519–528. https://doi.org/10.1017/S0033291715002019

Tang, Y., Hölzel, B.,K., & Posner, M. I. (2015). The Neuroscience of Mindfulness Meditation. *Nature Reviews. Neuroscience, 16*(4), 213-225. https://doi.org/10.1038/nrn3916

Torrente, F., López, P., Alvarez Prado, D., Kichic, R., Cetkovich-Bakmas, M., Lischinsky, A., & Manes, F. (2014). Dysfunctional Cognitions and their Emotional, Behavioral, and Functional Correlates in Adults with Attention Deficit Hyperactivity Disorder (ADHD): Is the Cognitive-Behavioral Model Valid? *Journal of Attention Disorders, 18*(5), 412–424. https://doi.org/10.1177/1087054712443153

University of Cambridge. (2017, October 23). Running on Autopilot: Scientists find Important New Role for 'Daydreaming' Network. *ScienceDaily*. Retrieved May 26, 2023 from www.sciencedaily.com/releases/2017/10/171023182609.htm

Voss, P., Thomas, M. E., Cisneros-Franco, J. M., & de Villers-Sidani, É. (2017). Dynamic Brains and the Changing Rules of Neuroplasticity: Implications for Learning and Recovery. *Frontiers in psychology, 8*, 1657. https://doi.org/10.3389/fpsyg.2017.01657

Made in United States
Troutdale, OR
01/07/2024